Archaeology
of the
Moundville
Chiefdom

A Dan Josselyn Memorial Publication

Archaeology of the Moundville Chiefdom

EDITED BY VERNON JAMES KNIGHT JR.
AND VINCAS P. STEPONAITIS

THE UNIVERSITY OF ALABAMA PRESS
TUSCALOOSA

The University of Alabama Press
Tuscaloosa, Alabama 35487-0380

Manufactured in the United States of America

∞
The paper on which this book is printed meets the minimum requirements of American National Standard for Information Sciences-Permanence of Paper for Printed Library Materials, ANSI Z39.48-1984.

Library of Congress Cataloging-in-Publication Data

Archaeology of the Moundville chiefdom / [edited by] Vernon J. Knight, Jr. and Vincas P. Steponaitis. — New ed.
p. cm.
Includes bibliographical references and index.
ISBN-13: 978-0-8173-5421-3 (pbk. : alk. paper)
ISBN-10: 0-8173-5421-2 (alk. paper)
1. Moundville Archaeological Park (Moundville, Ala.) 2. Mississippian culture—Alabama—Black Warrior River Valley. 3. Chiefdoms—Alabama—Black Warrior River Valley. 4. Indian pottery—Alabama—Black Warrior River Valley. 5. Social archaeology—Alabama—Black Warrior River Valley. 6. Black Warrior River Valley (Ala.)—Antiquities. I. Knight, Vernon J. II. Steponaitis, Vincas P.
E99.M6815A73 2007
976.1'43—dc22
2006017758

Contents

List of Figures

List of Tables

Foreword

CHRISTOPHER S. PEEBLES

MY ASSOCIATION WITH Vernon James Knight Jr., Vincas Steponaitis, and a score of other scholars who have worked at Moundville has been an unalloyed privilege and pleasure that has endured for almost 30 years. I am honored that Professors Knight and Steponaitis and our colleagues asked me to contribute this foreword. I would like to begin with a few assertions—assertions that I believe to be both accurate and true. First, fortune has looked with great favor on Moundville and the sites of the Moundville phase. Each and all are largely intact, few have been despoiled by looters or destroyed by other economic forces, and fewer still have succumbed to the ravages of natural forces. Second, excavations at Moundville and at other sites of the Moundville phase have been conducted in exemplary style, and the collections and archives from those excavations have been conserved with great fidelity. Third, those who produced the great bulk of the archaeological record for these sites not only must be counted among the most talented archaeologists of their respective eras, but they also all qualify as genuine polymaths. Fourth, the current generation of archaeologists who work at Moundville and in its environs are every bit as talented and productive as their intellectual ancestors. Finally, if the Moundville phase is taken as a single dynamic polity, one that occupies a few hundred thousand hectares and a few hundred years of the first one-half of our millennium, then more is known in more detail about this prehistoric society than any other similar archaeological manifestation in the Southeast.

That final assertion, if taken at face value, is certainly accurate. There are, however, some subtle relationships buried within it. One is that information is the raw material of knowledge; two, that piling up information does not necessarily lead to knowledge; three, that it takes imagination (conjectures, theories, theoretical models) to turn information into knowledge; four, that outside the realms of literature, metaphysics, and mathematics, all the imagination in the world is not very useful in the absence of information; five, that the chapters of this volume show that those who work at Moundville today have great imagination and also demonstrate the authors' keen appreciation of the archaeological record upon which their creative work rests. They also demonstrate, through their words and deeds, that these archaeologists are the legitimate heirs to a vast body of high-quality information left to them by the archaeologists who worked at Moundville over the last 150 years.

What other archaeological site can count as its first professional excavator a professor of chemistry, who also served as the director of the munitions bureau for the Confederate States of America, and who later became the president of the University of Alabama? How about the second excavator, a sybarite from Philadelphia, a graduate of Harvard, the child of a mother who gave a £5,000 pearl necklace (today's value more than $500,000) to one of her favorite debutantes, who gave up café life in Europe of the Belle Epoch for archaeology in the Southeast? Or two sequent state of Alabama geologists, one of whom was the president of the University of Alabama, the other the director of the Alabama Museum of Natural History, both of whom guarded the site of Moundville with their prestige and with their personal funds—in one instance even mortgaging his family's home to purchase part of the site for inclusion in a park planned by the state of Alabama? Then there was the electrical engineer who turned to archaeology, who oversaw the massive excavations at Moundville, who took part in the original archaeological surveys of the Black Warrior River valley, who supervised many of the TVA excavations in the Tennessee River valley, who was the first curator of the Museum of Atomic Energy at Oak Ridge, Tennessee, and who conducted a 50-year crusade to preserve the collections from most of the archaeological sites in Alabama, including Moundville. They are, in order, N. T. Lupton, C. B. Moore, E. A. Smith, W. B. Jones, and D. L. DeJarnette.

Their collective Moundville legacy is immense: hundreds of thousands of square feet of excavation, tens of thousands of archaeological features, millions of artifacts, and a superb archive of notes and drawings and photographs that documents their work. Moreover, either directly or indirectly, David Lloyd DeJarnette had a hand in the professional archaeological training of all the authors represented here (as well as one who ought to be included here, but cannot, because it has become his lot to serve as the adjutant general of the California National Guard, Maj. Gen. Tandy Key Bozeman, USAF).

Given the massive legacy left by more than a century of fieldwork, there came the time (in the 1960s) to turn all of that documentation into a site report for Moundville. There were Moore's publications and collections; there were notes and collections from the massive excavations conducted by the Alabama Museum of Natural History from 1929 through 1941; there were scattered collections and documents from other work that spanned 150 years. In large measure this was not a task for the imagination—except to the extent that one had to try to reconstruct the knowledge and skill each archaeologist brought to the task; to try to see what they did and did not see, record, and recover; and all the while to make allowances for the fact that each archaeologist learned on the job and became a better archaeologist as a result. This document became the framework—the context, the foundation—for the subsequent work at Moundville. Like most foundations, it was neither particularly elegant nor very visible, but it was important to the next steps in the research at Moundville.

These next steps have taken place in the context of a loose but highly collegian partnership among most of the individuals represented in this volume, plus a few, such as Tandy Bozeman, whose other duties precluded participation in this particular endeavor. Over the last twenty years this process has been iterative: trial formulations repetitively assayed against the archaeological record, modified, and in several cases discarded. In most instances, each new formulation built on these data has been founded on an earlier formulation; each application of a new theoretical model has strengthened some formulations and weakened others. In a few instances—one of which I will come to in a minute—new work has required that one give up cherished models. Taken together, the historical fabric of Moundville has been broadened and clarified with each cycle of research.

There were initial and tentative analyses of the Moundville burials and the settlement organization at Moundville in 1971. In 1978 Steponaitis and I contributed papers to the *Mississippian Settlement Patterns* volume, which advanced this earlier work markedly. In 1977 and

1978, a program of survey and testing was initiated to measure the size, chronological position, and duration of the major Moundville phase sites in the Black Warrior Valley. These data were used by Tandy Bozeman in his doctoral dissertation, which was completed under the supervision of Professor Albert C. Spaulding at the University of California, Santa Barbara. Based on his work, several models were constructed for the development of Moundville phase settlement organization. The chapter in this volume by Steponaitis has slain an element of one of my favorite settlement models and replaced it with the conclusion that in its later phases, Moundville was a necropolis and home for the elite but otherwise had no substantial living resident population. A second consequence of his current work is that my estimation of population growth for Moundville, at least in late Moundville II and Moundville III, is not correct.

In the late 1970s, using techniques developed in the late nineteenth century by Flinders Petrie for dating predynastic graves in Egypt, Steponaitis created a superb ceramic chronology for the Moundville site and phase. This chronology, which has been refined, expanded, and extended over the last decade, is the crucial framework on which all subsequent work has been hung. It gives the Moundville phase its truly historical dimension.

The initial burial analyses were refined and produced a reasonable model of "status in death" for Moundville. This analysis, where there were data to do so, was expanded to other Moundville phase sites. Later, when burials could be grouped by period, a developmental sequence was constructed for Moundville phase social organization. In the main, these models of Moundville social organization are still useful and generally correct, but given recent developments, these data are ripe for reanalysis and reconstruction.

Next, Mary Powell took on the skeletal population and drew a substantial sample of the more than 2,053 burials that had been recovered from the site for analysis. Not only did she look at the health and reproductive dynamics of this population but she also was able to examine it in the context of social ranking and through historical time. The summary that she has presented in this volume is only a small part of the work she has completed and reported thus far.

Her work, in turn, was an important element in the analysis of diet as measured by trace elemental and stable-isotope concentrations in human bone. Margaret Schoeninger and I completed an initial analysis of strontium levels in bone. The results of this work were suggestive of differences in dietary breadth, but far more needs to be done before one can trust our tentative conclusions. In her chapter, Schoeninger and our colleague Mark Schurr have used an analysis of stable carbon isotopes to show a decrease in maize consumption between Moundville III and the protohistoric Moundville IV. Another cherished part of my model of Moundville—increased maize consumption in Moundville IV as the cause for a marked decrease in health—has been destroyed.

Earlier work at Moundville had systematically collected and saved neither botanical nor animal remains. Margaret Scarry has conducted excavations at Moundville over the last 15 years with the recovery of these important bits of data in mind. She based her doctoral dissertation, a monograph, and several articles on the plant remains from her excavations. In turn, Lauren Michals is currently analyzing a large sample of faunal material from Moundville and environs for her dissertation.

There was little standardized and comparable information about the smaller Moundville phase sites prior to the 1977–1978 survey. Even with these data, there were no detailed data for the smaller ceremonial centers. Paul Welch partially closed this gap with his work at the White Mound and Village and Hog Pen Mound (an infelicitous name if there ever was one), Moundville III and I edifices, respectively. Again, the goals of his work have been to enrich the developmental record for the Moundville phase and to give greater specificity and verisimilitude to the economic models (mainly elements of a prestige-goods economy) that have been constructed for it. Lauren Michals has done much the same for the small domestic sites, and she too has reported her work in this volume.

Old and new excavations at Moundville have been combined to produce a detailed empirical model for its development as a settlement, as a paramount ceremonial center, and as regional necropolis. Over the last decade, Knight has been thinking about Moundville in social and symbolic terms. He has placed the symbols common to the Mississippian in their various archaeological contexts, thereby creating a semiotics of Mississippian society and ritual. Here, Jim Knight has presented an elegant and evocative model for the organization and social meaning of the mounds, plazas, and other social spaces at Moundville. His work has begun a line of investigation that will occupy his thoughts and the thoughts of others among us for the next decade.

Much remains to be done, even with the collections made 60 years ago at Moundville. Vin Steponaitis has described the ceramics, but precious little has been done with the other categories of materials. There are the copper, greenstone, chipped stone, bone, and shell artifacts; each of these classes of artifacts awaits a full and formal analysis and complete description and publication.

There is one final model for Moundville that requires restatement. I wish to emphasize it here so that it will not be extended or implied in situations where it is clearly inappropriate and unwarranted. One of the notions that I have held, explicitly and implicitly, for a bit more than 20 years is that the distribution of the Moundville phase settlements (and the Moundville population) can be treated as if they comprised an island ecosystem (in the sense and with all the analytical promise offered by Robert MacArthur and Edward O. Wilson, the latter yet another accomplished graduate of the University of Alabama, in their book *The Theory of Island Biogeography*). I have envisioned Moundville as an agricultural population firmly rooted in an oasis of very productive alluvial soils, watered but not destroyed by a quite predictable river, surrounded on each side by quite unproductive uplands thick with pine forests. Furthermore, I did not extend—at least in the specific, historical circumstances—the developmental models constructed for Moundville to other nearby Mississippian sites, specifically not to the sequent settlements on Lubbub Creek and the other Mississippian sites along the Tombigbee River. In fact, I have written quite the opposite from the first and last pages of the report on excavations in the Lubbub Creek Archaeological Locality to several publications thereafter. Thus I have been a bit surprised to read that I have either tried to extend the Moundville model to the Lubbub data and failed, or that I extended the model and had to be corrected, or that I had somehow changed my mind about the relationship between Moundville and Lubbub. The case is quite the opposite, and the several recent papers by Paul Welch on the differences between complex and simple chiefdoms make the case for why such an extension is neither appropriate nor warranted.

As I said in the beginning, the work at Moundville has been a collaborative effort; it has taken place across time and space and in an information-rich environment populated by a variety of theoretical models. For the last six years, ending in January 1994, I have had varying degrees of responsibility for information technology and resources at Indiana University, first as dean of academic computing and then as acting associate vice president of the university. One of the primary missions of my office was to support collaborative research mediated by information technology, research much like that reported here. One of the lessons I learned in that capacity was the great power and promise of teams and teamwork in any organization, even in research institutes. I found, like the Molière character who was speaking prose without knowing it, that those of us who have participated in this Moundville research project seem to have learned the importance of teams and collaborative research long before either became popular, either in the business world or in universities. My hope is that this teamwork will continue, unabated, for another 30 years.

Preface to the New Edition

AT THIS WRITING, thirteen years have passed since the 1993 Society for American Archaeology symposium that spawned the papers included in this volume. That symposium represented a significant break with previous syntheses of Moundville prehistory. In large measure, it had to do with realizing the full implications of an internal chronology introduced some years earlier. Among the chief insights resulting from this chronology was our growing awareness of two significant transitions in Moundville's historical trajectory. The first was the regional consolidation of the polity, which had the character of an event concurrent with the layout of the plaza, the major mounds, and the palisade. The second was the shift from a bustling, fortified town in the thirteenth century AD to a very dissimilar, vacant ceremonial center and necropolis in the fourteenth century.

In different ways, these conclusions had dawned on us by the late 1980s. One of us (VPS) had realized that the middens at Moundville were mostly early but the burials were mostly late. Thus the majority of people buried at Moundville could not actually have lived there. The other (VJK) had realized that only one of the mounds along the southern margin of Moundville's plaza was still occupied in the later part of the sequence. Thus mound building on the plaza periphery was early, but the site was partially abandoned later on. A new history of Moundville had to be written incorporating these insights. This history was realized in our introductory chapter, in which we decided to use the word "necropolis" for the first time in recognition of the fact that Moundville's late-period cemeteries were larger and more numerous than those of other large Mississippian centers. Our various collaborators were also busy employing new diachronic perspectives to shed light on other aspects of the Moundville chiefdom. In retrospect, given that Moundville archaeology is such an active scene, we think the book has held up pretty well, as the basic model it presents is still widely accepted.

Naturally, there have been advances since 1993 on several topics addressed in this book. For one thing, radiometric dates have accumulated rapidly. We have since decided to adopt a tree-ring calibrated phase chronology. The effect has been to collapse the Moundville sequence into a shorter span of calendric time than is given in Chapter 1. Following the results of an analysis by Knight, Lyle Konigsberg, and Susan Frankenberg (1999), the revised calendar ages of the phases are as follows:

West Jefferson phase	AD 1020–1120
Moundville I phase	AD 1120–1260
Moundville II phase	AD 1260–1400
Moundville III phase	AD 1400–1520
Moundville IV phase	AD 1520–1650

Our notion that Moundville was in some sense a planned community and that most of the mound construction there took place during a brief interval in the late Moundville I and early Moundville II phases is implicit in Chapters 1–3. We now have a bit more actual evidence of this construction chronology than we did at the time. From 1989 to 1998, Knight conducted new excavations in six mounds and obtained some 57 new radiocarbon dates bearing on episodes of mound construction. In that project, summit architecture was exposed on two mounds, and the contents of flank middens provided new data on elite activities. These topics have been explored in articles prepared by Knight (2004), Ed Jackson and Susan Scott (2003), and Julie Markin (1997), and in theses prepared by University of Alabama graduate students Elizabeth Ryba (1995), Robyn Astin (1996), Kristi Taft (1996), and Matthew Gage (2000). The idea that residential space at Moundville may have been formally partitioned at some point, as suggested in Chapter 3, served as a point of reference for a new study of household evidence at Moundville in a dissertation by University of North Carolina graduate student Greg Wilson (2005).

In the original symposium it was Paul Welch's assignment to provide a summary of the outlying settlements, a topic to which he had personally contributed the lion's share of the evidence with his work at the various single-mound centers. In a paper that became Chapter 8, Lauren Michals added a rare glimpse of a non-mound settlement belonging to the earliest part of the sequence. But one of the gaps in our picture of Moundville's hinterland was the lack of a good characterization of the numerous non-mound sites and their role in Moundville's rise, florescence, and decline. Fortunately a new generation has tackled this topic headlong, with important studies produced by University of North Carolina graduate student Mintcy Maxham (2000, 2004) and University of Alabama graduate students Scott Hammerstedt (2000), Jennifer Myer (2002), and Paul Jackson (2004). Mark Rees (2001) has conducted additional excavations at two of the single-mound sites as reported in his dissertation at the University of Oklahoma.

We are proud to say that Moundville research continues at a brisk pace. At this writing, John Blitz and his students have launched the Early Moundville Archaeological Project, which explores the idea that early differences in access to resources at the household level lies behind the emergence of social ranking that is so strongly marked later on. And the curated collections from former excavations continue to beckon. The future of Moundville research looks good from here.

VJK & VPS
January 2007

REFERENCES CITED

Astin, Robyn L.

1996 Mound M: Chronology and Function at Moundville. Master's thesis, Department of Anthropology, University of Alabama, Tuscaloosa.

Barry, Steven E.

2004 Lithic Raw Materials and Chipped Stone Tools: A Comparison of Two Sites in the Moundville Chiefdom. Master's thesis, Department of Anthropology, University of Alabama, Tuscaloosa.

Gage, Matthew D.

2000 Ground-Penetrating Radar and Core Sampling at the Moundville Site. Master's thesis, Department of Anthropology, University of Alabama, Tuscaloosa.

Hammerstedt, Scott W.

2000 Characteristics of Late Woodland and Mississippian Settlements in the Black Warrior Valley, Alabama. Master's thesis, Department of Anthropology, University of Alabama, Tuscaloosa.

Jackson, H. Edwin, and Susan L. Scott

2003 Patterns of Elite Faunal Utilization at Moundville, Alabama. *American Antiquity* 68(3): 552–572.

Jackson, Paul D.

2004 Coexistence of the West Jefferson and Moundville I Phases. *Journal of Alabama Archaeology* 50(1): 1–17.

Knight, Vernon James, Jr.

2004 Characterizing Elite Midden Deposits at Moundville. *American Antiquity* 69(2):304–321.

Knight, Vernon James, Jr., Lyle W. Konigsberg, and Susan R. Frankenberg

1999 A Gibbs Sampler Approach to the Dating of Phases in the Moundville Sequence. Unpublished manuscript.

Markin, Julie G.

1997 Elite Stoneworking and the Function of Mounds at Moundville. *Mississippi Archaeology* 32(2): 117–135.

Maxham, Mintcy D.

2000 Rural Communities in the Black Warrior Valley, Alabama: The Role of Commoners in the Creation of the Moundville I Landscape. *American Antiquity* 65(2): 337–354.

2004 Native Constructions of Landscapes in the Black Warrior Valley, Alabama, A.D. 1020–1520. Ph.D. dissertation, Department of Anthropology, University of North Carolina, Chapel Hill.

Myer, Jennifer L.

2002 Among the Fields: Mississippian Settlement Patterns in the Black Warrior Valley, Alabama. Master's thesis, Department of Anthropology, University of Alabama, Tuscaloosa.

Rees, Mark A.

2001 Mississippian Political Culture: Contrasting Historical Trajectories in Southeastern North America. Ph.D. dissertation, Department of Anthropology, University of Oklahoma, Norman.

Ryba, Elizabeth A.

1995 Summit Architecture on Mound E at Moundville. Master's thesis, Department of Anthropology, University of Alabama, Tuscaloosa.

Taft, Kristi Elaine

1996 Functionally Relevant Classes of Pottery at Moundville. Master's thesis, Department of Anthropology, University of Alabama, Tuscaloosa.

Wilson, Gregory D.

2005 Between Plaza and Palisade: Household and Community Organization at Early Moundville. Ph.D. dissertation, Department of Anthropology, University of North Carolina, Chapel Hill.

1. A New History of Moundville

VERNON JAMES KNIGHT JR. AND
VINCAS P. STEPONAITIS

WITHIN THE LAST DECADE there have been several advances in our understanding of the specifics of Moundville's developmental history. For example, critical segments of the regional chronology have been refined. Differences between early and late Moundville I phase communities have come into sharper focus. We have incipient chronologies of mounds and sheet midden deposits based on diagnostic sherds. The palisade has been firmly dated. We synthesize these and other refinements according to the following scheme: intensification of local production (AD 900–1050); initial centralization (AD 1050–1200); regional consolidation (AD 1200–1300); the paramountcy entrenched (AD 1300–1450); and collapse and reorganization (AD 1450–1650).

Moundville, located on the Black Warrior River in west-central Alabama, is not only one of the largest Mississippian centers in the Southeast but also one of the most intensively studied (Peebles 1981). During the late nineteenth century, the site was mapped by agents of the Smithsonian Institution (Steponaitis 1983b). In the first decade of the twentieth century, it was dug by Clarence B. Moore (1905, 1907). Between 1930 and 1941, excavations were continued on a grand scale by the Alabama Museum of Natural History using Civilian Conservation Corps federal relief labor (Peebles 1979). And since the 1950s, a number of smaller excavations have been undertaken, some of which continue to this day (Scarry 1986; Knight 1992). Only a fraction of the collections generated by this fieldwork have ever been thoroughly analyzed; even so, scholars using these materials have produced an impressive array of studies of social organization (Peebles 1974; Peebles and Kus 1977), political economy (Steponaitis 1978; Welch 1991; Welch and Scarry 1995), subsistence (Scarry 1986; Michals 1981; Peebles and Schoeninger 1981), health (Powell 1988), settlement patterns (Peebles 1978; Bozeman 1981, 1982), and chronology (Steponaitis 1983a).

Over the past ten years, new data and new insights coupled with refinements in chronology have led to substantial revisions in our understanding of Moundville's history. Our purpose here is to collate these recent advances into a new synthesis that draws heavily on, and provides a context for, the remaining chapters in this volume. First we describe Moundville and its setting, then we discuss the ceramic chronology, and finally we present our new interpretations of late prehistoric developments in the Black Warrior Valley.

THE MOUNDVILLE SITE

Moundville occupies a high, flat terrace of Pleistocene age on the eastern side of the Black Warrior River at Hemphill Bend, 24 kilometers (15 miles) south of the fall line, in an area where the alluvial valley of the Black Warrior cuts through the Fall Line Hills of Alabama. The terrace on which Moundville lies forms an abrupt bluff rising 17 meters (55 feet) above the river, well above the 100-year flood level. There are only a few such places in the alluvial valley of the Black Warrior where a high terrace directly abuts the river.

A schematic map of Moundville is shown in figure 1.1. Most previously published maps include only the prominent truncated mounds, some 20 in number, originally identified in the publications of C. B. Moore (1905, 1907). There are, however, additional low mounds, and we include those that have been confirmed. Also on this map we show the location of the Oliver Rhodes site, an area excavated during the Depression years that should be considered a part of the Moundville settlement, although it is on the opposite side of a small, unnamed stream. Our map offers what we believe to be a reasonable projection of the palisade line that effectively delimits the occupied area on the west, south, and east sides, where, as the map depicts, it perhaps terminates at Carthage Branch.

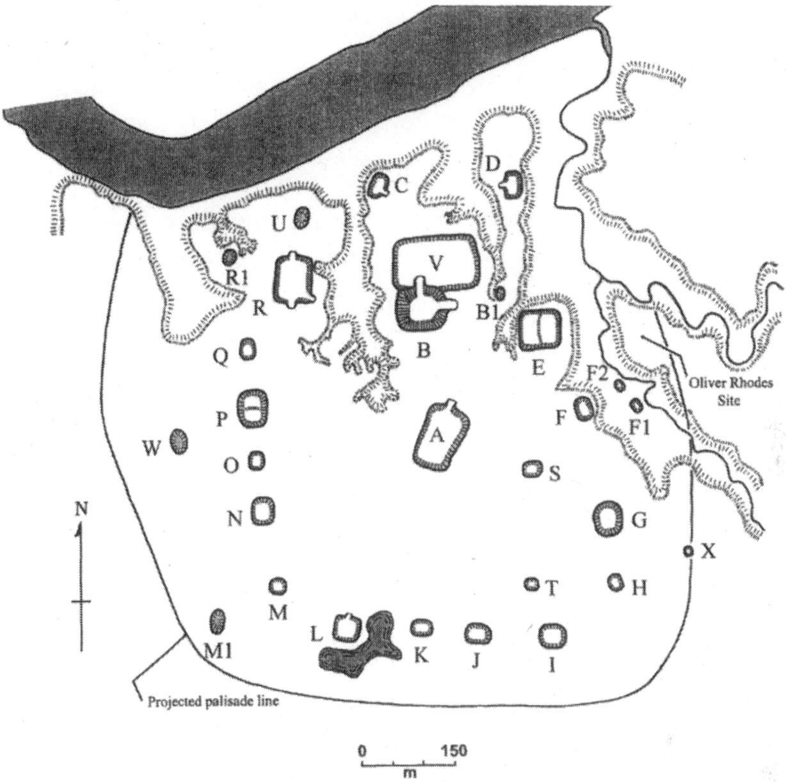

Fig. 1.1. Schematic map of the Moundville site.

The contiguous occupied area is approximately 75 hectares (185 acres) in extent. Within this zone we show the locations of 29 earthen mounds. The initial 22 letter designations were inherited from the work of Moore, and the lettering has been continued as additional mounds were recognized. Our figure for the number of mounds is perhaps conservative; a sketch map prepared by Nathaniel T. Lupton in 1869 shows peripheral mounds not presently accounted for (Steponaitis 1983a:144). Also, a topographic survey made by an engineering firm in April 1930 interprets three additional low rises as artificial mounds, which would bring the total to 32.

Present evidence suggests that for the most part, the extent of the occupied area is coincident with the palisade line, which we will discuss shortly. Moundville thus has the aspect of a compact, bounded settlement, in this respect similar to other fortified Mississippian centers. There are a few cases where Mississippian settlement areas are known to exist on the same terrace, but outside the palisade system. One example is the excavated tract known as the Picnic Area, which lies at the northwest margin of Moundville. Excavations there in 1991–1992 (chap. 4) revealed evidence of a small cluster of houses that largely predate the palisade. Another is a small mound site, the Asphalt Plant mound (1Tu50), that occupies the terrace just to the northeast of Moundville (Steponaitis 1992). This also predates the palisade, and as Welch argues in chapter 7, it probably was part of the early Moundville I phase community at Moundville.

We know that fortifications enclosed the Moundville settlement on three sides. The north side was protected by the river bluff, and deeply entrenched Carthage Branch to the northeast may have also played a role in the site's defenses. Slightly mounded remains of the palisade line along the southern boundary of the site were still visible to observers in the mid-nineteenth century (Steponaitis 1983b: 129–130). Regarding the precise position of this stockade, we have unambiguous information from modern excavations in just two localities. Excavations during 1991–1992 in the northwest riverbank section of Moundville, mentioned above, revealed evidence for multiple episodes of bastioned palisade construction. Closely corresponding evidence from the opposite side of the site was recovered during University of Alabama field schools (1978–1984) in the area east of Mound G (Vogel and Allan 1985). The palisade trenches in both areas reveal at least six episodes of renewal, some in place and others offset slightly from previous versions. Bastions, spaced 30–40 meters apart, were 4 meters wide and 7 meters deep, incorporating square towers.

A previous map prepared by Peebles (1971:81) was the earliest modern attempt to trace the palisade, and subsequent depictions (e.g., Morgan 1980:114) are based on Peebles's map. Peebles utilized unpublished information from Depression-era excavations that showed long trenchlike features in three localities: west of Mound O, west of Mound Q, and through the Oliver Rhodes site. He also used aerial photographs in his attempt to project the fortification line. Another set of linear features, discovered west of Mound P by John Walthall with a University of Alabama field school in 1976 (Allan 1984) was subsequently attributed to the palisade system. Unfortunately, it is difficult to tell how much of the latter evidence actually pertains to Moundville's fortifications. Neither the mapped features identified by Peebles from the 1930s records nor those excavated by Walthall in 1976 very much resemble the elaborate rebuilt bastion and curtain wall sequences discovered more recently.

Our evidence for the placement of the southern portion of the palisade line is admittedly tenuous. We base it on two scraps of evidence. First, Lupton's sketch map from 1869 shows the "remains of an irregular breastwork" that arcs distinctly south of Mound M1 on the southwest margin of the site and continues to the east (Steponaitis 1983b:144). Second, systematic augering in the area south of mounds I and J reveals a drop in the density of artifacts approximately 100 meters south of these mounds, a drop that may coincide with the palisade line in this vicinity (Steponaitis et al. 1994).

Most writers agree that the larger mounds at Moundville are deliberately arranged around the margins of a single plaza (e.g., Moore 1905: 5–6; McKenzie 1964:213; Peebles 1971:82–83; Steponaitis 1983a:4–6). This plan is basically quadrilateral, with mounds M through Q defining a western row, mounds I through L a southern row, and mounds F through H an eastern row. The northern boundary of the plaza, now encroached by the headward erosion of ravines, appears to be defined by mounds R, B, and E. Mound B, the largest mound of the group, is 17.3 meters high and contains an estimated 85,450 cubic meters of earth. In this plaza-periphery group, all of which are oriented roughly to the cardinal directions, there is an alternation between small mounds containing burials and larger mounds lacking burials. In the center of the plaza is Mound A, whose orientation is skewed to the east relative to the others. Also present inside the plaza-periphery group, near the east margin of the plaza, are two low mounds, S and T, whose purpose is unknown. North of the plaza-periphery group, isolated on ridges formed by deep ravines, are mounds C and D, both flat-topped earthworks known to contain high-status burials.

Other mounds lie outside the plaza-periphery group to the east and west. Two low, elongated mounds, U and M1, possess dense concentrations of burials and may be true burial mounds (Moore 1905:220–240, 1907:343). Mound F1, a small truncated mound on the opposite side of the site that was partially excavated during the 1930s, also contains numerous burials and thus appears to present a situation comparable to mounds U and M1. Its companion mound, F2, seems never to have attracted the attention of archaeologists, nor has mound B1, located northeast of Mound B. Mound R1, isolated on a ridge west of Mound R, is a low, unexcavated rise shown on maps as early as the 1930s but only recently confirmed through probing as being constituted of artificial fill. On the eastern margin of the site is Mound X, a basal remnant of a mound encountered during palisade excavations in this vicinity by a University of Alabama field school (Vogel and Allan 1985). This mound is of special interest because of its relation to the palisade, which postdates the mound and crosses over a portion of it. Like the Asphalt Plant mound, we attribute Mound X to the early Moundville I phase community at Moundville.

Mound W, completely excavated during the Depression era, is said to have been an occupied natural rise rather than a deliberate construction (Peebles 1979:4; Walthall and Wimberly 1978:121), based on examination of the excavation notes by Peebles. Because it was identified as a mound in the 1930s and is discussed in the literature by this name, we include it on our map.

Evidence of off-mound habitation, of variable density (Peebles 1973, 1978:381), is spread throughout the area around the plaza-periphery mound group and inside the palisade line. During the Depression-era excavations, much information was obtained about structure patterns, including ordinary houses and more specialized patterns interpreted as public buildings (McKenzie 1964; Peebles 1971:83). More recent excavations along the northwest riverbank (Scarry 1995) have provided additional data on residential structures. Peebles (1978:381) has suggested that "most day-to-day debris was discarded into the river and ravines"; while it is reasonable to suppose that some such dumping occurred, it should be noted that rich middens are also found within habitation areas on the level terrace. A century of cultivation may well have destroyed much of the sheet midden at the site. Occupational debris is also found inside the plaza-periphery group, but only in the immediate vicinity of the mounds. Limited test excavations in the central plaza by a University of Alabama field school in 1988 and auger testing by the University of North Carolina in 1993 (Steponaitis et al. 1994) show it to be basically free of cultural debris.

There is some evidence of artificial leveling of the plaza area by filling along its margins early in the construction history of the site. Recent excavations at the bases of mounds F and G showed artificial fills up to a meter in depth, apparently intended to build up surface depressions to the same level as the rest of the plaza. Similar fills may also be present on the west margin of the plaza, based on evidence from a small test excavation in the vicinity of Mound O.

CERAMIC CHRONOLOGY

Moundville's internal chronology was worked out in the late 1970s (Steponaitis 1980a, 1980b) and since then has been refined as additional evidence has accumulated (Steponaitis 1983a, 1992; Little and Curren

1995). The ceramic sequence now consists of five phases, spanning the period AD 900–1650 (fig. 1.2). All but the last of these phases have been further subdivided into early and late subphases, each about 75–100 years long. This degree of temporal control provides an unusually good opportunity to trace the history of Moundville and its surrounding sites.

The sequence begins with the West Jefferson phase (AD 900–1050), which was first delineated using evidence excavated from three small sites in the upper reaches of the Black Warrior drainage, about 90 kilometers northeast of Moundville (Jenkins and Nielsen 1974; O'Hear 1975). The pottery at this time was predominantly a plain, grog-tempered ware classified as Baytown Plain. Cord-marked, incised, and punctated decoration occurred in very small quantities. Late in the phase, shell-tempered pottery also started to appear. The only vessel forms made were bowls and jars, the latter often with loop handles.

The next three phases—consecutively numbered Moundville I, Moundville II, and Moundville III—were first set up as subdivisions of what had formerly been called the "Moundville culture" (Jones and DeJarnette 1936) and the "Moundville phase" (McKenzie 1966). They were initially based on two lines of evidence from Moundville: a seriation of gravelots and a stratigraphic analysis of midden deposits (Steponaitis 1983a). Subsequent excavations and analyses have generally confirmed the basic sequence and led to some refinements (e.g., chap. 4; Scarry 1995; Steponaitis 1992; Welch 1991, 1994). Particularly important has been the clear subdivision of Moundville I into early and late subphases (Steponaitis 1992:4–6), a distinction that was only vaguely perceived in the initial chronology (Steponaitis 1983a:132).

The span from Moundville I through Moundville III was a time of great diversity in vessel forms and decoration. The pottery was predominantly shell-tempered and comprised two major wares. One consisted of burnished, finely tempered bowls and bottles that were used for serving and storage; these nowadays fall into the types Bell Plain, Moundville Engraved, and Carthage Incised. The other consisted mainly of jars that were used for cooking; these vessels fall into the types Warrior Plain and Moundville Incised. The distinctions among phases can be seen in changing frequencies of these types, as well as in the appearance and disappearance of particular ceramic varieties, decorative modes, and attributes of vessel shape.

Specifically, the Moundville I phase was marked by relatively high frequencies of the decorated type Moundville Incised, with lesser amounts of Carthage Incised and Moundville Engraved. Jars typically had two handles and either folded or folded-flattened rims. Bottles were

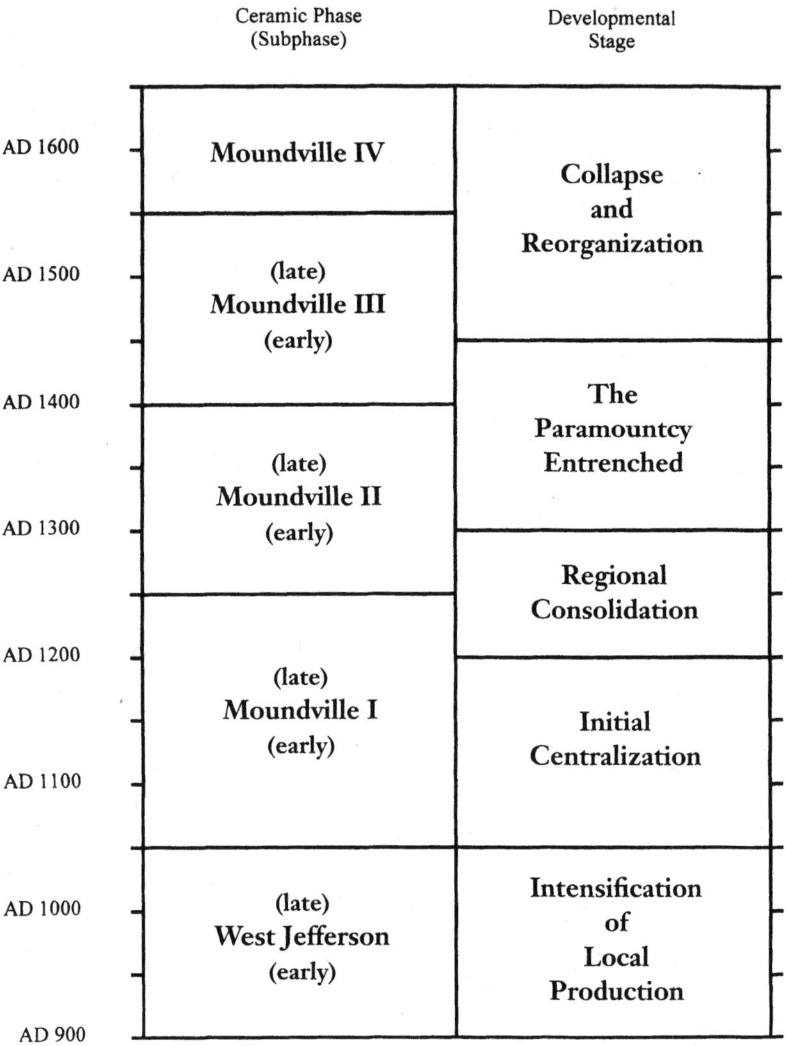

Fig. 1.2. Ceramic chronology and developmental stages used in chapter 1.

adorned with pedestals and had a slender, ovoid profile. Bowls existed in both restricted and shallow forms, the latter having the appearance of plates with straight, flaring rims. Over the course of this phase, grog-tempered pottery disappeared, Carthage Incised and Moundville Engraved gradually became more popular, and folded-flattened rims declined in frequency. In addition, early Moundville I assemblages often contained a distinctive kind of burnished ware—an early (and yet unnamed) variety of Bell Plain with a gray, finely textured paste—that fell out of use in late Moundville I times.

During the Moundville II phase, varieties of Moundville Engraved and Carthage Incised proliferated, while Moundville Incised declined in frequency and eventually disappeared. Common designs on the engraved wares included representational motifs as well as curvilinear scrolls made up of multiple, closely spaced lines. Such designs were often arranged around indentations in the vessel's surface. Bottles became subglobular in shape, usually with pedestal or slab bases. Bowls included hemispherical, cylindrical, and terraced rectanguloid forms. Jars typically had unmodified rims and either two or four handles.

Early in the Moundville III phase, Moundville Engraved and Carthage Incised continued to predominate among the decorated wares; late in the phase, however, the former type all but vanished. Among burnished wares, common shapes included subglobular bottles with simple bases, hemispherical bowls with beaded rims, short-necked bowls, and deep flaring-rim bowls. The number of handles found on jars continued to proliferate, with four, eight, and sometimes even more handles being used.

Our chronological sequence ends with the Moundville IV phase, until recently called the Alabama River phase and before that the Burial Urn culture (Cottier 1970; Curren 1982a, 1982b, 1984; DeJarnette 1952; Little and Curren 1995; Sheldon 1974). Although the Moundville IV ceramic complex showed stylistic links with its predecessors and retained shell as the dominant tempering agent, in many ways it was very different, encompassing a new suite of types. Carthage Incised continued to be made, along with the closely related type Pensacola Incised. New types included Alabama River Incised and Alabama River Appliqué. The major vessel types were short-necked bowls, flaring-rim bowls, and globular jars. Although this phase coincides with the period of initial Spanish exploration and colonization of the Southeast, European trade goods are rarely found in Moundville IV deposits.

A NEW VIEW OF MOUNDVILLE'S HISTORY

We now present a brief summary of Moundville's development. Our account incorporates the refinements to the cultural chronology discussed above and includes recent conclusions on a number of topics, several of which are treated in the chapters to follow. For detailed arguments and supporting data the reader is referred to those chapters and the citations therein. The history is set forth in terms of five developmental stages, which are given descriptive names as follows: (a) intensification of local production, (b) initial centralization, (c) regional consolidation, (d) the paramountcy entrenched, and (e) collapse and reorganization. Ceramically, the first stage coincides with the West Jefferson phase, the second with early Moundville I, the third with late Moundville I and early Moundville II, the fourth with late Moundville II and early Moundville III, and the fifth with late Moundville III and Moundville IV (see fig. 1.2).

Intensification of Local Production (AD 900–1050)

The terminal Woodland predecessor of Moundville culture in the Black Warrior Valley is the West Jefferson phase, first defined from excavations at the West Jefferson Steam Plant sites (Jenkins and Nielsen 1974), located above the fall line 70 kilometers to the northeast of Moundville. West Jefferson phase sites south of the fall line, closer to Moundville, are known primarily from survey data. These most often appear as large surface scatters, none of which, however, has been excavated as yet. From the existing information about these sites, it is our impression that the intensity of occupation seen here is not as great as in the corresponding period in the neighboring Tombigbee Valley to the west, where more information is available.

The big picture is a little clearer. Available evidence points to a general climate of social circumscription, endemic warfare, and resource stress afflicting a large section of the Southeast during terminal Woodland times. In several directions from the Black Warrior, certain river valleys harbored unusually large numbers of people in relatively large riverine settlements. The central Tombigbee Valley, the Guntersville Basin area of the Tennessee Valley, and the Alabama River Valley, for example, all possess terminal Woodland sites in great abundance according to survey data. Riverine settlements are closely spaced, site sizes are large, and midden development is extensive, as opposed to intermediate areas, which seem to have held decidedly fewer people. In each of the crowded valleys we find archaeological evidence for warfare. Subsistence stress due to local overcrowding is particularly well documented in the Tombigbee Valley.

Until we obtain better information on West Jefferson phase sites in the Black Warrior Valley, we can only speculate about the specific effects such broad-scale conditions may have had in an area with a seemingly more modest population. It is possible, for example, that a coalescence of West Jefferson phase peoples into a few relatively large villages was a response to endemic warfare. In any event, these were the dominant conditions under which local West Jefferson phase peoples began manifestly to intensify their production of both agricultural products and craft goods.

Our knowledge of West Jefferson subsistence economy is based primarily on data from the original West Jefferson Steam Plant sites in the upper Warrior Basin. These sites show a trend toward increased food production through time. Early West Jefferson phase peoples relied almost entirely on wild foods. A mobile settlement strategy employing warm-season floodplain villages and cold-season extractive camps has been suggested by Welch (1981). Later in the West Jefferson phase, around AD 950–1000, maize production intensified, while acorn and hickory nut procurement remained relatively stable (Scarry 1993a).

Evidence also exists for the intensification of craft production at West Jefferson phase sites, in particular the manufacture of shell beads. Microlithic tools commonly occur at large West Jefferson settlements. A study of microwear on these tools by Pope (1989) shows that most of them were used to drill shell. Here we call attention to the fact that shell pendants and beads, worn as jewelry and sewn onto garments, occur in burials of this era in various parts of the Southeast, in contexts that suggest that they constituted a standard of wealth (Steponaitis 1986:384, 1991). In this post-Hopewellian era, during which the exchange of valuables across the landscape was otherwise suppressed, the domestic production, display, and exchange of shell ornaments appear to have flourished in some areas. Locally in the Black Warrior Valley, we suspect that wealth in the form of shell beads was being manipulated by community leaders at this time, in their competitive efforts to attract followers, and that this activity prefigures the strategies of later elites.

It is not clear whether Moundville itself was occupied at this time. Typical grog-tempered West Jefferson series pottery is definitely scattered across portions of the site, and an apparent concentration of this material west of mounds O and P has been interpreted in the past as evidence of a small West Jefferson phase settlement (Walthall and Wimberly 1978:122–123; Steponaitis 1983a:151–152). However, no West Jefferson phase pit features have yet been documented anywhere at the site; moreover it is now reasonably well established that West Jefferson series pottery continued to be made and used at Moundville during the succeeding early Moundville I phase (Scarry 1995:234–235). This leads us to suspect at this point that Moundville was probably *not* occupied prior to about AD 1050.

Initial Centralization (AD 1050–1200)

The next period, which corresponds to the early Moundville I phase, is marked by the appearance of many of the material hallmarks of Mississippian culture: platform mounds, quadrilateral wall trench architecture, and shell-tempered pottery in a variety of new vessel shapes. Apparently some grog-tempered pottery identical to that of the local West Jefferson phase was still being made. Conspicuous changes are evident in such domains as the subsistence economy, settlement organization, and social structure.

During this period, dependence on corn became more pronounced, continuing the trend toward agricultural intensification begun during West Jefferson phase times (chap. 4). Other native crops, including squash, chenopod, maygrass, and sunflower, were also cultivated as minor components of the agricultural complex, and beans were introduced. Nut use, in contrast, declined precipitously from West Jefferson phase levels. In short, this period saw the emergence of a stable agricultural economy in the Black Warrior Valley, one in which corn contributed about 40 percent of the average caloric intake in the diet (chap. 6).

An abrupt change in settlement is also evident. Nucleated communities gave way to smaller and more dispersed farming settlements. Also, small, truncated mounds, probably the residences of an emerging elite, began to be built.

Most of the population of the Black Warrior Valley at this time was apparently living in small farming settlements to which we have applied the label "farmsteads," an example being the Oliver site reported by Michals (chap. 8). Survey and excavation data are not abundant, however, and other settlement types, as yet unrecognized, may also exist. Small clusters of houses dating to this period have been excavated at the Big Sandy Farms site (Ensor 1993) and at the northwest riverbank locality at Moundville (chap. 4). Individual houses have been identified in smaller excavations at several localities in the Moundville vicinity: north of Mound R, south of Mound E, and at the base of the Asphalt Plant mound. In this small sample, architectural diversity is pronounced, with rectangular single-set post houses, wall-trench houses, and small semisubterranean houses all counted as present, apparently juxtaposed in the same settlements. Because of the small scale of excavations to date we do not, however, possess a very good picture of what any of these settlements looked like in its entirety.

Small settlements were spread throughout the Black Warrior Valley. However, our impression is that occupation of the Moundville terrace was unusually dense. Judging from the distribution of diagnostic pottery, dwellings were concentrated along the edges of the terrace overlooking the Black Warrior River, as well as Carthage Branch and its tributaries (fig. 1.3A).

It is important that the only two mounds known to have been erected at this time in the Black Warrior Valley are found here as well. These are the Asphalt Plant mound (1Tu50) (Steponaitis 1992; see also chap. 7) and Mound X at the Moundville site. The locations of these mounds are shown in figure 1.3A, situated within what we visualize as a dispersed farming community. Although these mounds are relatively small, their construction still represents a substantial labor investment. They can be viewed, from one point of view, as tangible testaments to leadership. The apparent absence of contemporary mounds in other parts of the Black Warrior Valley is noteworthy, even though we presume the existence of local leaders up and down the valley, just as they must have existed in West Jefferson phase times. This suggests that even at this early stage in the region's political development, the Moundville locality was already filling the role of *primus inter pares* in the region.

Limited excavations at the Asphalt Plant mound revealed that its occupants, whom we reckon as leaders of a small-scale ranked society, were engaged in a traffic of raw materials, particularly nonlocal rocks and minerals (chap. 8; Steponaitis 1992). The mound sites must have served as central nodes of authority for leaders who employed the ritual of mound building and the accumulation and distribution of exotic goods as key elements of their efforts to expand and consolidate their authority in a competitive setting. This initial centralization of authority, moreover, may have been helped along by a need to lighten the burden of chronic interregional strife. Despite these developments, however, we do not believe that regional consolidation had yet been effectively achieved.

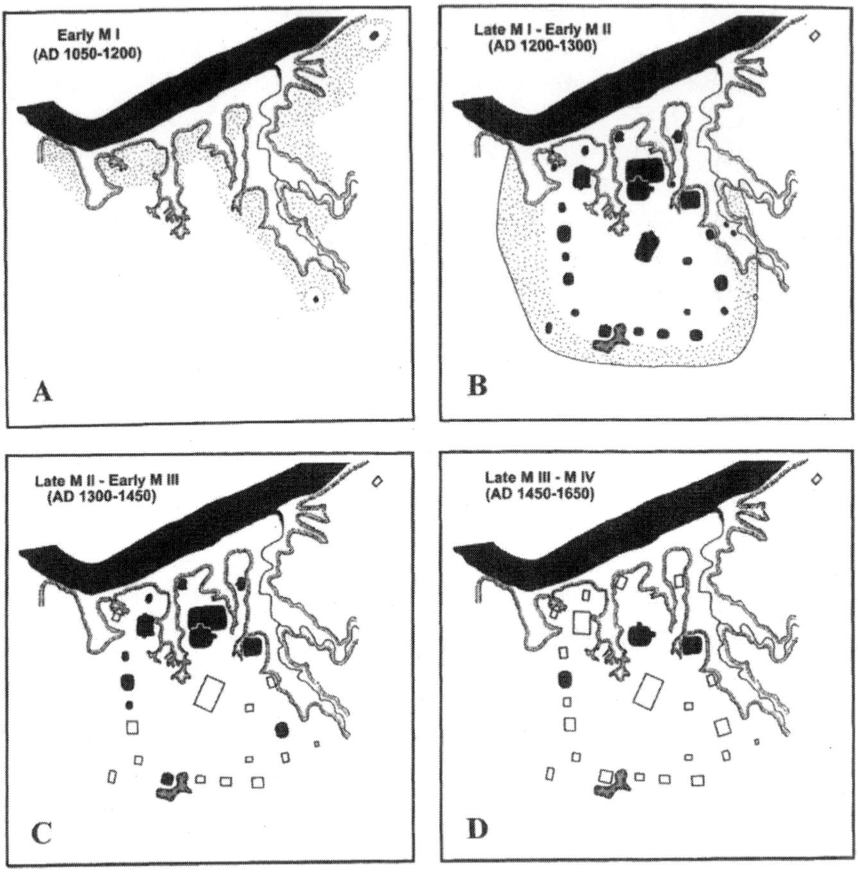

FIG. 1.3. Settlement changes at Moundville. *A*, Early Moundville I. *B*, Late Moundville I–early Moundville II. *C*, Late Moundville II–early Moundville III. *D*, Late Moundville III–Moundville IV. Occupied mounds are black; abandoned mounds are open rectangles; domestic occupation area is stippled.

Regional Consolidation (AD 1200–1300)

During the late Moundville I phase, certainly by AD 1250, a paramount center was constructed at Moundville, marking the political consolidation of an area minimally including a 40-kilometer segment of the Black Warrior Valley below the fall line at present-day Tuscaloosa. The event of regional consolidation is seen archaeologically in a number of ways.

Working with the curated collections from the 1930s, we have recognized that every mound for which we have sherd data has a strong

Moundville I phase component (Knight 1989, 1994). This suggests, contrary to previous scenarios (cf. Steponaitis 1983a, 1991), that construction of all of the major mounds was begun at roughly the same time, probably between about AD 1200 and 1250 (fig. 1.3B). According to present indications it was during this time that the basic plan of the center was established, including the layout of the central plaza and the positioning of central and peripheral mounds. Built into this configuration were an east-west bilateral symmetry, a pairing of residential mounds with mortuary temple mounds, and a ranking of social space (chap. 3; Peebles 1971).

The palisade was also first erected at this time. Recent excavations in the northwest riverbank area (chap. 4) provide direct radiocarbon dates of palisade features, indicating that the palisade was built initially around AD 1200 and remained in use, with approximately six rebuildings, until about AD 1300. With its construction, people began to move in large numbers inside the palisade walls, and thereafter virtually all domestic activity took place within its confines. The presence and maintenance of this elaborate work is strong testimony to a concern for military security during this period.

Thus, Moundville now assumed the character of a large, palisaded town, drawing in residents from a broad area. We estimate the resident population of this period as somewhat less than 1,000 people. Most of the sheet midden around the plaza dates to this time (chap. 2). In off-mound areas between the plaza and palisade there were compact arrangements of square wattle-and-daub houses with wall trench construction. Houses averaged about 19 square meters in floor area, which suggests they were inhabited by nuclear families. Cylindrical or bell-shaped storage pits were no longer used, which suggests that foodstuffs were stored above ground (chap. 4).

We wish to emphasize that the whole character of the Moundville settlement changed at this point. Prior to AD 1200, the settlement was unstructured and was spread out along the riverbank and the banks of Carthage Branch. With these changes, the settlement not only grew much larger but also became highly structured and formal, with public and domestic architecture carefully arranged around the quadrilateral plaza. The settlement was imposed on the landscape, in a flurry of coordinated activity in which plaza margins were artificially leveled to accommodate mounds, and existing constructions were cleared away to accommodate the new architecture. The most telling example of this is the case of Mound X, an early Moundville I phase construction that was decommissioned in order to clear the path of the palisade along the eastern margin of the new community.

Another indicator of regional political consolidation was the construction of several second-order mound centers elsewhere in the Black Warrior Valley. Earlier mound sites were abandoned, and at least three new ones, the Jones Ferry, Poellnitz, and Hog Pen mounds, were built in the area north of Moundville (chap. 7). All of these are single-mound sites with minor off-mound occupation areas, probably inhabited by only a few people, despite the obvious large-scale communal labor involved in raising these earthworks. We suggest that they were occupied by elite subordinates to the paramount at Moundville, and served as secondary administrative nodes to focus local ritual and productive activity and to facilitate the flow of tribute to the primary center. Most of the people in the hinterlands of the polity presumably lived in dispersed farmsteads.

In the economic sphere, changes continued to occur. Agricultural production increased to the point that maize provided about 65 percent of calories in the diet (chap. 6). Moreover, plant remains of this period provide the first clear evidence of the provisioning of the elite by commoners. Corn cupules and nutshells, the by-products of food processing, are much more abundant at rural sites than in elite residential areas at Moundville, indicating that plant foods were being brought to the paramount center in processed or partially processed form to reduce their bulk for transport (Scarry and Steponaitis 1992). Another indication of the distinctiveness of elite foodways is the relative abundance of burnished service pottery over utilitarian cooking and storage pots in elite midden deposits (Welch and Scarry 1995). Such elevated frequencies of service ware are found in deposits north of Mound R. Clearly, by the late Moundville I phase, mobilization of foodstuffs as tribute, as modeled by Welch (1991:179–183), was already an integral part of Moundville's political economy.

As is evident in several contexts at Moundville, the acquisition of nonlocal goods and raw materials also intensified during this interval. One indication, from the analysis of domestic deposits in the northwest riverbank area (chap. 4), is that the relative abundance of nonlocal chert, greenstone, and mica increased from the early to the late Moundville I phase. A second indication comes from the analysis of grave goods from seriated burials from throughout the center, among which the per capita frequency of such exotic materials as copper and marine shell also peaked during the period under consideration (Peebles 1987a;

Steponaitis 1991). Finally, some information is becoming available for mound contexts. In deposits on the flanks of Mound Q, evidence for elite craft production has been found, increasing substantially during early Moundville II times. This evidence includes sandstone saws for the manufacture of stone palettes, greenstone adze blades, pottery trowels, and microblades made from imported chert. The materials being worked include sheet copper, galena, and pigments of various kinds (Knight 1992), probably used in nondomestic social settings and potentially incorporated into a prestige goods economy (see Welch 1991).

In summary, we interpret the available evidence for the period AD 1200–1300 as testimony that the entire region was consolidated at the outset into a single polity with a primary center at Moundville and several second-order administrative centers. At the primary center lived nobles who received tribute in the form of foodstuffs from the hinterlands. At this center both the elite and nonelite engaged, in different ways, in the production and exchange of crafts involving nonlocal raw materials, some of which, as exotic goods meant for display, were funneled into a prestige goods economy involving exchange relationships with other polities.

The arrangement of public architecture at the Moundville site suggests a sociogram, in which the placement of mounds around the plaza reflects ranked status relationships among kin groups (chap. 3). If so, a fixed rank ordering had been imposed on these kin groups by incorporating that order into a sacred landscape, an act that implies considerable power at the center. Such power, vested in the office of a paramount chief, would also have been necessary to enforce this undoubtedly contested view of social reality once it had been imposed. And the most revealing measure of the extent of this power is in the immense amount of labor that had to be mobilized to level the plaza, construct the earthworks, and build the palisade.

The Paramountcy Entrenched (AD 1300–1450)

Despite the strong indications of political consolidation in the previous period, we have only indirect traces of the presumed paramount chiefs and their close kin. It is only in the following period, which we characterize as an entrenched paramountcy, that a chiefly cult symbolism became elaborated and that we find certain burials decked out with luxury goods and costumery bearing this symbolism. A good case can be made that the paramounts themselves were buried in mounds C and D on the northern margin of the site. In our ceramic chronology, this period encompasses the late Moundville II and early Moundville III phases.

Peebles, in his analysis of the social hierarchy of the Moundville site (Peebles 1974; Peebles and Kus 1977), defined a "superordinate dimension" among the burials at the site, which is to say the presumed nobility, marked by the inclusion of exotics as grave goods, most commonly marine shell beads, copper gorgets, copper ear spools, notched stone paint palettes, mineral-based pigments, and galena crystals. At the apex of the hierarchy, as Peebles reconstructs it, are burials that also possess copper-bladed axes, only seven of which are known from Moore's excavations in mounds C and D. One such burial, fancifully described by Newell Wardle (1906) as the "Great Chief of Mound C," contained bracelets and anklets of copper-covered beads, three sheet-copper gorgets, a pearl necklace, a sheet-copper hair ornament secured by a bison horn pin, and an amethyst pendant in the form of a human head, in addition to a copper-bladed axe. We now believe that most if not all of these lavish burials belong specifically to the period being discussed.

Just as Moundville's rulers began to distance themselves radically by symbolic means from their followers, most of Moundville's resident population vacated the center, presumably moving out onto dispersed farmsteads in the peripheral alluvial valley. Such a remarkable evacuation is witnessed by the scarcity of middens dating to this time, in stark contrast to the previous period (chap. 2). Supporting evidence is to be found in the domain of architectural style. The domestic architectural form characteristic of the post–AD 1300 era in this region, possessed of large-diameter wall posts, hipped roof construction with interior supports, and entrance trenches, is entirely missing among the numerous houses excavated at Moundville to date, which emphasize the earlier, flexed-pole, narrow wall trench form of construction. The palisade also ceased to be rebuilt at this time and was henceforth no longer present. Almost as rapidly as Moundville had become a town, it ceased to be one, leaving, we propose, only the elite and their retainers as permanent residents.

There are several possible explanations for this out-migration. For one, we find it conceivable that the dispersal involved a conscious decision by the elite to enhance the sanctity of the center by emptying it, by which action they would further distance themselves from the affairs of commoners. A second possibility is that it may have been a practical solution to soil depletion and the exhaustion of wood resources within Moundville's immediate catchment, caused by the unprecedented concentration of people during the preceding period (Scarry and Steponaitis 1992). A third alternative, bearing in mind that the act of amassing behind the walls of a fortified town bespeaks a desire for security, this subsequent dispersal may have been conditioned by a lessened threat of attack. It may, of course, have been a combination of such factors.

With this move, Moundville now became a necropolis, a center of mortuary ritual for the region as a whole. As residential spaces were vacated across the site, a series of cemeteries were established to fill the vacuum. At this time the resident population of the center was small, and most of those buried at Moundville had not actually lived there. This is most strikingly shown by the inverse relationship between chronologically diagnostic sherds from midden deposits and seriated burials (chap. 2). Diagnostic sherds, reflecting the accumulation of domestic refuse, drop precipitously in frequency after the Moundville I phase, stabilizing at about one-fourth of the previous level during Moundville II and III. The frequency of burials, in contrast, is relatively low during the Moundville I phase but increases greatly during Moundville II, peaking during the Moundville III phase. Essentially, after about AD 1300 there are far more burials at the site than would be predicted by the off-mound middens and architecture. Moreover, very few burials of this period are known from the outlying sites. The only known exception is the small cluster of burials at the Mill Creek site, a farmstead at the northernmost reach in the distribution of Moundville phase sites (cf. chap. 7).

Certainly by AD 1400, if not earlier, according to our sherd data (Knight 1989, 1994), many of the mounds at the primary center had been abandoned (fig. 1.3C). As our schematic map shows, the general tendency was for mounds on the southern margin of the plaza to be abandoned first. There was, additionally, a change in the way certain mounds were used. By AD 1400 the smaller mounds around the plaza periphery that had previously been used for mortuary purposes had virtually ceased in that function, as the focus of mortuary ritual, including that of the elite, shifted to off-mound cemeteries. Other mounds, in contrast (notably B, E, G, P, Q, and R), show evidence of vigorous occupation and continued construction throughout the period.

During this period long-distance exchange declined somewhat, although, as amply witnessed by the furnishings of elite burials, the prestige goods economy continued to function. Much of the iconographically rich material at Moundville traditionally attributed to the classic Southern Cult, largely from elite burials, probably dates to this time, particularly, in our estimation, to the fourteenth century AD. We make this estimate with some trepidation, however. Very little of this material has been directly dated, and some of it may be somewhat earlier. Iconographically, images found in chiefly cult paraphernalia contain possible references to warfare, either literal or figurative, emphasizing trophy heads, scalp forms, and weapons. These are juxtaposed with cosmological images, including a variety of center symbols and supernatural creatures. At this time engraved pottery bearing representational art also makes its first appearance, a class of special artifacts showing a range of themes that is congruent with the chiefly cult symbolism displayed in other media. Pottery vessels engraved with this art are very abundant at the primary center, where they are by no means restricted to elite contexts, and they also occur in lesser frequency at the outlying sites. This conspicuous broadening of the social contexts in which this iconography appears may be called a communalization of the chiefly cult symbolism (Knight 1986:682). Such pottery was produced at the primary center until about the middle of the fifteenth century AD.

Beyond Moundville, additional secondary mound centers were established, while others continued to be occupied. Welch (chap. 7) lists seven second-order mound sites that were probably occupied during the late Moundville II phase, both north and south of the Moundville site, and an eighth that was added during early Moundville III. These additional centers must have been needed to serve and administer an increased rural population, expanded no doubt by the virtual emptying of the primary center. None of these were large sites, and indeed there is no sign of a nucleated settlement in the Black Warrior Valley. Presumably the majority of people continued to live in farmsteads.

In summary, the most fundamental signature of the period AD 1300–1450 is that the primary center was once again radically transformed, from a thriving town to a largely vacant ceremonial center, chiefly residence, and necropolis. The lavish burials found mostly in the northern part of the Moundville site, with their cult regalia, combine with the virtual emptying of the center to suggest that the nobility were now both symbolically and physically distancing themselves from others. Perhaps paradoxically, however, more people than before came to have access to, or at least contact with, the esoteric religious symbolism of chiefship via the designs engraved on common service pottery. The tributary economy was in full swing, as numerous second-order administrative centers mobilized the labor and the agricultural surplus of a farmstead-based population numbering perhaps 10,000 people.

Another key to understanding this period is the beginning abandonment of certain mounds at the primary center, particularly in the southern half of the site. If we have correctly interpreted the situation, it is evident that the fixed rank order of social groups imposed on the landscape in the initial layout of the site, some two centuries earlier, was not immune to disagreement. Those that had the least to gain from such a fixed arrangement were the lower-ranked groups, assigned spaces on the opposite side of the plaza from the shrines and residences of the ruling elites. As these ruling elites consolidated their power, engaging in ritual activity and continued enlargement of mounds on the north end of the site, others simply stopped contributing. It is, perhaps, the first sign of troubles that were to come.

Collapse and Reorganization (AD 1450–1650)

The latter part of the fifteenth century in the Black Warrior Valley is marked by further signs of stress within the chiefdom. Several additional mounds at the primary center were abandoned during this period (fig. 1.3D), leaving only mounds P, B, and E on the northern side of the site with any signs of continuing construction or occupation. In the off-mound areas only a small tract southwest of Mound G is known to have been occupied. During these waning years the Moundville site was still being used for mortuary ritual, but on a much smaller scale. Mortuary mounds were no longer receiving the tombs of the elite, and substantially fewer burials were being placed in the off-mound cemeteries (Steponaitis 1983a: fig. 36).

Many of the outlying mound centers, in contrast, continued to see further occupation and episodes of mound construction extending into the sixteenth century. The largest of the outlying mounds, Snows Bend, reached a height of 3.5 meters. At the White site, where we have more plentiful data, there is considerable evidence for the provisioning of the local elite at this late date (Welch 1991). At the same time, cemeteries began to be established at some of the outlying secondary mound centers. Such cemeteries are well documented for the Snows Bend and White sites (DeJarnette and Peebles 1970; Welch 1991). Also, nucleated village-sized settlements began to reappear for the first time in the Black Warrior Valley since West Jefferson times (discounting the special case of Moundville), both in conjunction with secondary mound sites, as in the case of White, and separately, as in the case of the Powers site (chap. 7). All of these phenomena point to an increasing independence and self-sufficiency among the outlying communities during AD 1450–1550, at the expense of the center.

Most, if not all, of the secondary mound sites, however, were abandoned by approximately the middle of the sixteenth century. Here, on the threshold of the historic era, stirrings of activity at the primary center can still be detected on the summits of mounds P, B, and E, although earthen additions to these mounds had probably ceased entirely. Among these three mounds we have the best information for Mound E. Mound E appears to have had a relatively small occupation of a portion of its summit during the middle to late sixteenth century, with no additional earth construction. Our available evidence suggests that all of the mounds at Moundville were abandoned by the end of this century.

The late sixteenth century in the Black Warrior Valley heralds the Moundville IV phase. It has long been recognized that this time of urn burials was one of radical reorganization and change (Sheldon 1974). By this time most of the people in the valley were living in a few moundless, nucleated villages. No longer was there any inkling of an organizational level above that of the village, and the trappings of Mississippian hierarchy disappeared. Dependence on maize dropped significantly in favor of wild foods, perhaps as a result of soil exhaustion (chap. 6). Whereas earlier Moundville populations were reasonably healthy (Powell 1988), human skeletal remains of this period show elevated occurrences of cribra orbitalia and porotic hyperostosis (Hill-Clark 1981). Schoeninger and Schurr (chap. 6) attribute these conditions to a high pathogen load exacerbated by malnutrition. The Moundville IV phase villages continued to be occupied until about AD 1650, at which time the valley was finally depopulated due to the external pressures of broad-scale conflict. The Black Warrior had become Potagahatchie, the "river at the boundary," a buffer zone between warring proto-Creeks to the east and Choctaws to the west (Knight 1982a).

To reiterate, at the beginning of the period AD 1450–1650, the Moundville site already had become a specter of itself, the greater part of it abandoned. Nonetheless it is without doubt significant that a few of the most important mounds at the center, Mound B in particular, were still being occupied during the middle to late sixteenth century. This may well signal the existence of a nominal chief and some degree of political unity, although there are few signs of the strongly hierarchical social and political system of previous centuries. The political situation at this time, we believe, may have been similar to that of the Chickasaw at the beginning of the eighteenth century, according to the account of

Thomas Nairne (Nairne 1988). In which case, a hereditary paramount was recognized among the town chiefs, who was perhaps the personification of unity among the towns, although, like the present monarchs of England, he had no real political power.

There is no sidestepping another matter: De Soto's incursion into this region in the autumn of AD 1540. According to our chronological alignments, this event falls near the end of the Moundville III phase. Peebles (1986:33, 1987b:24) has forcefully argued that Moundville's decline as a hierarchical system antedates the expeditionary age and was in no sense a product of it, and with this position we are in general agreement. There is still room for debate, however, on the precise state of affairs described by the chroniclers of the De Soto expedition, particularly in view of the fact that Hudson and his colleagues (Hudson et al. 1990:183–191) chart the course of De Soto's expedition through the very heart of our area of concern, visiting the late Moundville III phase mound sites at White, Grays Landing, Wiggins, Burnette, Snows Bend, and even Moundville itself. They interpret the documents as describing a somewhat unstable but still unified polity little different from other diminutive polities along their route. This chiefdom was called Apafalaya, and it had a chief of the same name. Several other placenames of the region are mentioned in the chronicles, leaving little doubt that Apafalaya's inhabitants spoke a Western Muskogean dialect.

Hudson and company do not suggest that De Soto's army encountered a Moundville chiefdom anywhere near its height, which arguably makes it irrelevant that the chronicles do not mention a large ceremonial center having 29 mounds. They suggest that the decline undergone by the Moundville polity prior to the entrada was the product of the common internal instability of Mississippian political systems, whereas, in contrast, the postcontact Moundville IV phase, with its reorganization and evidence of nutritional stress, exhibits "fundamental structural changes" very likely attributable to the European contact (Hudson et al. 1990:188–191).

At issue here is not whether the Moundville political system went into decline from internal causes prior to the sixteenth century. All concerned agree that it did. The question, rather, is whether the former Moundville chiefdom was totally decentralized in AD 1540 as Peebles sees it, or whether it was still a minimally functioning chiefdom unifying a district of several towns, as Hudson would have it.

We have offered our own account above, grounded on current archaeological knowledge, of the conditions prevailing during the late

Moundville III phase, which we suggest is the appropriate unit for a calendar date of AD 1540. This was indeed a time of decline, during which there is evidence of increasing independence among the scattered communities of the Black Warrior Valley. But we are impressed by the evidence, only recently recognized and previously unsuspected, of De Soto-era occupation on the summits of some of the major earthworks at Moundville, which we think bespeaks a lingering importance attached to the all but defunct ceremonial center. Thus we have suggested the hereditary head-chiefship among the early eighteenth century Chickasaw towns as an analogy appropriate to these conditions. In regard to the chronicles of De Soto and their accounts of the province of Apafalaya, conceding that they are not as clear as one would like, they do seem, by our reading, to be describing at least a nominally centralized political situation not out of line with our impressions of the late Moundville III phase. In this respect our position is close to that of Hudson and his colleagues. Having said this, we take no position on the many specific correlations proposed by those researchers between named towns in the De Soto accounts and specific late Moundville III phase archaeological sites.

CONCLUSION

For more than 25 years, beginning with the work of Christopher Peebles (e.g., 1971, 1983; Peebles and Kus 1977), the Moundville system has played a prominent role in discussions of Native sociopolitical complexity in North America. At first, discussions centered on defining aspects of hierarchy in Moundville's spatial organization, settlement pattern, and burial population. An empirical basis was thus established for claims about the Moundville phenomenon in relation to a neoevolutionary theoretical framework. By the end of the 1970s a robust internal chronology for Moundville had been achieved, based on changes in pottery (Steponaitis 1980a, 1980b). This achievement, along with the acquisition of new subsistence and site survey data in the Black Warrior Valley, allowed discussion of an expanded range of topics having a distinctly historical dimension. It now became possible, for example, to engage Moundville data in theoretical discussions of the rise and decline of hierarchical societies and to track the internal development of the system's political economy (e.g., Welch 1986; Peebles 1986, 1987b; Steponaitis 1991).

In the last decade, research on several fronts by several researchers has reached the point where additional issues can be addressed and others recast, resulting in a total picture of Moundville's historical development that is a significant refinement, we believe, over previous constructions of the recent past. Those previous models portrayed Moundville's development as a steady climb to a Moundville III phase climax, followed by a relatively abrupt collapse. We have now, in essence, inverted that schema. We now see the peak occupation of the center as being early in its history during the late Moundville I phase, coinciding with the initial political consolidation of the region, followed by a protracted decline.

Although we have not trumpeted our theoretical views in this summary, it should be obvious that our sympathies are consistent—at least in a very general sense—with the partisans of practice theory as expressed by Bourdieu, Giddens, and others. This direction, currently in vogue, is provoking questions of how elites actively work to win and consolidate power over followers, including the deliberate manipulation of architectural space. This brand of social theory also points to issues of factionalism and resistance to authority, and the effect of these, along with material factors, in the decline and collapse of hierarchical societies. We look forward to the role that our currently burgeoning knowledge of the Moundville system and its sociopolitical history will ultimately play in such discussions.

2. Population Trends at Moundville

VINCAS P. STEPONAITIS

AT MOUNDVILLE, MOST MIDDEN DEPOSITS date to the Moundville I phase, but the vast majority of burials date to the Moundville II and III phases. Relative abundances of sherds suggest that Moundville's resident population peaked between AD 1050 and 1300 and then precipitously declined. Between AD 1300 and 1550, the site was inhabited principally by elites and became a center of mortuary ritual for the region as a whole. Most of the dead buried in Moundville's cemeteries during the Moundville II and III phases were apparently brought in from outlying settlements.

Moundville is not only one of the largest Mississippian centers in the Southeast but also one of the most intensively studied. Yet despite many decades of sustained research, one basic question has received surprisingly little attention: How did the size of Moundville's resident population change through time?

The few previous attempts to model population change at Moundville proceeded from the assumption that the people buried at the site also lived there (e.g., Steponaitis 1983a). Thus, the relative number of burials in each phase was taken as a rough index of population. This reasoning suggested that population was small during the West Jefferson (AD 900–1050) and Moundville I (AD 1050–1250) phases, increased during Moundville II (AD 1250–1400) and Moundville III

(AD 1400–1550) phases, then declined precipitously by the start of the Moundville IV (AD 1550–1650) phase. The most frequently cited estimate of the site's maximum population was 3,000 residents (Peebles 1983:190, 1986:29, 1987a:27, 1987b:9–10).

Although this scenario was reasonable given the information available at the time, recent reexamination of midden evidence has called it into question (Steponaitis 1992). Specifically, the problem is this: The great majority of sherds deposited at the site appear to date to the Moundville I phase, significantly earlier than most of the burials. If one assumes that these sherds represent habitation debris, then Moundville's resident population must have peaked early in the site's history, and its later burial population must have consisted largely of individuals who lived elsewhere.

My goal here is to review what is known about midden deposits at Moundville and to discuss more fully the implications of this evidence. I begin by presenting the available data on the chronological distribution of middens. Next, I consider the chronological distribution of burials. Finally, I draw these lines of evidence together in formulating a new interpretation of Moundville's population history.

CHRONOLOGICAL DISTRIBUTION OF MIDDEN DEPOSITS

In view of Moundville's long history of investigation, surprisingly little information exists on the chronology of its middens. This lack is attributable to two factors: First, many of the early excavators sought only burials and large artifacts and did not care much for sherds. Second, even though many of the later excavators did recover sherds, these collections have never been fully analyzed and reported. Hence, I can rely only on the older excavations for which sherd counts have been published and the more recent ones from which I have personally examined at least a sample of the ceramics. Among these are the Roadway and Riverbank excavations conducted by the Alabama Museum of Natural History (AMNH) and the suite of test excavations conducted by the University of Michigan Museum of Anthropology (UMMA).

I focus here on middens that seem to be associated with off-mound residential areas, rather than middens associated directly with mounds (such as those found on summits or flanks). I exclude the latter from consideration because many mounds were nonresidential and also because the summits of residential mounds did not comprise a large proportion of the site's inhabited area when the population was at its peak (cf. chap. 3).

Let us now discuss each of the relevant excavations, presented in the order in which they were originally carried out.

AMNH Roadway Excavation (1939)

One of the last, and by far the most ambitious, of the Depression-era projects at Moundville was the Roadway excavation, so named because it followed the projected path of the paved road that is now used by visitors to the site (Peebles 1979). The excavations took place within a sinuous transect 15 meters wide and 2.4 kilometers long, which cut across the central plaza as well as areas to the east, south, and west of the mounds (fig. 2.1). In all more than 10,000 square meters were opened; the work yielded dozens of structures, hundreds of burials, and more than 100,000 artifacts from refuse deposits that were encountered along the way.

The collections from this excavation have never been fully studied (cf. Welch 1989). Fortunately, there does exist a published tabulation of all the sherds that were found, classified according to types (Wimberly 1956). Although this tabulation takes no account of vertical or horizontal provenience within the excavations, it can still be used to gauge the overall abundance of sherds dating to different phases and hence the relative intensity of occupation at different times. Whatever these data lack in spatial resolution is more than offset (for present purposes) by the size and spatial extent of the collection; no other excavation, before or since, has ever sampled so much of the site and systematically recovered so many sherds.

When one examines the relative frequencies of shell-tempered types from this excavation, one finds that they closely match the pattern typical of Moundville I phase assemblages. This is not to say that Moundville I is the only phase represented; later components are certainly present also. But it is clear that Moundville I is by far the dominant phase represented. There is no other plausible explanation for the high frequency of Moundville Incised among decorated types and the correspondingly low frequencies of Bell Plain and Moundville Engraved. A recent look at a sample of these sherds strongly supports this conclusion (Welch 1989).

For the purposes of reconstructing trends in population, it would obviously be helpful to know how much of this collection dates to each

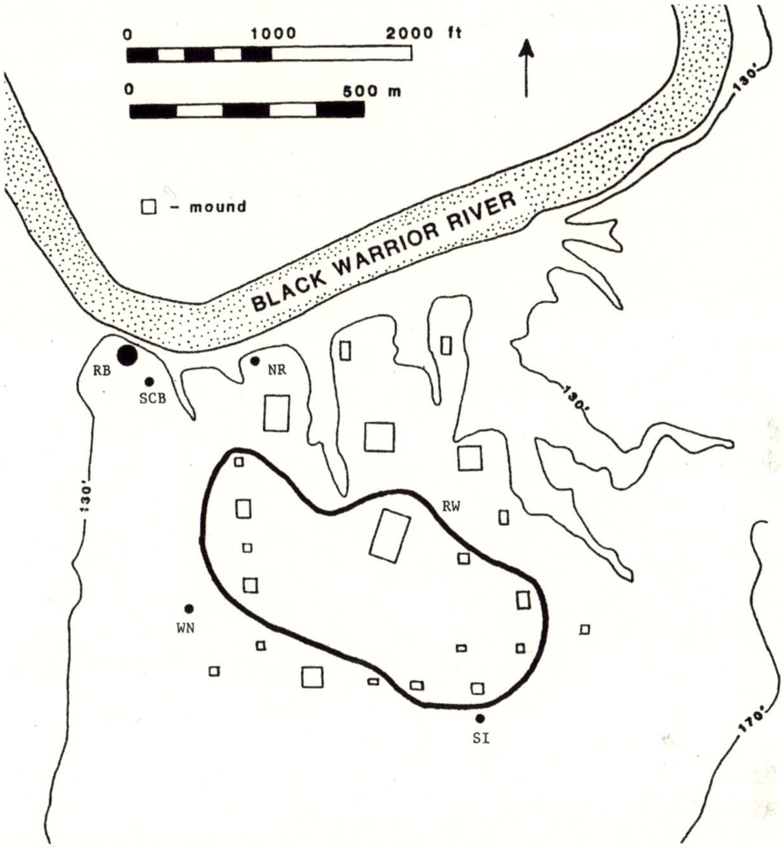

Fig. 2.1. Excavations at Moundville with chronological information on middens. *RW*, Roadway. *NR*, north of Mound R. *SCB*, south of Conference Building. *SI*, south of Mound I. *WN*, west of Mound N. *RB*, Riverbank.

phase in the sequence. One can obtain such estimates using an elegant statistical technique devised by Kohler and Blinman (1987). This technique relies on least-squares regression to partition chronologically mixed collections into their constituent components. The basic idea is simple. One begins by constructing a model assemblage for each phase that might appear in the mixture. The regression equation treats each such phase as an independent variable, the mixed assemblage as the dependent variable, and each pottery type as an individual "case" or "observation." The least-squares criterion is then used to find the linear combination of phase assemblages that best fits the mixed assemblage in question. If the type frequencies in the model assemblages are expressed as proportions and the frequencies in the mixed assemblage are expressed as counts, then the regression coefficient (or slope) associated with each phase (or independent variable) represents an estimate of the number of sherds from that phase in the mixed collection.

The model phase assemblages used in the present case are shown in table 2.1, and the results of the regression analyses are presented in table 2.2. Of the 95,742 shell-tempered and grog-tempered sherds in the Roadway collection, Kohler and Blinman's method estimates that 1.1 percent date to the West Jefferson phase, 73.4 percent date to the Moundville I phase, and only 25.5 percent date to the Moundville II and III phases combined.

Before interpreting these figures, one must control for the differing spans of the phases in question. This is best accomplished by dividing the number of sherds from each phase by the duration of that phase in years. The resulting ratios are estimated deposition rates, expressed as the average number of sherds deposited per year (table 2.2). To the extent that refuse accumulation correlates with numbers of people, these estimates suggest that Moundville's population increased by a factor of 50 between the West Jefferson and Moundville I phases, then decreased by a factor of 4 in the Moundville II–III phases.

Despite the uncertainties that beset these estimates, one conclusion seems beyond doubt: The vast majority of habitation refuse encountered during the Roadway excavation was deposited during the Moundville I phase, prior to AD 1250.

UMMA Test Excavations (1978–1979)

In the late 1970s, the University of Michigan Museum of Anthropology tested four different localities at Moundville: north of Mound R, south of the Conference Building, south of Mound I, and west of Mound N (fig. 2.1). These excavations were carried out by Margaret Scarry (1981a, 1986), under the general direction of Christopher Peebles. Although the principal goal was to recover plant-food remains, valuable chronological data (in the form of diagnostic sherds and dates) were obtained as well. Let us now consider the chronology of each locality in turn.

NORTH OF MOUND R. This excavation consisted of two adjacent 2 × 2-meter units, which were taken down to sterile subsoil. The cultural deposits here were 2 meters thick and rich in artifacts. Broadly

Table 2.1.
Model Phase Assemblages and Actual Sherd Counts from the Roadway Excavation at Moundville

	Model Phase Assemblages			
Type[a]	West Jefferson[b]	Moundville I[c]	Moundville II–III[d]	Roadway Excavation[e]
Bell Plain	0	59	1,487	8,918
Mississippi Plain	94	1,075	3,500	79,442
Carthage Incised	0	14	82	1,752
Moundville Engraved	0	0	167	397
Moundville Incised	1	157	74	4,116
Baytown Plain	8,266	0	0	1,078
Benson Punctated	5	0	0	16
Alligator Incised	4	0	0	16
Mulberry Creek Cord Marked	5	0	0	7
Total	8,375	1,305	5,310	95,742

a. Type names from early publications were translated to their approximate modern equivalents as follows: Moundville Black Filmed is counted as Bell Plain, Warrior Plain as Mississippi Plain, Moundville Filmed Incised as Carthage Incised, Moundville Filmed Engraved and Moundville Engraved Indented as Moundville Engraved, McKelvey Plain and West Jefferson Plain as Baytown Plain. Nonlocal types and those predating the West Jefferson phase were excluded from consideration. Also excluded were several rare types that do not appear to have been consistently sorted in all assemblages.

b. Based on the combined assemblages from sites 1Je31, 1Je32, and 1Je33 (Jenkins and Nielsen 1974).

c. Based on the total shell-tempered sherd counts from Bessemer (DeJarnette and Wimberly 1941:81). This site was chosen over other known Moundville I components largely because its pottery was originally sorted according to the same typology later used in classifying the Roadway material. The Bessemer collection also contains some 1,200 grog-tempered sherds; although some of them may well date to the early Moundville I phase, most can be attributed to the preceding West Jefferson component and thus were ignored for present purposes.

d. Based on assemblages from the Moundville II and Moundville III levels in the midden north of Mound R at Moundville (Steponaitis 1983a). The two phases are here combined because they contain virtually identical type frequencies (i.e., they differ only at the level of varieties). Keeping these phases separate in regression analysis would inevitably lead to problems of collinearity (see Kohler and Blinman 1987).

e. After Wimberly 1956.

Table 2.2.
Estimated Rates of Sherd Deposition in the Roadway Assemblage at Moundville

Phase	Phase Duration (years)	Estimated Sherds in Assemblage[a] (*N*)	(%)	Estimated Rate of Deposition (sherds/year)
Moundville I	200	74,621	73.4	373.10
Moundville II–III	300	25,958	25.5	86.53
West Jefferson	150	1,101	1.1	7.34

a. Estimates derived by means of the least squares method of Kohler and Blinman (1986), using the data in table 2.1. The regression equation is $y = 1{,}101.4\,x_1 + 74{,}621.4\,x_2 + 25{,}957.6\,x_3$, where y is the Roadway assemblage, x_1 is the model West Jefferson assemblage, x_2 is the model Moundville I assemblage, and x_3 is the model Moundville II–III assemblage ($R^2 = 0.995$; $p < .001$). The dependent variable (y) consists of sherd counts, while the independent variables (x_1, x_2, x_3) are expressed as proportions.

speaking, three stratigraphic zones were encountered. The uppermost 40 centimeters consisted of midden with scattered pits and hearthlike features, but no definite floors or distinct living surfaces. The next 30 centimeters consisted of similar refuse deposits, except that these were interspersed with occasional traces of sand floors. Finally, the lowest 130 centimeters comprised a series of closely superimposed sand floors, separated by lenses of refuse.

An extended discussion of the pottery from this excavation has appeared in print (Steponaitis 1983a) and need not be reiterated here. Suffice it to say that the lowest zone dated to the Moundville I phase (principally late Moundville I), the next zone dated to the Moundville II phase, and the uppermost zone dated to Moundville III. Thus, even though refuse from all three phases was present, nearly two-thirds of this deposit accumulated during Moundville I times.

SOUTH OF CONFERENCE BUILDING. This test also consisted of two adjacent units, each 2 × 2 meters in size. Though not nearly as deep, the cultural deposits were similar in character to those north of Mound R. On top was a plowzone 20 centimeters thick (Zone I); below that was dark, rich midden about 25–35 centimeters thick (Zone II); and at base was a layer of superimposed sand floors (Zone III), containing three puddled-clay hearths (Scarry 1986:161–168).

The shell-tempered pottery from this excavation comprises an almost pure Moundville I assemblage (table 2.3). The only later diagnostic is a single sherd of Moundville Engraved, var. *Hemphill*, suggesting a slight Moundville II or III phase admixture. Jar attributes exhibit a classic stratigraphic sequence (table 2.4): from bottom to top, the percentages of standard jars and unmodified rims increase, while the percentages of neckless jars, folded-flattened rims, and folded rims decrease. Based on the predominance of standard jars, the nearly equal and high frequencies (overall) of both folded and folded-flattened rims, and the healthy representation of Moundville Engraved, the deposit would seem to date principally to the middle-to-late portion of the Moundville I phase.

Table 2.3.
Ceramic Assemblage, South of Conference Building

Type, Variety	Zone I[a]	Zone II[b]	Zone III[c]
Shell-tempered			
Bell Plain, *Hale*	72	115	18
Mississippi Plain, *Hull Lake*	3		
Mississippi Plain, *Warrior*	387	466	63
Carthage Incised, *Summerville*		1	
Carthage Incised, *unspecified*	3	1	
Moundville Engraved, *Hemphill*		1	
Moundville Engraved, *unspecified*	11	4	1
Moundville Incised, *Carrollton*	3	1	
Moundville Incised, *Moundville*	5	23	4
Moundville Incised, *unspecified*		5	
Grog-tempered			
Baytown Plain, *Roper*	8	13	4
Alligator Incised, *unspecified*	3	1	2
Benson Punctated, *unspecified*	1		
Sand-tempered			
Baldwin Plain, *unspecified*	2		1
Nonlocal			
Harrison Bayou Inc., *Harrison Bayou*		1[d]	
Total	498	632	93

a. Includes TUA level 1 and TUD level 1.

b. Includes TUA levels 2–4 and TUD levels 2–3.

c. Includes TUA levels 5–9 and TUD levels 4–5, as well as features 1, 5, and 8.

d. Partial vessel.

Table 2.4.
Attributes of Shell-Tempered Jar Rims, South of Conference Building

	Zone I		Zone II		Zone III		Total	
	(*N*)	(%)	(*N*)	(%)	(*N*)	(%)	(*N*)	(%)
Basic shape								
Standard jar	10	83.3	20	74.1	1	50.0	31	75.6
Neckless jar	2	16.7	7	25.9	1	50.0	10	24.4
Secondary shape feature								
Unmodified rim	7	58.3	8	29.6	0	0.0	15	36.6
Folded rim	2	16.7	11	40.7	1	50.0	14	34.1
Folded-flattened rim	3	25.0	8	29.6	1	50.0	12	29.3

Note: All but one of the descriptive terms used here are defined by Steponaitis (1983a:47–78); the exception is "unmodified rim," which refers to unthickened jar rims, that is, ones that are neither folded nor folded-flattened. For the correlation between stratigraphic zones and excavated levels, see notes to table 2.3.

The four dates obtained from this excavation are generally consistent with the pottery (Scarry 1986: table 5.11). One radiocarbon assay from the base of Zone II yielded an uncorrected age of 875 ± 80, or AD 1075, a bit on the early side but not unreasonably so, given the standard error. Three archaeomagnetic dates from hearths in Zone III fell within a range from AD 1120 TO 1230.

SOUTH OF MOUND I. A single 2 × 2-meter unit was opened south of Mound I, approximately 30 meters inside the presumed location of Moundville's palisade (Scarry 1981a, 1986:161). The cultural deposits were about a meter deep but not as rich in domestic refuse as those north of Mound R or south of the Conference Building. Among the features encountered were a hearth, a wall trench, and a line of postholes, clearly indicating that houses stood here. The entire deposit was excavated in arbitrary 10-centimeter levels, and no clear stratification was observed.

For present purposes, we can treat the pottery from the various levels as a single assemblage (table 2.5). Leaving aside the few grog-tempered and sand-tempered sherds from earlier components, all the shell-tempered diagnostics point to an occupation during the Moundville I phase, possibly lasting into early Moundville II. Rim modes can be used to refine this estimate even further (table 2.6). The

Table 2.5.
Ceramic Assemblage, South of Mound I

Type, Variety	All Levels[a]
Shell-tempered	
Bell Plain, *Hale*	63
Mississippi Plain, *Hull Lake*	5
Mississippi Plain, *Warrior*	466
Carthage Incised, *unspecified*	2
Moundville Incised, *Moundville*	9
Moundville Incised, *unspecified*	1
Grog-tempered	
Baytown Plain, *Roper*	3
Sand-tempered	
Baldwin Plain, *unspecified*	3
Total	552

a. Includes TUB levels 1–10.

very low percentage of neckless jars and the complete absence of folded-flattened rims suggests that this occupation began in late Moundville I times. All in all, this area seems to have been inhabited sometime between AD 1150 and 1300, with no hint of anything later.

WEST OF MOUND N. A single 1 × 1-meter test unit was excavated about 130 meters west-southwest of Mound N, in an area thought to be near the palisade (Scarry 1980:11–12; also see Scarry 1986: fig. 5.6). The cultural deposits here were about 45 centimeters deep and contained a relatively low density of artifacts.

The recovered sherds, though sparse, again seem to indicate an early occupation (table 2.7). All the diagnostics in this small assemblage are consistent with the Moundville I or early Moundville II phase.

AMNH Riverbank Excavation (1991–1992)

The most recent midden excavations took place in the winter of 1991 and 1992 and were located on the terrace edge near the Conference Building in the northwest portion of the site (chap. 4). The work was done in advance of a riverbank stabilization project, which ultimately destroyed much of this locality. Some 1,825 square meters were manually or mechanically stripped and mapped, and the exposed features were

Table 2.6.
Attributes of Shell-Tempered Jar Rims, South of Mound I

	All Levels	
	(*N*)	(%)
Basic shape		
Standard jar	20	95.2
Neckless jar	1	4.8
Secondary shape feature		
Unmodified rim	12	57.1
Folded rim	9	42.9
Folded-flattened rim	0	0.0

Note: All but one of the descriptive terms used here are defined by Steponaitis (1983a:47–78); the exception is "unmodified rim," which refers to unthickened jar rims, that is, ones that are neither folded nor folded-flattened. These counts include TUB levels 1–10.

Table 2.7.
Ceramic Assemblage, West of Mound N

Type, Variety	All Levels[a]
Shell-tempered	
Bell Plain, *Hale*	3
Mississippi Plain, *Warrior*	42
Moundville Engraved, *Havana*	1
Moundville Engraved, *unspecified*	2
Moundville Incised, *Moundville*	2
Moundville Incised, *unspecified*	1
Unclassified	1
Total	52

a. Includes TUE levels 1–6.

excavated. The area was found to contain some 16 house patterns, a segment of the palisade showing several episodes of rebuilding, a variety of shallow pits, and a few burials. All the structures and virtually all the refuse dated to Moundville I and the very beginning of Moundville II; the only significant later features were a number of intrusive burials from Moundville II or III times. As we shall soon see, this pattern of superposition nicely reflects Moundville's history in microcosm.

Discussion

All told, the various off-mound excavations undertaken over the last 60 years have yielded surprisingly consistent results. In every case, the greatest bulk of the midden encountered dated to Moundville I or (perhaps) early Moundville II times. The only places that yielded significant later deposits were portions of the Roadway and the locality north of Mound R.

Indeed, judging from the excavations just considered, some of the deepest and richest middens formed along the northern edge of the site, closest to the Black Warrior River. This area was clearly a major focus of settlement during the Moundville I phase, and it continued being used, albeit more sporadically, in later phases as well. The Roadway excavations, located farther south and away from the river, also encountered many middens. Moundville I sherds were found throughout these excavations, but Moundville II and III sherds were principally concentrated in two locations: west of Mound P and east of Mound S (Welch 1989:6).

CHRONOLOGICAL DISTRIBUTION OF BURIALS

Having just reviewed the chronology of Moundville's middens, let us now turn to another important source of information on Moundville's population history, the temporal distribution of burials. Moundville's many excavations since the turn of the century have yielded data on more than 2,000 burials, found virtually everywhere across the site (Moore 1905, 1907; Peebles 1971, 1979). Many of these burials contained grave offerings, such as pottery, beads, celts, and other implements.

Since 1978, I have been able to date many of these burials based on the associated pottery (for a description of the method, see Steponaitis 1983a:133–149). As of this writing, 505 burials can be placed within temporal spans consisting of one or two adjacent phases. If we partition the burials that span two phases equally between them, then we arrive at a corrected estimate for each phase (table 2.8). These estimates suggest that only about 7 percent of the burials were interred during Moundville I, 38 percent during Moundville II, 53 percent during Moundville III, and less than 2 percent during Moundville IV. It should be noted, incidentally, that the complete absence of burials during the West Jefferson phase may be more apparent than real, since burials of

Table 2.8.
Chronological Distribution of Dated Burials at Moundville

Phase	Length of Phase (years)	One- or Two-Phase Spans[a] (*N*)	One- or Two-Phase Spans[a] (%)	Estimates for Single Phases[b] (*N*)	Estimates for Single Phases[b] (%)	Estimated Rate of Deposition (burials/year)
Moundville IV	100	2	0.4	9.5	1.9	9.5
Moundville III–IV	250	15	3.0			
Moundville III	150	149	29.5	267.5	53.2	1.78
Moundville II–III	300	222	44.0			
Moundville II	150	59	11.7	190.5	37.7	1.27
Moundville I–II	350	41	8.1			
Moundville I	200	17	3.4	37.5	7.4	0.19
West Jefferson	150	0	0.0	0.0	0.0	0.00

a. Includes all burials that can be dated to a one- or two-phase span by direct association with diagnostic pottery; individuals within multiple interments are counted separately. Rows designated by a range spanning two phases include burials that date within that range but cannot be placed more precisely.

b. Single-phase estimates based on the data at left. Burials that span two phases are divided equally between the two.

this period generally do not contain pots as grave accompaniments (Jenkins and Ensor 1981; Ensor 1979; Welch 1990).

There are, of course, other ways of arriving at such phase-specific estimates. One could, for example, rely only on the burials that can be dated to single phases; one could also divide the chronologically ambiguous burials proportionally rather than equally between the phases to which they might date. Yet no matter which method one chooses, all estimates point to the same, inescapable conclusion: The vast majority of burials at Moundville—something on the order of 90 percent—date to the Moundville II and III phases. Even if all the borderline cases were assigned to Moundville I, the total for this phase would not exceed 13 percent.

Correcting for differences in phase duration (table 2.8), we see that the rate at which burials were deposited increased 670 percent between Moundville I and Moundville II and another 40 percent between Moundville II and Moundville III, after which it declined precipitously.

MOUNDVILLE'S POPULATION HISTORY: SYNTHESIS AND SPECULATIONS

It now remains to construct a plausible interpretation of Moundville's population history by reconciling the two, seemingly contradictory patterns we have observed: most of the middens are early, but most of the burials are late (fig. 2.2). The question is, What do these patterns mean?

The simplest and most plausible explanation for the midden pattern is that Moundville's resident population peaked early in the sequence, during the Moundville I phase, and declined substantially thereafter. Recent data suggest that most of the mounds were constructed during the late Moundville I or early Moundville II phase (AD 1200–1300) (Knight 1989, 1992; Welch 1989). The decline in population seems to have occurred just after this period of mound construction, when Moundville established itself as a major regional center (cf. Steponaitis 1992). Prior to this change, Moundville probably contained a cross-section of the region's inhabitants, including many commoners as well as the elite. After AD 1300, however, it is reasonable to suppose that the inhabitants were mostly elite: high-ranking families together with some retainers and assorted functionaries. The Moundville of AD 1300–1500 was not strictly speaking a vacant ceremonial center, but

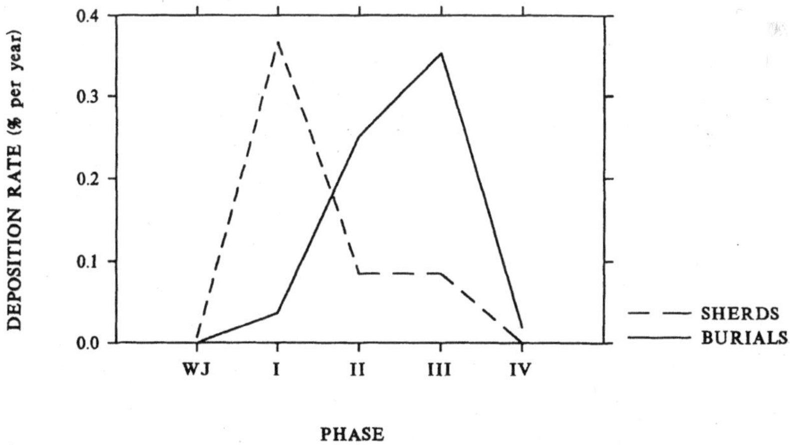

Fig. 2.2. The deposition rates of sherds and burials at Moundville. Data are taken from tables 2.2 and 2.8; to facilitate comparison, deposition rates have been reexpressed in units of percent per year.

neither was it a densely settled town. Rather, it contained a modest resident population that probably fluctuated through time with the vicissitudes of politics and the demographic fortunes of particular kin groups connected with the mounds (chap. 3). Whatever the case, by circa AD 1550 Moundville was virtually abandoned as a settlement. The few Moundville IV sherds that occur suggest an ephemeral occupation, perhaps nothing more than occasional visits to a sacred place that had formerly been a political and religious center of a major chiefdom.

Yet if middens are the best index of Moundville's population, then how do we interpret the great increase in burials that occurred during Moundville II and III, when the number of residents declined? The only good explanation is that most of the people interred at Moundville after AD 1300 did not actually live there. Moundville was, after all, not only a political capital but also a ritual center. In this light, it is not at all difficult to imagine that people from outlying communities may have been brought to Moundville for burial. Indeed, the cemeteries at Moundville are the only ones known in the Black Warrior Valley for the period between AD 1050 and 1450. The two other cemeteries that have thus far been discovered in the valley date to the Moundville III phase, close to the time when Moundville was abandoned (chap. 7; DeJarnette and Peebles 1970; Welch 1991).

There are other possible explanations for the observed pattern, but none is as convincing. For example, one alternative is that the paucity of Moundville II–III midden reflects a change in refuse-disposal practices. Although Moundville I refuse may have accumulated around residential precincts, Moundville II–III refuse may have been collected and dumped into the ravines and river along the northern edge of the site (Peebles 1978:381). The idea is interesting, but there is no compelling reason to believe it is true. For one thing, Moundville II–III middens do exist on the site, even in places far from the riverbank. Indeed, some of the richest and deepest Moundville III middens are those on the flanks of mounds (e.g., Knight 1992; cf. Smith and Williams 1994:30). If any refuse were given special treatment, one would think it would be that associated with these sacred structures. The fact that mound-related trash accumulated where it was dropped argues strongly against any major movement of refuse.

One might also argue that the lack of Moundville I burials is an archaeological illusion, caused by proportionally fewer burials of this phase having datable pots as grave goods. This proposition can be evaluated by examining the abundance of vessels in single-component cemeteries at outlying sites. The two known outlying cemeteries in the Black Warrior Valley—Snows Bend (DeJarnette and Peebles 1970) and White (Welch 1991)—both date to Moundville III. These sites yielded a total of 75 burials, 43 percent of which included pottery. Although no outlying Moundville I cemeteries have yet been found in the Black Warrior Valley proper, three Moundville-related cemeteries of this age have been excavated in the Tombigbee Valley nearby (Atkinson et al. 1980; Jenkins and Ensor 1981; O'Hear et al. 1981); here, 56 burials were uncovered, of which 32 percent contained pottery. The early cemeteries do have a slightly lower percentage of burials with pots, but the difference is so small that it cannot account for the dramatic patterns observed at Moundville.

Finally, we must consider the possibility that the observed patterns are simply the result of sampling error. Because Moundville has never been thoroughly investigated with any sort of probabilistic or systematic design, the biases in our existing sample are admittedly hard to gauge. It may be, for example, that past excavators missed major concentrations of Moundville I burials or major deposits of Moundville II–III midden. Yet there are several factors that make this explanation seem unlikely. First, there has been no deliberate bias toward recovery of early middens or late burials; indeed, all but the most recent excavations took place before the current chronology was worked out. Second, the fact that the chronological trends for burials and middens run in opposite directions argues against our simply having missed one or another phase entirely. Third, the magnitude of the differences in those trends is so great that it is hard to imagine how sampling error alone could account for them. All in all, I see no credible alternative to the historical scenario I have proposed.

Up until now, we have considered only the relative size of Moundville's population at different points in time. The question remains, can we also say anything about its absolute size? I can answer this question only by indulging in speculation, loosely constrained by the few bits of evidence that exist.

The first way of approaching this problem is to work backward through time. If my scenario is correct, Moundville was inhabited during its later phases (Moundville II and III) by a contingent of elite families, religious functionaries, and their retainers. All these individuals were presumably linked to particular mounds or sets of mounds, which were maintained by corporate subclans or cult institutions (see chap. 3 and Knight 1986, 1990). Let us assume that on the average 20 individuals were associated with each of the principal mounds; some may have lived on the mounds, while others may have lived nearby. We know that at least 4 of the mounds at the site (I, J, K, and X) were not used much, if at all, after Moundville I times (Knight 1989; Steponaitis 1992). Let us also exclude from our estimate Mound V, which is probably an extension of Mound B, as well as the low outliers that probably are associated with major mounds of the plaza-periphery group. If we assume that the 15 remaining mounds were all used simultaneously during Moundville's later history (almost certainly an unrealistic assumption), we arrive at an estimated population of 300 individuals for the Moundville II and III phases. Recalling that the estimated sherd-deposition rate in the Roadway excavation was four times greater before AD 1250 than after (table 2.2), we can plausibly assume that the earlier population was also four times greater. This reasoning yields an estimate of 1,200 residents for the Moundville I phase.

Alternatively, one can derive an estimate using data on house densities and total habitable area. At present, the only large exposure at Moundville with houses that can be accurately dated is the Riverbank excavation. There, a total of 16 house patterns were uncovered in an area of 0.1825 hectare. (This count includes structures 1 through 6 in the PA tract and structures 1 through 6 in the ECB tract, described by Scarry in chapter 4. Among the latter, Structure 5 was rebuilt twice and Structure 6 was rebuilt four times, yielding a total of 16 discrete patterns.) Many of these house patterns overlapped, and all dated to the 250-year interval between AD 1050 and 1300 (chap. 4). If we assume that a wooden-post house lasted an average of 10 years (cf. Warrick 1988), then the average density of contemporaneous houses can be calculated as $D = NL/AT$, where D is the average density of houses at any time, N is the number of house patterns observed, A is the area excavated, T is the duration of the interval over which the houses were occupied, and L is the average longevity of a house. Using the Riverbank figures just cited, the formula yields an estimated average density of 3.5 contemporaneous houses per hectare. Assuming 5–8 people per house (chap. 4), this household density translates into an average of 17.5–28 persons per hectare. If one excludes the mounds and the plaza, the total habitable area within and immediately around the palisade is about 60 hectares. Extrapolating from the Riverbank to the entire site thus produces an overall population estimate for the Moundville I phase of 1,050–1,680 residents.

Although the two estimates just derived for Moundville's peak population are consistent with each other and are of the same order of magnitude as the previously cited estimate of 3,000, we have every reason to be suspicious, if not downright skeptical, of all these numbers. We still know very little about the distribution of residential areas at Moundville, the longevity of houses, or, for that matter, the numbers of people associated with houses or mounds. Indeed, the little we do know suggests that areas along the river were among the longest and most heavily occupied portions of the site; if so, then extrapolating from the Riverbank to the site as a whole is bound to yield estimates that are too high. What we can say is this: Moundville may have had a population, early in its history, of 1,000–1,700 people. But the underlying calculations entail some tenuous assumptions, which if wrong would probably tend to inflate the results. Frankly, I would be very surprised if Moundville's permanent residents much exceeded 1,000, even during Moundville I times.

Whatever the case, much more in the way of excavations and collections research needs to be done before Moundville's population history is well understood. My hope is that the evidence and hypotheses presented here will serve as a useful baseline from which this future work can proceed.

ACKNOWLEDGMENTS

I wish to acknowledge with thanks the help of Jim Knight and the other contributors to this volume, without whose puzzled looks, probing questions, shared insights, and substantive corrections the ideas in this chapter might never have made it this far.

3. Moundville as a Diagrammatic Ceremonial Center

VERNON JAMES KNIGHT JR.

SOME ETHNOGRAPHICALLY DOCUMENTED ceremonial centers have spatial layouts that are diagrammatic of basic aspects of social organization. The Moundville site shows regularities in its layout that suggest that its plan is a sociogram. An analogy for interpreting these spatial regularities comes from an ethnographic account collected by Frank Speck concerning spatial relationships among Chickasaw corporate kin groups in a ceremonial context.

The Moundville site appears to have a greater degree of formality in its architectural layout than is seen at many other large Mississippian mound centers. Although much is still to be learned about the public architecture at Moundville, various symmetries and polarities are easily perceptible. A review of these regularities in this chapter will provide grounds to claim that Moundville's formal layout is that of a diagrammatic ceremonial center. Moreover, I hope to show that an ethnographic analogy can be applied to the case in order to invest these patterns with meaning.

I take as my starting point the generalization that "site plans act as communicative or mnemonic devices expressing or reaffirming through symbolic associations relations between groups, or positions held by individuals within a culture's framework" (Lawrence and Low 1990:466). Such a process works at different levels of specificity. Certain ceremonial centers, in fact, seem to owe their elementary spatial layout to a sort of chart or map of important social distinctions, perhaps grafted to a cosmological plan.[1] These may be called diagrammatic ceremonial centers. We can define them more exactly as central places in traditional societies in which the layout of public architecture or monuments calls deliberate attention to key social and cosmological distinctions, in a maplike manner.[2] A key word here is "deliberate," for this is a special case, apparently neglected in the theoretical literature on the built environment, where social relations are not merely imprinted on the landscape but where political forces actively create the site plan on monumental scales.

SUBTERFUGES IN THE IDIOM OF SPATIAL FORM

Before proceeding to the case at hand, I wish to call attention to a theoretical issue, taken from the ethnography of spatial form, as follows: Even though social structure and community space may, so to speak, share the same coordinate system, there are good reasons to doubt that the spatial idiom gives a necessarily accurate reading of social reality, particularly where community space can be manipulated by interest groups.

A convenient illustration of this principle is offered by Lévi-Strauss (1963:132–163), who pioneered the structural analysis of traditional village plans with his comparison of Winnebago, Trobriand, Bororo, and Eastern Timbara village layouts. His often-cited Bororo village offers a classic example of the use of symmetry and polarity in village layout to recreate the elementary segmentations of social organization in a tribal society, in a very maplike manner. Lévi-Strauss develops the terms "diametric dualism" and "concentric dualism" to analyze this and comparable cases. In the Bororo village we see a central men's house and dance platform contrasted against a concentric ring of houses arranged by clan. Superimposed on this are the diametric dualisms of a moiety organization and a more obscure upstream versus downstream distinction that runs perpendicular to the former. All would seem tidy and satisfying, a case where one might simply read the main contrasts of Bororo social structure directly from the settlement structure. But Lévi-Strauss emphatically denies this possibility. He says that the spatial layout is an utter misrepresentation of the empirical social structure. In the first place the clans are ranked, and in the second, marriage is partly regulated by the existence of three, not two, endogamous marriage classes.

These, he says, are features that are actually masked or disguised—even contradicted—by the concentric arrangement.

Lévi-Strauss exposes here a profound quandary: the social elements that are objectified in community space by diametric and concentric dualisms, despite the allusion to balance, can in actuality be radically out of balance. These same social elements are referred to in other contexts using terms such as "superior" versus "inferior," "elder" versus "younger," "noble" versus "commoner," or "strong" versus "weak" (Lévi-Strauss 1963:139). Such "logical subterfuges," as Lévi-Strauss calls them, lead him to question the whole theory of dual organization.

The reasons for this apparent masking and obfuscation in spatial orders are not difficult to discern. Space is limited to three dimensions. Spatial orders can project only a limited number of symbolic discriminations and still remain orderly, uncluttered, and coherent. But the social hosts that make use of these spaces are organized, in contrast, by complex overlays of statuses and roles that typify social structure, symbolically expressed in manifold ways. The implications of this for our problem are clear. No matter how obvious and redolent the patterning is (contra Hodder 1986), in the absence of an ethnographic anchorage there can never be any straightforward way to read social organization from its spatial objectifications at a prehistoric ceremonial center. Consider the testimony of a distinguished symbolic anthropologist: "As Dumont has powerfully argued for the case of India, the organization of thought and social relations is imprinted on the landscape. But, if only the physical aspect is susceptible of study, how to interpret this pattern would seem to pose an insoluble problem" (Douglas 1972:521). We must expect a priori that the architectonics of centers must bear the load of multiple referents (not necessarily logically compatible) and flexible uses.

If we accept the principle that formal spatial arrangements tend to ignore certain elementary social orders and distinctions in favor of others, we must also ponder what it must mean to monumentalize these condensed and arbitrary representations of social reality. What does it mean to magnify them, to fossilize them permanently on the domestic and ceremonial landscape? Can these representations be manipulated in nontraditional ways by an interest group?

If we decide, together with Kus (1981:212, 1982:54), that spatial representations of social forms can be consciously exploited, then it seems fair to suggest that the creation of diagrammatic ceremonial centers is, in part, a political effort to insure the intergenerational stability of a particular, arbitrary vision of social reality. The dimensions of that reality—its hierarchies, levels, oppositions, contrasts, and polarities—once designated and monumentalized in public architecture, from that point onward contribute to the recreation of that reality, as people participate in the center as a part of their social environment. Thus Lawrence and Low (1990:471, citing the work of Hillier and Hanson), speak of how "Built forms not only express but direct and shape social processes concerned with stability and controlling behavior." As Harré observes, "The very fact of order, when recognized by human beings, is, in itself, the source of a message that all is well. Orderliness of the physical environment broadcasts a kind of continuous social Muzak whose message is reassurance" (1978:144).

In acknowledging this potential for political exploitation, however, we also have to recognize that the built environment can become an arena for resistance to domination (Smith and David 1995). From this point of view, spatial meanings are in fact negotiated over the long term. I prefer to view the progressive abandonment of mounds in Moundville's later history (chap. 1) as just such a struggle between political domination and resistance.

ARCHITECTURAL PATTERNING AT THE MOUNDVILLE SITE

Twenty-nine mounds are present at the Moundville site within an occupied area of about 75 hectares (fig. 1.1; see chap. 1). The mound arrangement has a compact appearance, and with its orderly rows of mounds defining its central plaza, this compactness gives Moundville a striking visual aspect that is often remarked upon. Fifteen prominent mounds on four sides define a unitary central plaza roughly in the shape of a parallelogram, as suggested in figure 3.1, with the east and west boundaries canted slightly to the northwest.[3] For convenience of discussion I shall refer to these mounds as the plaza-periphery group.

What is known to date about the plaza comes from limited test pitting, controlled surface collection, and auger testing. The preliminary impression is that of a well-defined and bounded space essentially sterile of cultural deposits, with margins somewhat interior to the plaza-periphery mounds that border it. The existence of two small mounds, S and T, at or near the plaza boundaries, plus an apparent sweathouse and other nonmounded buildings excavated on the plaza's southern edge just north of Mound L (Peebles 1983:190–191), leaves little doubt that

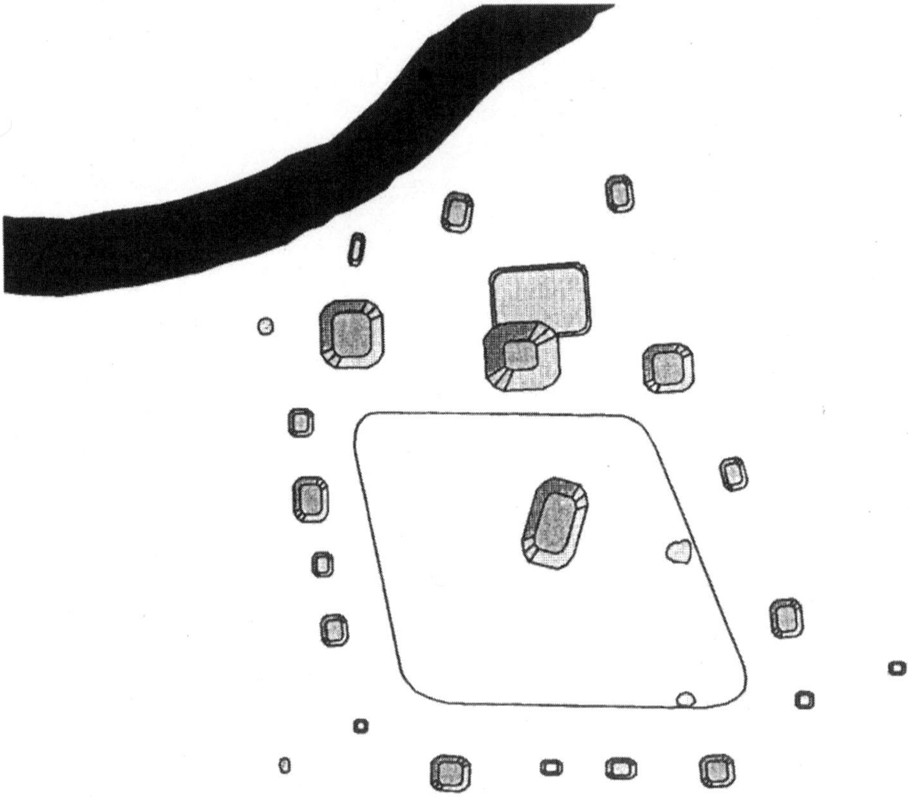

Fig. 3.1. Approximate plaza outline.

there is a band of architecture surrounding the plaza margins just interior to the plaza-periphery mound group.

Two mounds appear to have a literally central importance to the architecture of the site. Mound A, the second largest mound of the group by volume, lies in the center of the plaza. It is the obvious axis of the whole arrangement, the apparent center of gravity of the group.[4] Why Mound A was built on a ground plan askew from that of the rest of the group is not known, but it might be significant that Mound A's orientation and ramp are aligned with minor mound B1. Opposite

Mound A on the north plaza margin lies Mound B, by far the most imposing of the mounds at Moundville.[5] Mound B appears to lack burials, and although its proportions are unique it is probably best thought of as the functional equivalent of the elite residential mounds of the plaza-periphery group.

In the overall layout one may see an obvious bilateral symmetry, defined by a canted line bisecting mounds A and B and neatly dividing the southern tier of mounds between mounds J and K (fig. 3.2). Christopher Peebles, commenting on this symmetry, states that "the arrangement of mounds, buildings, artifact distributions, and burials [of] one half [is] virtually a mirror image of the other." This, he suggests, is strong evidence of a planned community with an underlying symmetrical structure of spaces and activities (1983:190). Peebles recognizes additional elements in the spatial patterning of public architecture. First, in the plaza-periphery group there is an alternation of small and large mounds around the plaza. These two size classes of mounds had different uses. The small ones, highlighted in figure 3.2, contain high-status burials, sacrificial skull interments, decapitated skeletons, and infant burials. They are probably temple mounds. The larger ones lack burials and were presumably residential substructures (1971:82; 1983:190). Second, particular mounds appear to be paired with their mirror-image counterparts on the opposite side of the plaza. Thus, residential Mound E is the image of Mound R, mortuary Mound F is the image of Mound Q, Mound G is the image of Mound P, and so forth. Peebles sees a significance in the alignment of these pairings across the plaza, suggesting that they follow the line of the winter solstice (1971:82).[6] These observations on the uses of the mounds draw heavily on the investigations reported by Clarence B. Moore in "Certain Aboriginal Remains of the Black Warrior River" (1905) and "Moundville Revisited" (1907). This is necessarily the case, because mound investigations at Moundville more recent than Moore's have been rare and limited in scope. Moore himself does not discuss the alternation of larger mounds not having burials with smaller ones having burials, but a close reading reveals that he was certainly aware of the distinction (Moore 1905:199),[7] presumably declining comment because of his customary reluctance to generalize.

Based on the evidence of Depression-era excavation records, Peebles also suggests that this same bilateral symmetry is revealed in other domains, including the spatial distribution of effigy vessels and pigments of certain colors (Peebles 1971:83, 1983:190). The present availability of better chronological controls, plus recourse to the orig-

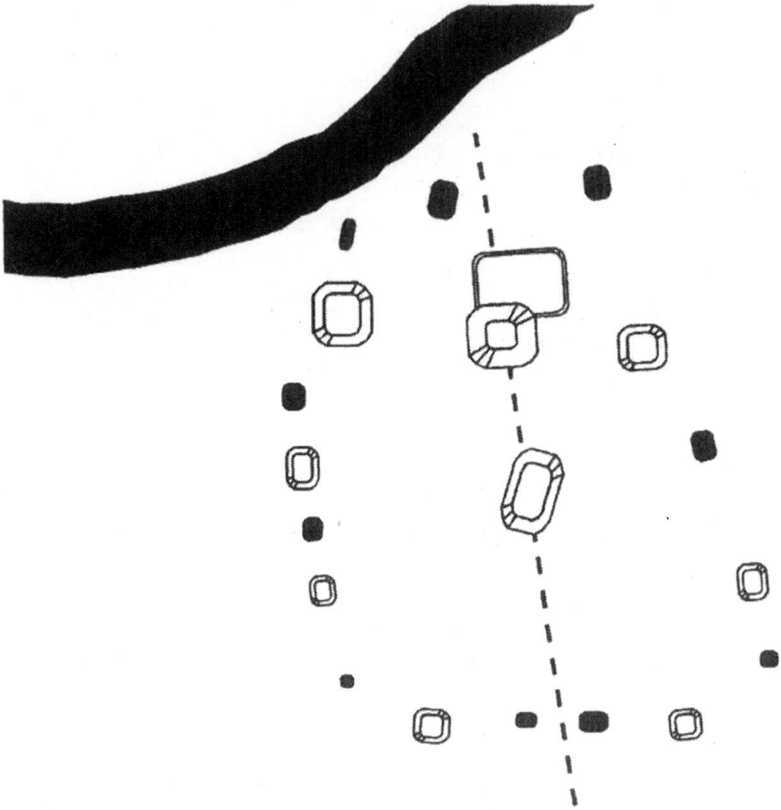

Fig. 3.2. Bilateral symmetry of the plaza-periphery group. Mounds containing burials are darkened, showing alternation and pairing with larger mounds without burials. Minor mounds omitted for clarity.

inal collections, will allow a more rigorous exploration of these intriguing patterns.

Along with the evidence for an underlying east-west bilateral symmetry, there is evidence for an underlying north-south polarity. The larger mounds of the plaza-periphery group are found in the northern section of the site. High-status burials also tend to be found in the northern section. Nonmounded public architecture is documented near the northeast and northwest margins of the plaza, and the two mounds yielding the most richly endowed burials, C and D, are also the northernmost mounds at the site. Peebles summarizes this as a structured utilization of "status space" (1971:83, 87; 1978:381), generally degrading from north to south.

In support of the idea that there is an order to be seen in the mound arrangement, it is instructive to compare mound volumes as one progresses around the plaza (fig. 3.3). The volumes of the alternating mounds without burials decrease in perfect regularity as one moves around the plaza either clockwise or counterclockwise from center north, beginning with Mound B at center. Moreover the intermediate mounds with burials in every case have volumes smaller than either of the mounds bracketing them. If size equates in some way with importance, these observations sustain both the notion of bilateral symmetry and the independently confirmed position of the north end of the site as the high-status pole in a ranked delineation of status space.

Returning to the phenomenon of a patterned distribution of mortuary versus elite residential mounds in the plaza-periphery group, I propose that there is more to the pattern than a regular alternation. In my reading of this phenomenon, each elite residential mound is paired with at least one adjacent mound showing a mortuary use. This sug-

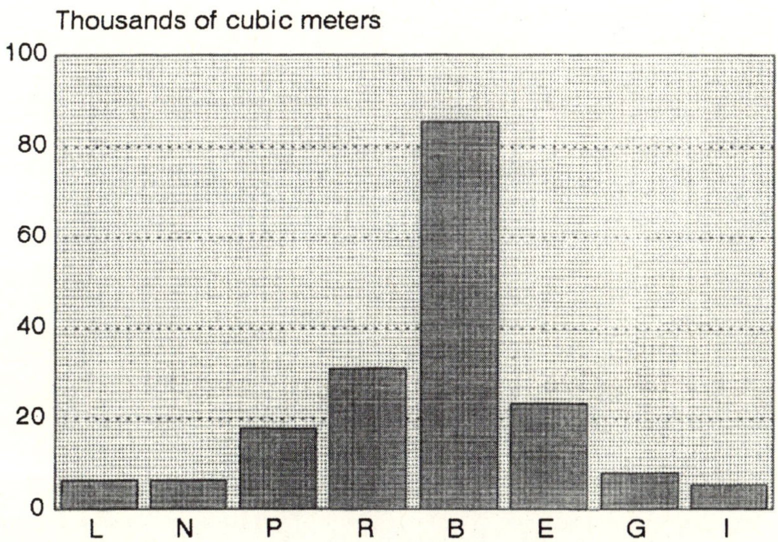

Fig. 3.3. Volume of plaza-periphery mounds not containing burials, showing regular size decrease clockwise and counter-clockwise from Mound B on the center axis. Volume data are from estimates made by Walter B. Jones in the 1930s.

gests that the basic building block of the Moundville mound group, so often repeated throughout the Mississippian sphere, is the functional pairing of a noble residence with an ancestral mortuary temple. It seems reasonable to suppose that each such pair at Moundville is an architectural manifestation of one of the primary corporate segments of the Moundville community.

These propositions, of course, assume that Peebles is correct in thinking that there is evidence at Moundville for a coherent, underlying town plan. The idea that these various symmetries and polarities in the layout of public architecture at Moundville are real and indicative of a cognized order absolutely depends on a demonstration of the contemporaneity of this architecture at some point in Moundville's development. That argument is both complicated and frankly premature pending a full published account of the evidence, but it is necessary for the present to state the following preliminary indications: first, that the full mound and plaza arrangement was in contemporaneous use during a time interval that I would estimate as being roughly AD 1250–1300, coincident with the maximum residential population of the site and with the existence of its palisade; second, that the mortuary temple architecture on mound summits fell entirely out of use by at least AD 1400 and perhaps earlier; finally, that entire groups of mounds were abandoned by about AD 1400 and that others had only ephemeral use from that point to the sixteenth century (i.e., the late Moundville III phase), by which time the use of the mounds by elites was very spotty across the site.[8]

Thus, the formal allocation of architectural space around the plaza early in the history of the Moundville community may have been guided by a ranking of important corporate segments within that community. But if the architectural space on the plaza margins was formally segmented, there is unfortunately no evidence to tell us exactly how these segments were configured. Using possible mound pairings as a guide, there are several conceivable solutions. Figure 3.4 illustrates one of these and is offered here without any particular assurance of its correctness. Nonetheless it will serve to show that the layout is comprehensible in these terms. The rankings are indicated by number relative to Mound B and correspond to the relative mound volumes given in figure 3.3.

This highly conjectural drawing may be used to illustrate three further points. First, any such reconstruction must be based on the known public architecture of the site—in this case emphasizing the architecture that happens to be marked by mounds. But we already know that there is additional public architecture that is not mounded, so far encountered

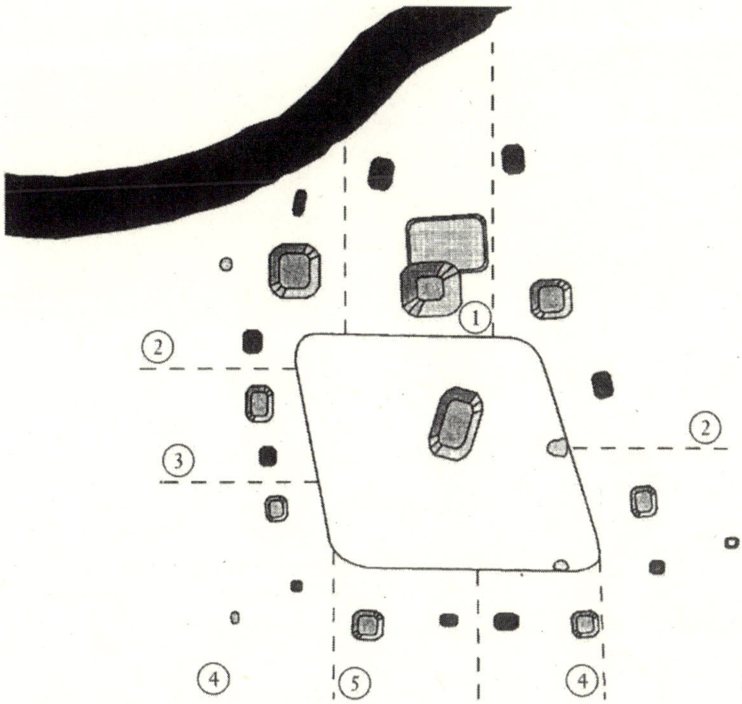

Fig. 3.4. A hypothetical segmentation of social and architectural space. Numbers represent rank ordering with respect to Mound B.

in various discontinuous off-mound excavations during the Depression era (Peebles 1983:190–191). There is no way of knowing what fraction of the total configuration of public architecture this represents. There is every reason to think that a knowledge of the full range and spatial arrangement of these public buildings would result in a different picture. Second, the mounds may not be strictly paired, in the sense that certain of the elite residential mounds, perhaps the most important among them, may have had more than one subsidiary mound associated with them. In figure 3.4, I have depicted residential mounds R and E as each associated with more than one subsidiary mound, and there is also evidence for nonmounded public architecture in the near vicinity of these major mounds. A functional differentiation of this auxiliary, special-purpose architecture might be expected in such cases. Third, the illustration also emphasizes that the proposed mound pairs may have been tied to broader residential segments of the community, also distributed according to a segmentary principle.

AN ETHNOGRAPHIC ANALOGY

It may be confidently assumed that Mississippian mounds and mound clusters were corporate facilities (Knight 1981). That is, each monument was within the dominion of some definite corporate group. Which leads to the following question: What kind of corporate groups were these?

To provide an answer I appeal to an ethnographic analogy. In 1904 a young Frank Speck, under the influence of Franz Boas as a Columbia graduate student, was sent to Oklahoma Territory, whence he returned with a diagram, reproduced here as figure 3.5.[9] It was obtained from a Chickasaw informant named Ca'bi'tci, and it purports to show the formal arrangement of named house groups (corporate subclans)[10] in a "camp square," which was a temporary field encampment of an otherwise dispersed community, convened for the purpose of holding an important council (Speck 1907). It shows the subclans arranged by rank around a rectilinear space, divided bilaterally according to the well-known dual organization, and centered on a council fire symbolized in the Chickasaw manner by a cross-in-circle motif. The north-south dividing line between the two divisions is in this case a creek, but was sometimes an imaginary line.

Clans in the Native Southeast were formally ranked, and the ranking of the subclans is manifested here by a spatial order: the highest ranking subclans in each division were assigned positions on the north-central axis, while the remaining subclans were arrayed by descending rank both clockwise and counterclockwise around the margins of the camp square. If the analogy can be supported, we can propose that the corporate segments putatively arrayed around the perimeter of Moundville's plaza were ranked kin groups and, more specifically, corporate subclans manifesting a dual organization.

In evaluating this analogy, I will employ three criteria: its goodness of fit, its relevance, and its generative quality, that is, to what degree it may yield new and unanticipated insights (cf. Wylie 1985:96–105).

Goodness of Fit

Moundville's layout and Ca'bi'tci's diagram share (a) a rectangular plaza, (b) bilateral symmetry on a north-south axis, (c) a center reference point of apparent ceremonial importance, (d) arrangement of basic community segments by rank around the plaza, and (e) a ranking of these segments both clockwise and counterclockwise starting from a position at

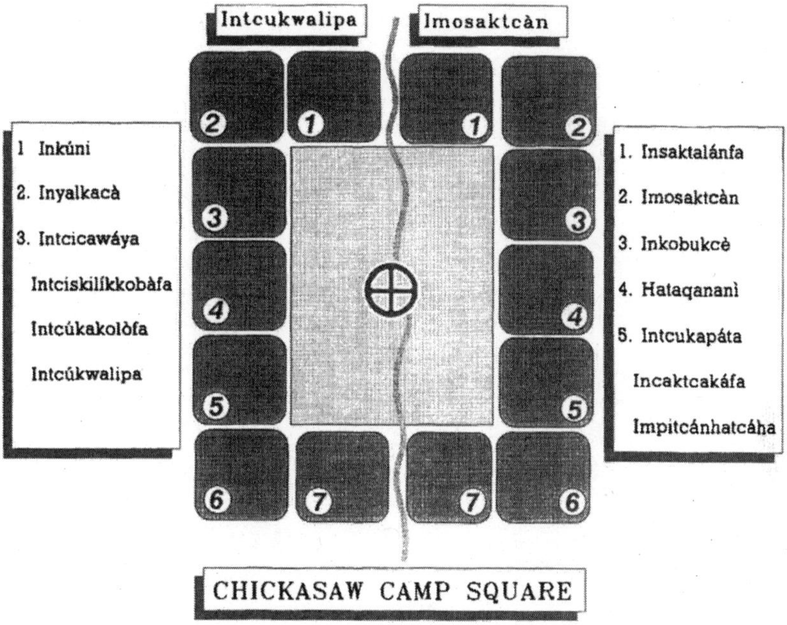

Fig. 3.5. Diagram of a Chickasaw camp square, according to Ca'bi'tci, an informant of Frank G. Speck (Speck 1907). The ranking of house groups (subclans) is shown in the margin. The cross-in-circle motif represents a council fire. The relative rank of the house groups without a number is not specified.

center north. Ca'bi'tci's plan is a projection in a spatial idiom of certain fundamental social distinctions in one Chickasaw community, emphasizing the relative rank of hereditary kin segments. A literal application to Moundville would allow us to interpret the mound pairs around the plaza as marking ranked, corporate subclans of the Moundville community, a form of organization I have already argued is appropriate for a Mississippian context (Knight 1990).

One important mismatch between the two contexts is the central placement of Mound B at Moundville, the most prominent mound of the plaza-periphery group, directly on the site axis. The highest ranking house groups in Ca'bi'tci's schema, in contrast, are located to one side or the other of the central axis. The possible significance of this anomaly will be discussed presently.

Relevance

An obvious fact about this analogy is that Native testimony recorded in 1904 is being applied to a phenomenon dating to the thirteenth century. Thus the time gap is a hefty 700 years. There can be no supportable claim that Moundville was ethnically Chickasaw, despite the Western Muskogean place-names found among towns in the Moundville area visited by De Soto's army in 1540 (Swanton 1939:51; Hudson et al. 1990:183–191).[11] Nonetheless, there are archaeological reasons for thinking that the Moundville region and the Chickasaw heartland in western Mississippi were culturally connected at least as early as the twelfth century. The material culture of the Chickasaw-area Lyon's Bluff sequence (circa AD 1100–1400) is similar to that at Moundville of corresponding age.[12] This uniformity of material culture beyond the spatial boundaries of the Moundville phase proper led Jenkins and Krause (1986:92) to include the Lyon's Bluff sequence within the broader "Moundville variant," a concept that emphasizes strong and long-standing cultural ties at a scale larger than an archaeological phase. Later protohistoric changes in material culture in the Chickasaw-area sequence also have counterparts in the Central Alabama area (Marshall 1977; Solís and Walling 1982). In sum it can be concluded that traditional cultural connections between the two adjacent regions, insofar as the archaeology reveals them, are of a strength and sufficient time depth not unfavorable to the present thesis.

Perhaps of more importance to the analogy's relevance is the slightly disturbing lack of corroboration, noted by Swanton (1928:196), of the camp-square arrangement by any other Chickasaw source. Even James Adair, who spent many years among the Chickasaw in the eighteenth century, does not mention a camp square of this sort. Moreover, Speck's informant in 1904 was obviously relating an idealized, anachronistic schema pertinent to some earlier time, perhaps even relating to events prior to the Removal in the early nineteenth century. So how shall we evaluate the credibility of this evidence?

Regarding the informant himself, little may be said. Speck does not tell us how old Ca'bi'tci (a.k.a. Josiah Mikey) was at the time of his statement. He does seem to have been something of an authority on Chickasaw myths, traditional ceremonies, and ritual practices (Speck 1913:292). But lacking more specific information on his special qualifications, it might seem prudent to dismiss Ca'bi'tci's testimony as plausibly a distorted or even fabricated item of memory culture. However, there are other lines of evidence that in the absence of direct corroboration do tend to lend credence to the account.

First, it may be readily observed that this Chickasaw camp square is very much the analog, both in its form and purpose, to the formal camp circles of the Plains tribes. Like the Chickasaw camp square, the Plains camp circles were used exclusively as models for temporary encampments; they were in the form of a sociogram, with the space around the perimeter formally allocated to clans by order of their rank; and the whole was bisected by a line marking the dual organization of clans. The only significant difference is the shape: the Chickasaw example is quadrilateral whereas the Plains examples are circular, and this basic difference mitigates against the possibility that the origin of this account lay somehow in Ca'bi'tci's potential early exposure to Plains cultural practices. Naturally Speck noticed this strong similarity, and he commented on it (1907:51). It reinforced his general view that Chickasaw culture, being the westernmost representative of the "Muskogean stock," was "something of a gradation between this and the Great Plains group" (1907:50), a view that might today find some support in the context of Plains-Southeastern comparisons of folklore and ceremonial culture (e.g., Lankford 1987:244; Hall 1989).

Second, it is not irrelevant that Chickasaw ethnography provides us with additional examples in which social distinctions were formally expressed in a spatial idiom. Reminiscent of Ca'bi'tci's schema is the layout of a Chickasaw war camp in the early eighteenth century, as described by Thomas Nairne. This war camp, like Plains camp circles, was apparently oriented to the direction of the trail being followed, judging by references to the front and back of the camp and the order in which it was set up. It featured a sacred fire in the center, and the warriors were arranged around it according to a rank principle. First were the "Chief Officers" plus their attendants, next the "other Capt[ain]s" and their attendants, whose fires formed a line "in the front" of the camp. The other warriors made their camps indiscriminately "behind" them in a crescent, and they could not encamp until after the various officers and their attendants had already established their camps and received fire by rank from the sacred fire in the center (Nairne 1988:42).[13]

In a different ritual context, the quadrilateral plan and sacred center of Ca'bi'tci's diagram are reproduced in the ceremonial ground prepared for the installation of a Fane Mingo, a special Chickasaw status of familial guardian. Again according to Nairne, this was a square ceremonial ground with an adjacent arbor, in the center of which was drawn a cross-in-circle design to signify the sun (1988:40–41).

We should ask, are there any other documented contexts in Chickasaw ethnography in which space was formally allocated specifically according to kin group rank, as in the Ca'bi'tci diagram? Champagne (1992:45), commenting on the organization of seating in a Chickasaw council square, says that "the iksas sat in the council square according to phratry and iksa rank." This statement is apparently based on Schoolcraft, who, after listing the rank order of the clans and the offices associated with them, relates the manner in which the head chief, or "king," called a council of clan chiefs to assembly. "When they convened, the king would take his seat. The runners then placed each chief in his proper place" (1851:1:311).[14]

It is difficult to evaluate whether any of the various assemblies of Chickasaw communities that occurred during the nineteenth century in Oklahoma Territory could have been organized according to a formal camp square—and therefore at a period not very remote from the time of Ca'bi'tci's account. Unfortunately Speck does not tell us the range of assemblies supposed to have been organized in this manner, but he does indicate clearly that it was a flexible model that could govern different kinds of assemblies. For example, it could be applied on two different scales. For a council of war involving a single community, the camp square would be laid out with the house groups arranged as in the diagram, with a stream serving as the boundary line between divisions. For a council held with another tribe, the layout would be retained, but with certain differences. There would be only an imaginary dividing line, and both of the divisions of the Chickasaw community would encamp on the same side of the line, while the other group encamped on the other side of the line. The camp square was said to be established halfway between the parties (Speck 1907:54).

The reference to a community war council assuredly alludes to a pre-Removal situation, but there were other post-Removal assemblies of otherwise dispersed communities that might have been organized on this model. A prime candidate would be the camp assemblies called for ball games (Graebner 1945:337). Graebner, based on WPA interviews during the 1930s, also notes the social importance of Christian camp meetings, the latter "attended by large numbers of [Native] frontier folk, who tarried as long as three weeks at the regular camp grounds which were equipped with cabins for the women and children." Speck (1907:56) noted that "at certain times during the summer, communities gather together to secure quantities of fish. . . . Such gatherings are frequently the occasions of dancing and gaming." The Chickasaws for a time may have adopted the green corn ceremony from their neighbors (see Swanton 1928:262), but the data on this subject are ambivalent. Adair does mention a possible analog, which he calls a "great solemn feast of love," apparently held by one or more towns during the spring at a camp separate from the town proper. According to Adair this lasted several days and involved dancing, feasting, and the single-pole ball game (Adair 1968:21–22).

The apparent prominence of organized camp assemblies of various sorts among the Chickasaw, during the latter nineteenth and perhaps the early twentieth centuries, leaves open the possibility that Ca'bi'tci may have been speaking as much from experience as from oral tradition. At any rate, he may not have been any farther removed from such events as, let us say, Fletcher and LeFleshe were from their subject matter in their famous ethnographic accounts of Omaha culture in the days of the buffalo hunts.

Generative Quality of the Analogy

I have mentioned previously that the one important mismatch between Ca'bi'tci's diagram and Moundville's layout is very revealing. In the Chickasaw camp square, the highest ranking subclans of each division straddle the center line on the north end of the plaza. But at Moundville, the largest elite residential mound of the plaza-periphery group, Mound B, has, in the terms of Ca'bi'tci's diagram, been taken out of the binary system entirely and moved over to a position on the central axis. I think it is reasonable to suggest that Mound B, the largest and tallest of Moundville's mounds, was the residence of the paramount and that this shift to a central position is in effect a statement setting up a diametric relationship between the paramount and the rest of the community. It can therefore be read as the inaugural substitution of a class relation, symbolically at least, for a rank relation. But here is the intriguing thing: as a statement of class opposition it conveys the impression of a subtle strategy to merge a class distinction into an old, culturally familiar order. Indeed the entire remainder of the imposed structure is not a denial but instead an affirmation of kin-based organic solidarity and reciprocity, the very antithesis of class. This says something, I suspect, about the creative strategies that emergent elites are obliged to pursue as they extol, on the one hand, the powers of a divine chief and semidivine nobles but at the same time are forced to come to accommodation with deeply rooted cultural structures governed by principles of reciprocity and balance.[15]

CONCLUSION

Diagrammatic ceremonial centers, where they occur in traditional societies, are centers in which public architecture is deliberately arranged in such a manner as to evoke and reinforce key social distinctions. The center itself constitutes a map of these distinctions, a sociogram. Commonly the pattern also incorporates a cosmological reference, investing the social dimension with a timeless and divine aspect. A functionalist argument would see diagrammatic ceremonial centers, particularly monumental ones, as devices for stabilizing societal relationships over generations.

Because of the limitations of the idiom—space—the social order that receives emphasis in these central places is an arbitrarily condensed and simplified vision of reality. Their symbolic meanings are open to manipulation by interest groups. Ethnography serves as a caution to remind us that important aspects of social organization may actually be ignored or contradicted by the spatial symbolism (cf. Lévi-Strauss 1963:132–163). These factors conspire to make it virtually impossible for an archaeologist to simply read social organization directly from the architectural arrangement. Confident archaeological interpretation of the meaning of such a center requires either a developed ethnographic context or a compelling ethnographic analogy.

I have taken the latter course, and the reader is left to judge whether or not the analogy is a compelling one. In applying it, I have tried to make my criteria and justifications plain.

I suggest that Moundville is a diagrammatic ceremonial center, in which pairs of mounds around the periphery of the plaza represent a fixed rank ordering of local kin groups and in which the placement of Mound B on the central axis reveals the paramountcy as symbolically transcending a reciprocal dual organization. By my reconstruction, at least for the brief time during which the formal plan was at the full, Moundville's planners effectively legislated the relative rank of kin segments (which formerly may well have been negotiable) by monumentalizing that ranking in a ceremonial space. It was an attempt by an emergent nobility to make a newly transformed social order tangible, inviolable, immovable, sacred.

NOTES

1. The degree to which a ceremonial center may be a sociogram, a cosmogram, or both is without doubt broadly variable, as is the degree to which it may be residential or vacant. Although this is an important topic, I cannot broach it here.
2. Modern, ethnographically informed studies of diagrammatic ceremonial centers include those of Isbell (1976) for the sixteenth-century Inca and the Desana of Columbia, DeBoer and Blitz (1991) for the Chachi of Ecuador, Dillehay (1990) for the Mapuche of Chile, and Kus (1981, 1982) for the Merina of Madagascar. Huffman (1981) has made creative use of ethnographic analogy in his interpretation of ceremonial space at prehistoric Great Zimbabwe in southern Africa, as has DeBoer (1997) in a perceptive recognition of a spatial grammar among Ohio Hopewellian earthworks. Lathrap and his colleagues (1977) use Lévi-Strauss's settlement plan of the modern Ge as their model for interpreting the plaza, central public architecture, and surrounding settlement area of Real Alto, a Valdivia ceremonial center in Ecuador. Isbell's article "Cosmological Order Expressed in Prehistoric Ceremonial Centers" (1976) is a pioneering attempt to apply ethnographic insights to interpret the spatial layout of prehistoric Chavín centers.
3. This is not the only possible interpretation. Morgan (1980:114), for example, visualizes a main plaza flanked by three subsidiary plazas. But the interpretation favored here has the advantage of both consensus and better intelligibility.
4. A more precise axial point for the site may be hypothesized as being located at the center of the southern portion of Mound A's summit.
5. According to Morgan (1980:xxxi), Mound B ranks third in size among Mississippian earthworks, surpassed by Monks Mound at Cahokia and Mound A at Etowah.
6. Despite an investigation by Hardman (1971:163–165), a completely satisfactory demonstration of solstitial or equinoctial alignments in the architecture of Moundville is yet to be made. Hardman's reconstruction bears little resemblance to Peebles's.
7. Moore's return to Mound Q in his 1906 season—the only mound he felt the need to reinvestigate—is illuminating. According to the pattern, this mound should have yielded burials, but it did not. Moore, however, gives other reasons for suspecting the presence of burials in this mound, an issue that was not resolved until definite mortuary evidence was found in 1992.
8. Current excavations begun by the author in 1989 and continuing to the present (1996) are focused on developing a mound chronology that will determine the points during which various mounds were in use contemporaneously. The new program of work is also an attempt to clarify apparent distinctions in the uses of public architecture on the mound summits.
9. Speck's material on the Creeks and Chickasaws was incidentally obtained in 1904 and 1905 while doing fieldwork among the Yuchi in Oklahoma. The

materials not pertaining to the Yuchi were published as three separate contributions. This fieldwork was sponsored by the American Museum of Natural History and the Bureau of American Ethnology.

10. Speck (1907:51) understood these named groups to be identical with clans, but Swanton (1928:197) corrected the mistake, pointing out that Speck's informant meant to refer to localized "house groups" pertaining to only one community. House groups were essentially the local, small-scale, corporate manifestations of the clan system within a single Chickasaw community. They were named in the same manner as the broader clans and were likewise separated into two divisions.
11. Western Muskogean may be classified as a language that includes Chickasaw as one of its dialects.
12. I am relying on the conclusion of Atkinson (1987), Hudson (Hudson et al. 1990), and others that the Chickasaw settlements at first contact lay within the area subsumed by these archaeological phases.
13. For corresponding material on the formality of war-camp layouts among the Choctaws and Creeks, see Romans (1775:65) and Gatschet (1884:167), respectively. Gatschet repeats the comparison with Plains camp circles.
14. According to Swanton (1928:191), Schoolcraft's information on this point was "prepared . . . by a United States Indian agent from information obtained from several old Chickasaw chiefs shortly after the period of their emigration from Mississippi."
15. Compare Pauketat's statement on why the trappings of divine chiefship at Cahokia do not immediately appear after the political consolidation of the American Bottom during the Lohmann phase: "The common sense of the populace would still have been rooted in a rank hegemony [as opposed to a class hegemony], even though substantial cosmic powers may have been recognized to be a component of political office. Thus, the materialization of an ideology touting elite separateness would have presented the consciousness of the nonelite with an unacceptable challenge to common sense and subordinate ideologies" (1994:175–176).

4. Domestic Life on the Northwest Riverbank at Moundville

C. MARGARET SCARRY

OUR DEPICTIONS OF MOUNDVILLE tend to emphasize glamorous political, economic, and ritual activities. Considerably less has been said about mundane domestic activities. Recent excavations on the riverbank on the northwest edge of Moundville uncovered residential deposits dating to the Moundville I phase (AD 1050–1250). This chapter first describes the results of the riverbank excavations and then uses the data from the riverbank combined with information from earlier excavations to examine several aspects of domestic life at Moundville.

Moundville and its associated sites have been the subjects of archaeological investigations for more than 100 years. As a result, we have a reasonably good understanding of the social, political, and economic organization of Moundville and the polity it dominated. Despite this, there are some curious gaps in our knowledge. Notably, our depictions of Moundville's history emphasize the grand picture. We know considerably less about the domestic arrangements and mundane activities of the people who lived at Moundville and elsewhere in the Black Warrior Valley.

Recent excavations on the northwest riverbank of the Moundville site exposed houses, fortifications, and burials. Except for the burials, most of the remains date to the Moundville I phase (AD 1050–1250). Thus, they provide data about the period when construction of the mound-and-plaza complex was begun and Moundville gained political dominance over the valley (chap. 3; Steponaitis 1991:197–198). The new evidence complements previous evidence about Moundville's development and provides insights about domestic life in a dynamic period. In the following pages, I summarize what was found near the riverbank and use the data to examine several aspects of daily life at the paramount center.

THE RIVERBANK EXCAVATIONS

The people who built Moundville selected a high terrace overlooking the Black Warrior River for their mound-and-plaza complex. This location provided a commanding view of the river. Unfortunately, today the steep riverbank is eroding in several places, and valuable archaeological resources are being lost.

In 1991, the United States Army Corps of Engineers, Mobile District, began a project to stabilize the riverbank on the northwest edge of Moundville, where erosion was threatening both archaeological deposits and the Nelson B. Jones Conference Building (see areas labeled PA and ECB on figure 4.1). To prevent further erosion, the existing bank had to be cut back and reangled. In the fall and winter of 1991–1992, a crew from the Alabama Museum of Natural History Division of Archaeology conducted excavations to mitigate the impact of the stabilization project.

PREVIOUS RESEARCH NEAR THE NORTHWEST RIVERBANK

The area on the northwest periphery of Moundville had received considerably less attention than the central mound-and-plaza complex. Insofar as we could determine from the records stored at Moundville Archaeological Park, past investigations of this area were limited to four brief excavations.

In March 1948, Steve B. Wimberly and Lewis Larson conducted test excavations before construction of the picnic shelter that is now known as the Nelson B. Jones Conference Building. (Their notes are on file at Moundville Archaeological Park.) Wimberly and Larson found six burials, several parallel "stockade" trenches, and portions of trenches for bastions that connected to the main palisade lines.

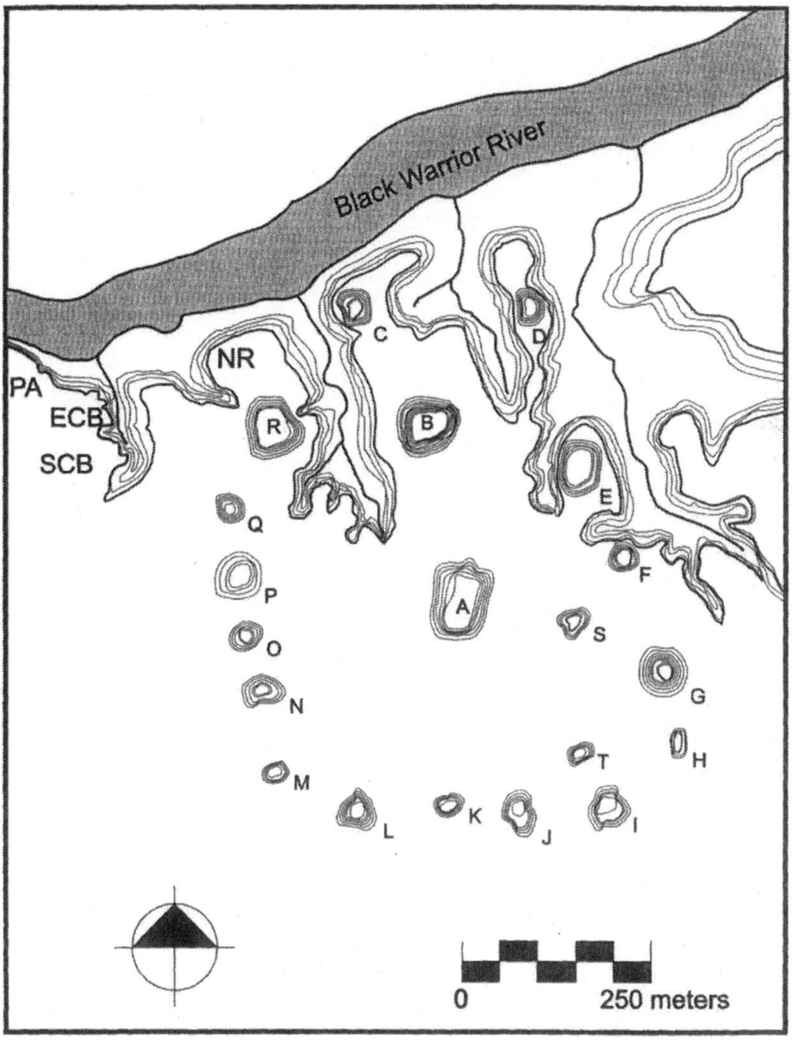

Fig. 4.1. Location of excavations in Moundville I deposits at Moundville. Courtesy Office of Archaeological Services, University of Alabama Museums.

Later that year, Wimberly, Larson, and Charlie Lott excavated an area a few meters southeast of the new picnic building prior to the construction of a drainage ditch for that structure. They found a single poorly preserved burial but little else.

A year later in August 1949, E. C. Chapman and Charlie Lott excavated a small patch of "kitchen midden" due east of the Conference Building. A brief note by Chapman describes the midden as containing abundant sherds, as well as animal bones, mica, and stones. He gave the distance from the Conference Building but provided no other information about the nature or circumstances of the excavation.

Besides the excavations done in the late 1940s, one other small excavation was conducted near the Conference Building. In 1979, a field crew that I directed as part of the University of Michigan's Moundville Archaeological Project placed two test units on a knoll south of the Conference Building (area labeled SCB on figure 4.1). In an area of 2 × 4 meters, we found two superimposed floors, each of which had a puddled-clay hearth. Ceramics from the units and paleomagnetic samples from the hearth indicated that the materials associated with the floors dated to the middle to late part of the Moundville I phase (Scarry 1986:161–168; chap. 2). Abundant mica in a pit that originated above the floors suggested that at some point the area might have been the locus of craft activities.

1991–1992 RIVERBANK EXCAVATIONS

The area investigated during the 1991–1992 excavations extended about 100 meters along the bank—from the edge of a ravine on the east to the edge of the terrace on the west—and extended 40–50 meters in from the bank. Within this area, we investigated two large tracts (fig. 4.2). One tract lay east and north of the Conference Building. Following tradition, which designates excavation areas at Moundville by reference to either nearby mounds or other landmarks, we called this tract ECB (east of the Conference Building). The other tract was on the terrace northwest of the Conference Building, in an area that had held picnic tables for the use of visitors to the site. This tract we called PA (Picnic Area). We treated each tract as a separate excavation area and adjusted the field methods to accommodate the nature of the deposits and to maximize data recovery in the time allotted for the project (see Scarry 1995 for detailed discussions of the information summarized below).

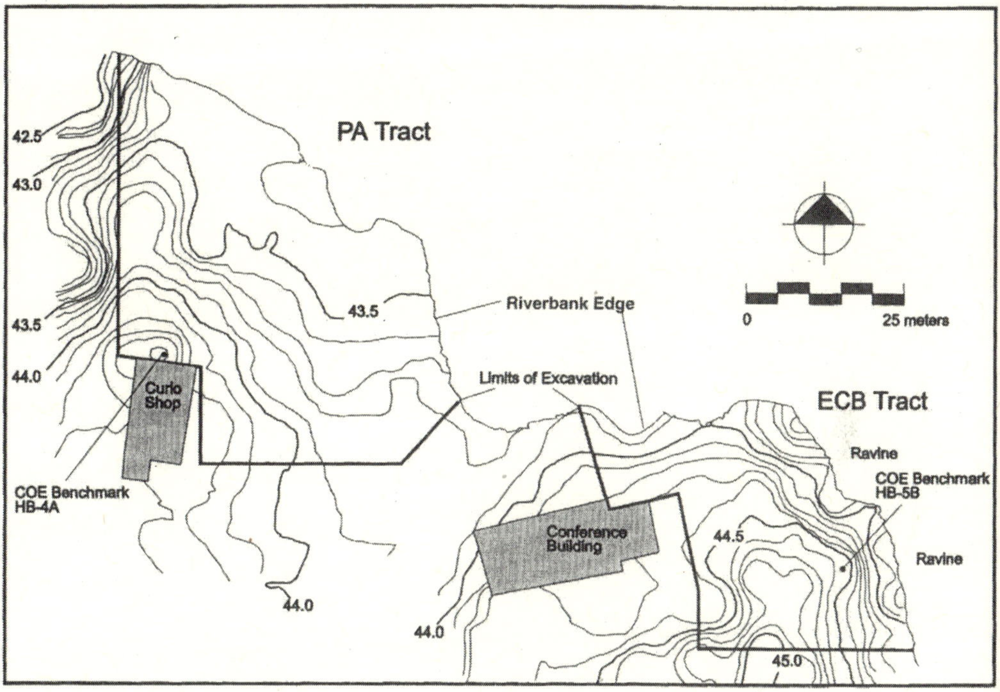

Fig. 4.2. Topographic map of the PA and ECB tracts. Courtesy Office of Archaeological Services, University of Alabama Museums.

The PA Tract

The PA tract encompassed an area of approximately 1,375 square meters. To explore the deposits, the crew excavated nine test units, each 1 × 1 meter, and dug shovel tests at 10-meter intervals across the tract. Because there appeared to be little intact midden, we decided to forego hand excavation of the surface deposits. Instead, the plowzone was mechanically stripped from the entire tract. The crew mapped all features found beneath the plowzone and then excavated a selected sample of them. Most unexcavated features were small circular stains that probably were either isolated postholes or roots.

The occupation of the PA tract was neither heavy nor complex, but it was nonetheless interesting (fig. 4.3). Remnants of six domestic structures, representing four distinct households, were present. There were no formal refuse or storage pits associated with the structures. Irregular patches of

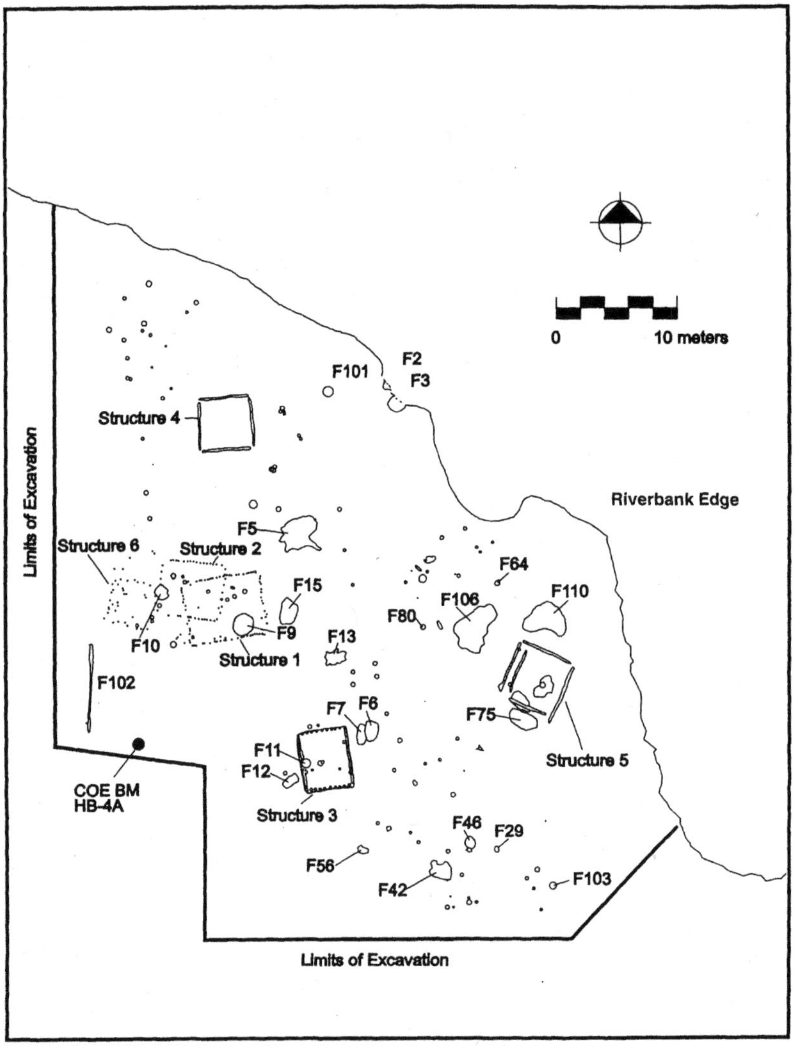

Fig. 4.3. Archaeological features and structures in the PA tract. Courtesy Office of Archaeological Services, University of Alabama Museums.

midden that had accumulated in depressions near the houses produced debris that provided evidence about when the structures were occupied and about the activities of their residents. Artifacts and radiocarbon dates indicate that houses were built in the Moundville I phase (AD 1050–1250) and that the area was most heavily used during the early part of the phase.

Although they ranged in size from 14 square meters (Structure 6) to 32.5 square meters (Structure 1), the houses had similar floor plans. All were rectangular, single-room structures. None had internal roof supports, and there was no evidence for partitions or screens. The two structures whose floors were intact had puddled-clay hearths near their centers. One house (Structure 5) had double trenches along its south and west walls. These may have been a result of repairing or rebuilding the structure, but it is also possible that the innermost trenches supported posts for benches rather than walls.

Although the houses had similar internal layouts, they were built differently. Structures 1, 2, and 6 were constructed using singly set posts to support the walls. Structure 3 was built in a rectangular basin. Its north and south walls were constructed using singly set posts, and the east and west walls were constructed with the posts set in wall trenches. Structures 4 and 5 were constructed by setting the posts for all four walls in trenches. Both were rectangular and had open corners between the trenches.

Radiocarbon dates from materials associated with the structures suggest that the differences in construction techniques are chronological (table 4.1). Two radiocarbon assays were run on material from the floor of Structure 3, the semisubterranean structure. The averaged calibrated date from these samples is AD 1030–1146. Two radiocarbon assays also were obtained from charcoal found in features associated with the singly set post structures 1, 2, and 6. One charcoal sample came from Feature 9, the other from Feature 15. The two samples gave identical dates; calibrated, these fall within the period AD 1044–1151. Given that the standard errors of the dates for the two structure types overlap (see table 4.1), I feel it is unwise to assign temporal priority to one house form or the other. The important point is that the dates place both the semisubterranean structure and the singly set post structures within the first half of the Moundville I phase.

The wall-trench structures appear to have been built slightly later. A radiocarbon assay was run on a sample from Feature 110, a midden-filled depression just north of Structure 5. The calibrated age for the sample is AD 1221–1256. This suggests that the structure was occupied in middle to late Moundville I times. No materials suitable for dating were recovered from Structure 4, but its similarity in form to Structure 5 suggests that it too dates to the latter half of the Moundville I phase.

The ceramics from the PA tract are consistent with the radiocarbon dates. The assemblage as a whole fits comfortably within the Moundville I phase; Moundville Incised is the most abundant decorated type and there are very few diagnostic sherds from later phases. More important, the ceramics from the semisubterranean and singly set post structures conform to our expectations of what an early Moundville I assem-

Table 4.1.
Radiocarbon Dates from the Riverbank Excavations at Moundville

Feature Number	Context	Lab Number	^{14}C Age BP	^{13}C-adjusted Age BP	Uncalibrated Date	Calibrated Date[a] (Age Range)	Average Date (Age Range)
ECB tract							
19	Structure 4, pit within structure	Beta 53382	810±120	720±120	AD 1230±120	AD 1286 (1214–1393)	
66	Structure 6, pit within structure	Beta 53390	3400±70	3400±70	1450 BC±70	1688–1644 BC (1760–1534)	
45	Pit intruding palisade trench	Beta 53388	710±80	670±80	AD 1280±80	AD 1297 (1280–1397)	AD 1262 (1213–1284)
		Beta 53389	910±70	880±70	AD 1070±70	AD 1163–1206 (1038–1258)	
169	Palisade trench north of structures	Beta 53393	1130±110	1100±110	AD 850±110	AD 904–982 (781–1025)	
159	Bastion trench	Beta 53392	1300±90	1270±90	AD 680±90	AD 695–772 (661–883)	
173	Palisade trench	Beta 53768	820±90	780±90	AD 1170±90	AD 1263–1275 (1165–1293)	
29	Southern palisade trench	Beta 53767	690±60	650±60	AD 1300±60	AD 1302–1381 (1287–1397)	
26	Burial 8, burial pit	Beta 53383	670±90	640±90	AD 1320±90	AD 1305–1386 (1284–1411)	AD 1285 (1262–1297)
		Beta 53766	800±60	770±60	AD 1180±60	AD 1265–1277 (1217–1289)	

73	Burial 9, burial pit	Beta 53391	540±80	490±80	AD 1460±80	AD 1433 (1406–1469)	
PA tract							
9	Pit associated with structures 1, 2, and 6	Beta 53770	1000±90	940±90	AD 1010±90	AD 1044–1151 (1001–1213)	
15	Midden-filled depression associated with structures 1, 2, and 6	Beta 53398	980±70	940±70	AD 1010±70	AD 1044–1151 (1020–1209)	
Str. 3	Floor Structure 3 semisubterranean structure	Beta 53400	880±70	840±70	AD 1110±70	AD 1215 (1075–1278)	AD 1030–1146 (1002–1155)
		Beta 53401	1130±70	1100±70	AD 850±70	AD 904–982 (886–1018)	
110	Midden-filled depression associated with Structure 5	Beta 53771	850±80	820±80	AD 1130±80	AD 1221–1256 (1158–1283)	
5	Isolated midden-filled depression	Beta 53768	610±70	580±70	AD 1370±70	AD 1334–1402 (1302–1426)	

a. Dates calibrated using version 3.0.3 (1993) of the radiocarbon program CALIB (Stuiver and Reimer 1993).

blage should look like, and the ceramics from one of the wall-trench structures fit expectations for a late Moundville I assemblage.

In a recent article, Steponaitis (1992:4–6) suggested that differences between the ceramic assemblages from Site 1Tu50, a single-mound site called Asphalt Plant by Welch (chap. 7), and those from Moundville I components at Bessemer and Moundville are chronological and reflect changes that took place between early Moundville I (i.e., Asphalt Plant) and late Moundville I (i.e., Bessemer, Moundville north of Mound R, and Moundville Roadway) (see table 4.2). At the Asphalt Plant mound,

Table 4.2.
Frequency of Ceramic Types from Selected Contexts in the PA and ECB Tracts

	Total Sherds[a] (*N*)	Mississippi Plain (%)	Moundville Incised[b] (%)	Bell Plain (%)	Carthage Incised (%)	Moundville Engraved (%)
Early Moundville I						
1Tu50[c]	607	82.7	1.8	15.0	0.5	
Oliver (1Tu459)[d]	1,035	80.3	3.5	15.7	0.1	
Late Moundville I						
Moundville SCB[e]	1,187	77.4	3.5	17.3	0.4	1.4
Moundville NR[c]	2,799	58.1	3.8	34.8	0.5	2.4
Moundville Roadway[c]	97,561	81.4	4.3	9.1	1.8	0.4
Bessemer[c]	997	74.0	6.7	10.7	1.4	2.7
Moundville PA tract	1,843	80.4	3.3	15.1	0.7	0.5
Structures 1, 2, and 6	270	84.4	1.1	13.7		0.7
Structure 3	196	91.3		8.7		
Structure 5	195	86.2	2.6	11.3		
Moundville ECB tract	3,614	73.7	4.7	18.8	1.5	1.3
Structure 4	103	60.2	7.8	30.1	1.0	1.0
Structure 6	215	74.4	5.1	18.6	1.0	1.0
Northern Palisade	134	66.4	9.0	24.6		
Feature 45	279	65.9	6.5	24.7	0.4	2.5
Southern Palisade	142	78.2	0.7	19.0	0.7	1.4

a. Grog-tempered Late Woodland sherds and nonlocal shell-tempered sherds not included.

b. Barton Incised sherds are included with Moundville Incised.

c. Data from Steponaitis 1992: table 2.

d. Data from Michals (chapter 8, this volume).

e. Data from Steponaitis (chapter 2, this volume).

grog-tempered and sand-tempered sherds, which are typically associated with Late Woodland components, constitute about 8 percent of the assemblage. The shell-tempered ceramics from the site are predominantly plain; there are relatively few Moundville Incised sherds, even fewer Carthage Incised, and no Moundville Engraved. Steponaitis (1992:6) argues that the Asphalt Plant assemblage is "what we might expect from a component dating to the *early* part of the Moundville I phase, perhaps somewhere between AD 1050 AND 1150."

Grog-tempered sherds are more abundant in the assemblages from the early structures in the PA tract than in the Asphalt Plant assemblage. Grog-tempered sherds constitute 27 percent of the ceramics associated with the singly set post structures and 52 percent of those associated with the semisubterranean structure. For the latter, it should be noted that approximately 25 percent of the grog-tempered sherds come from two, nonlocal Baytown Plain, var. *Addis*, carinated bowls. These vessels probably came from the lower Mississippi Valley and date to Mississippian, not Late Woodland times. Setting aside the *Addis* sherds, the relatively high frequencies of local grog-tempered sherds might seem to suggest there was a Late Woodland (West Jefferson) component in the PA tract, but this does not appear to have been the case. In all contexts, including the floor of the semisubterranean structure, the grog-tempered wares were found intermingled with shell-tempered ceramics. There were no pure Late Woodland features.

The shell-tempered ceramics from the early structures in the PA tract fit Steponaitis's predictions for an early Moundville I assemblage (table 4.2) and are consistent with the dates that place them in the early part of the Moundville I phase. Two Moundville Engraved sherds were recovered from the singly set post structures, but they account for less than 1 percent of the ceramics from the structures. In all other respects, the proportions of shell-tempered types from the semisubterranean and the singly set post structures are quite similar to those from the Asphalt Plant mound. The forms of the jar rims from the early structures also suggest an early Moundville I placement for these houses. Jars with folded rims were made during the Moundville I phase but not thereafter, and jars with folded-flattened rims appear to have been made primarily in the early part of the phase (Steponaitis 1983a:102, personal communication 1993). Folded-flattened rims account for 71 percent and folded rims for 18 percent of the jar rim sherds from the semisubterranean and singly set post structures.

No ceramics were recovered from Structure 4, but the ceramics from Structure 5 are consistent with the date that places the wall-trench structures later in the Moundville I phase (table 4.2). Compared to the ceramic assemblages from the structures with earlier dates, the assemblage from the wall-trench structure contains a much smaller proportion of grog-tempered sherds (6 percent) and more than twice as many Moundville Incised sherds. Folded-flattened rims (30 percent) account for a smaller proportion of the jar rim sherds, and folded rims (25 percent) constitute a larger proportion. The absence of Carthage Incised and Moundville Engraved sherds combined with the moderate presence of grog-tempered sherds and folded-flattened jar rims suggests to me that the wall-trench structure dates more toward the middle of Moundville I than toward the very late end of the phase.

Besides ceramics, the deposits in the PA tract produced debitage from both local Tuscaloosa-gravel chert and from nonlocal cherts (table 4.3). Most of the nonlocal stone was Fort Payne chert, which probably came from northern Alabama (Futato 1983:154–158). Debris from all stages of knapping, utilized flakes, and formal tools are present but not abundant. The composition of the chert assemblage suggests that the manufacture and use of flaked-stone tools was not a prominent activity. The residents of the PA tract do not appear to have specialized in the manufacture of flaked-stone artifacts. Neither do they seem to

Table 4.3.
Quantities of Selected Stone and Minerals from the PA and ECB Tracts

	Local Chert (*N*)	Nonlocal Chert (*N*)	Fine Gray Micaceous Sandstone (*N*)	Greenstone (*N*)	Mica (g)
Moundville PA tract	83	57	76	5	8.5
Structures 1, 2, and 6	9	2	6	1	
Structure 3	25	1	2		
Structure 5	3	17	3		8.0
Moundville ECB tract	81	165	44	48	77.3
Structure 4	3	2	1	1	1.2
Structure 6	6	16			8.8
Northern Palisade	5		2		0.1
Southern Palisade		2			0.2

have engaged in any form of craft production that required flaked-stone tools. Rather, the assemblage is what we would expect to find if they made tools only as needed for domestic use.

Modest quantities of fine gray micaceous sandstone, greenstone, and mica also were recovered from the PA tract (table 4.3). Fine gray micaceous sandstone, obtained from the Pottsville formation 30 kilometers north of Moundville, is the material from which palettes were made (Steponaitis 1992:8). Greenstone from the Hillabee formation in east-central Alabama (Gall 1993) was used primarily to make celts. The closest source of mica, more specifically muscovite, is in the Appalachian Mountains of northeast Alabama (Jones 1939:202–203). The mica from the PA tract consisted of small fragments of unworked or scrap material. The purpose or purposes for which it was used are unclear. It is possible that the pieces were manufacturing debris and that some of the residents of the area engaged in craft production involving mica; ornaments made of this material have been found in burials at Moundville (e.g., Moore 1907:395). Alternatively, Paul Welch (personal communication, 1992) has suggested that the mica may have been used to make a glitterlike pigment.

The stone assemblage recovered from the early Moundville I structures and their associated features is relatively undistinguished. The only nonlocal materials are three pieces of Fort Payne chert and a greenstone celt fragment; the celt fragment and two of the pieces of the chert came from deposits associated with the singly set post structures. Eight pieces of fine gray micaceous sandstone were recovered, but none had been worked.

The later Structure 5 produced a stone assemblage that is quite distinct from that of the earlier Moundville I structures. Nonlocal chert is more abundant than local chert, and modest quantities of mica are present. Three pieces of fine gray micaceous sandstone, two of which had saw marks, were recovered from midden deposits associated with the structure. The later residents of the PA tract seem to have had more access to nonlocal and esteemed local materials. Moreover, the mica and worked sandstone provide what little evidence there is for craft production associated with structures from the PA tract.

Overall, the evidence indicates that the PA tract was a residential area during the Moundville I phase. Within that period, people changed the way they built their houses, began to make a greater variety of pottery, and gained increased access to nonlocal stone. Some residents may also have become involved in craft production. Throughout the phase, however, the area seems to have been used solely for domestic activities. There is no evidence for special-purpose buildings or ceremonial activities from the PA tract.

Although the radiocarbon dates and ceramics from the structures indicate that the primary occupation of the PA tract was during the Moundville I phase, there is some evidence for occasional use of the area after that time. Feature 5, an isolated midden-filled depression located near the center of the tract, produced a calibrated radiocarbon date of AD 1334–1402 (table 4.1). Most of the ceramics from this feature were Moundville I types, but the presence of two beaded-rim sherds indicates that it probably contained some later material as well. There are also a few late sherds from the plowzone and from Feature 3, located on the edge of the riverbank.

The ECB Tract

The ECB tract encompassed an area of approximately 450 square meters. In this area the crew removed most of the overburden by hand. Features that extended beneath the plowzone were mapped and excavated. Initially, six 1 × 1-meter units, which formed an east-west trench, were excavated. Subsequently, 63 additional units were opened to follow features and explore the deposits within the impact area.

Although the ECB tract was considerably smaller than the PA tract, its occupation and use were more complex and varied (fig. 4.4). Within the ECB tract, we found structures and patches of midden associated with them, multiple rebuildings of a palisade system, and 10 burials (including 7 that were excavated in 1948). Artifacts and radiocarbon dates indicate that the structures and the palisade were constructed during the Moundville I phase and that the area was most heavily occupied during the latter part of the phase. The burials clearly postdate the use of the area for residential purposes.

Six structures, two of which had been rebuilt, were present in the ECB tract. As in the PA tract, there were no special-purpose buildings; all the structures were rectangular, single-room houses. Except for Structure 5, which had a center post, there was no evidence for internal supports, partitions, or other furnishings in any of the houses. Three of the structures (1, 2, and 3) were too incomplete for reliable estimates of floor area to be made. The other three ranged in size from 10.5 square meters (the initial building of Structure 5) to about 20 square meters (Structure 6).

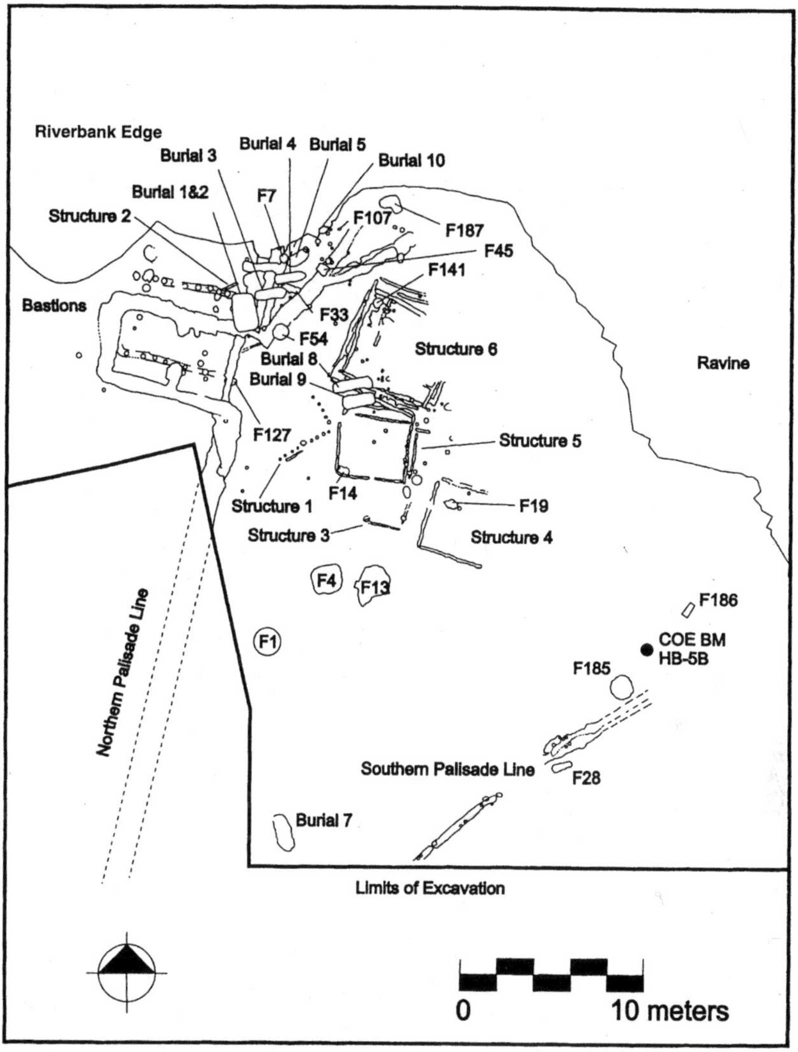

Fig. 4.4. Archaeological features and structures in the ECB tract. Courtesy Office of Archaeological Services, University of Alabama Museums.

Structures 1 and 2 were aligned with one another but not with the other structures or the palisade. These two houses probably date to the early to middle part of the Moundville I phase. Structure 1 was built using singly set posts to support its walls. We have no direct evidence as to when this structure was occupied. We recovered no artifacts or materials suitable for radiocarbon dating that were clearly associated with Structure 1. The similarity of this structure to structures 1, 2, and 6 in the PA tract suggests, however, that it may have been built and occupied in the early part of the Moundville I phase. Structure 2 was largely obliterated when the palisade was built. All that remained of the structure were portions of the northwest and southeast wall trenches. Again we have no direct evidence pertaining to the dating of this structure. The evidence suggests, however, that the palisade-and-bastion system was built during the Moundville I phase (see below). Since Structure 2 predates the palisade, it seems likely that it was occupied in early to middle Moundville I times.

The close packing of the other houses (structures 3–6) and their alignment with the palisade suggests they were occupied while the fortifications were standing. Based on their positions relative to one another, however, it seems unlikely that all four households were occupied simultaneously.

Materials from pits associated with two of the closely spaced wall-trench structures were submitted for radiocarbon dating (table 4.1). One sample was collected from Feature 66, which was located within Structure 6. The date produced by this sample, 1450 BC ± 70, is clearly spurious. The other sample was collected from Feature 19, a pit located within Structure 4. This sample produced a calibrated date of AD 1286. This places the feature and presumably the occupation of the structure in the very late Moundville I or early Moundville II phase.

The ceramic assemblages from the ECB tract as a whole and from the two houses (structures 4 and 6) from which reasonable numbers of sherds were recovered point to a late Moundville I date for the bulk of the occupation. Shell-tempered ceramics constitute 95 percent of all sherds recovered from the ECB tract and 96 percent of the sherds from the two structures. Folded-flattened and folded rims—forms found only on Moundville I jars—account for 13.4 percent and 25.6 percent respectively of the jar rim sherds from the ECB tract. Moundville Incised, Carthage Incised, and Moundville Engraved ceramics are all more abundant than in the PA tract and occur in proportions comparable to their representation in other late Moundville I assemblages (table 4.2). Finally, there are few sherds that are diagnostic of the Moundville II or III phases, and those that are present were recovered from the plowzone or from features not associated with the structures or the palisade.

The deposits associated with the structures in the ECB tract produced modest quantities of chert debitage, a dozen triangular projectile points, two drills, and a microblade. As in the PA tract, there is nothing to suggest that chert tools were used for anything other than routine domestic chores. It is worth noting, however, that though the tools and flakes were used for mundane purposes, most were made from nonlocal chert (table 4.3).

Besides chert, the ECB stone and mineral assemblage included fine gray micaceous sandstone, greenstone, mica, a galena crystal, and copper scraps (table 4.3). Fine gray micaceous sandstone was less common in the ECB tract than in the PA tract, and greenstone (primarily celt fragments and polished chips from celts) and mica were much more abundant in the ECB tract. Concentrations of mica were found associated with structures 3 and 6 and in several patches of midden (features 13, 185, and 187) not directly associated with any particular structure. A galena crystal was found in Structure 6, and several copper scraps were found in midden deposits on the edge of the ravine (features 185 and 186). Together with the abundance of nonlocal chert, the greater quantities of greenstone and mica in the ECB tract and the presence of galena and copper suggest the late Moundville I residents of that area had more access to imported materials than did the early Moundville I residents of the PA tract.

Both the northwest and southeast sections of the ECB tract contained trenches from palisades that had been modified and rebuilt repeatedly (fig. 4.4). The curtain walls of the palisades were set in trenches that ranged from 30 to 50 centimeters wide. Posts in the curtain walls were 25–35 centimeters in diameter and were set 20–40 centimeters apart. We found no evidence that the palisade walls were plastered. But assuming that the palisade was for defense, it seems unlikely that the spaces between the posts were left open.

The northern palisade line included a bastion that had been rebuilt at least once. Both the initial bastion and its replacement extended 6–7 meters from the main curtain wall. They were 4 meters wide and at least the later one was open to the inside. Protrusions about halfway along the bastion trenches may have held posts that supported crosswalks or roofs.

It is difficult to determine the exact sequence of the curtain walls in the northern palisade line. As is evident from the map of the ECB tract (fig. 4.4), the curtain walls near the riverbank were moved several times. What is not obvious from the plan view, however, is that most of the trenches had held at least two sets of posts. In all, the palisade section near the riverbank was rebuilt at least six times. The westernmost trench (Feature 31) held the initial wall, which ran more or less perpendicular to the riverbank. Subsequent walls were reangled, and moved to the east. The final walls for the northern section were placed in the trenches designated features 169 and 174. South of the bastion, the alignment of the curtain wall seems to have changed little over the life of the palisade. The wall itself, however, was rebuilt or repaired at least three times. The dashed lines extending from Feature 173 to the southwest indicate the continuation of this curtain wall. The projection is based on Wimberly and Larson's field notes and on an exploratory unit excavated just south of the Conference Building.

Besides the curtain walls and bastions in the northwest section of the ECB tract, there was another palisade line in the southeast corner of the tract (fig. 4.4). This southern palisade, which had been rebuilt at least once, appears to have been part of a different (or at least radically modified) system from that formed by the curtain walls and bastions near the riverbank. The angle of the southern line suggests that it did not connect to the northern section.

We obtained radiocarbon assays on six samples from contexts associated with the palisades (table 4.1). Two samples produced dates that seem improbably early. A sample from Feature 159, the second bastion trench, gave a calibrated date of AD 695–772. A sample from Feature 169, the east fork of the last curtain wall near the riverbank, gave a calibrated date of AD 904–982. Since we found traces of a wall-trench structure under the palisade, and 93 percent of the ceramics from the palisade trenches near the riverbank are shell-tempered, there seems little doubt that the palisades were constructed sometime after the beginning of the Moundville I phase. Thus, the early dates from features 159 and 169 are inconsistent with other evidence about the age of the palisade.

Three samples from the northern palisade line yielded radiocarbon dates that are consistent with our understanding of the chronology of Moundville. A sample from Feature 173, the curtain wall that runs south from the bastion, produced a calibrated date of AD 1263–1275. Two samples from Feature 45, a pit that intrudes the curtain wall designated Feature 46, produced an averaged calibrated date of AD 1262.

The dates from Feature 173 and Feature 45 both fall on the cusp between the Moundville I and Moundville II phases. The date from Feature 45 is particularly interesting. Feature 45 was a refuse-filled pit that clearly intruded Feature 46; the curtain wall must have been gone when the refuse was deposited. Feature 46 was one of the last curtain walls built near the riverbank. Thus most, if not all, of the palisade in the northwest section of the ECB tract seems to date to the Moundville I phase.

The southern palisade line appears to have been built after the system near the riverbank was dismantled. A radiocarbon sample from Feature 29 produced a calibrated date of AD 1302–1381. This suggests that the southern palisade line was in place during the Moundville II phase.

The ceramic assemblage from the northern palisade trenches is consistent with the radiocarbon dates (table 4.2). The pottery looks like a Moundville I assemblage; 93 percent of the sherds are shell-tempered, Moundville Incised is the dominant—and virtually the only—decorated type, folded and folded-flattened rims are present, and there are no diagnostics from later phases. Although trench fill might contain some later intrusive material, most of the artifacts should be from midden that was present when the trenches were dug and/or from midden used to fill the trenches after the posts were pulled. Hence, the midden and the artifacts it contains should be earlier than the fill event. The ceramic assemblage from the palisade trenches near the riverbank suggests that the system dates to the Moundville I phase.

Likewise, the ceramics from Feature 45, the refuse pit that intrudes the northern palisade line, are consistent with the radiocarbon dates. The ceramics from the pit are in accord with a late Moundville I or early Moundville II date for the feature. The Moundville Incised sherds include varieties (*Snows Bend* and *Carrollton*) that occur at that time but not much earlier or later. There are no folded-flattened or folded rim sherds that would indicate an earlier Moundville I date. Likewise, there are no varieties or modes that are diagnostic of later Moundville II–III assemblages.

The ceramic assemblage from the southern palisade line contains no late varieties. In fact, the assemblage looks like a late Moundville I assemblage. This would seem to indicate that the southern palisade was in place in early Moundville II rather than later in the phase.

If we put the various clues together, it is possible to place the palisades in time with a fair degree of certainty. Three lines of evidence are pertinent: (a) indications of when the palisade was erected, (b) data for estimating how long the palisade in its various manifestations was standing, and (c) information about when the palisade was dismantled.

There is sound evidence that before the palisade was built, the ECB tract was occupied by people whose material culture we classify as Moundville I. We found the remnants of a rectangular wall-trench house intruded by the northern palisade trenches. Evidence from the PA tract suggests that this was not the earliest building technique for Moundville structures. Moreover, the palisade trenches themselves contained early Moundville I ceramics. These data suggest that the palisade system near the riverbank was not built before the beginning of Moundville I and that it was probably not built until sometime around the middle of the phase.

Once erected, the palisade was repaired and modified at frequent intervals. We can estimate the duration of the palisade by multiplying the number of trenches by estimates of post use-life. In doing this, we are assuming that the palisade was rebuilt only when posts began to rot, that each trench represents a building episode, and that the palisade stood continuously.

The use-life of posts varies depending on the type of wood selected and the conditions of the soils in which the posts are set. Susan Prezzano (1992:253–256) presents data that indicate that the use-life of palisade posts at Iroquois sites in New York was between 5 and 8 years. Robert Lafferty (1973) uses an estimate of 15–20 years for posts in the palisades he studied. Gloria Cole and Caroline Albright (1983:159–162) report that posts would last 20 years in the ground in the Tombigbee Valley. Evidence from Vogel and Allan's (1985) excavations of a section of palisade on the northwest edge of the plaza indicates that the residents of Moundville used pine logs for the palisade posts. Since pine posts are rot resistant (Panshin and Zeeuw 1970:458–459), 10–20 years would seem to be a reasonable estimate for the use-life of the palisade posts. It should be noted that although we use the extremes of this use-life to discuss the temporal placement and longevity of the palisade, we believe the actual use-life was probably closer to 10 years than to 20.

Counting trenches visible only in cross section, the curtain walls near the riverbank were rebuilt six times. If the use-life of posts was 10–20 years, then the palisade line near the riverbank may have been in place for 60–120 years. The later, southern palisade line has two trenches, and by our estimates could have been in place for 20–40 years.

For the northern line, radiocarbon assays, ceramics, and intrusive burials provide evidence about when the palisade was dismantled. The radiocarbon dates and pottery from Feature 45, the pit that intruded one of the final curtain walls near the riverbank, suggest that the northern palisade line was gone by very late Moundville I or early Moundville II times. The intrusion of the palisade trenches by Moundville II–III burials clearly indicates that the northern palisade line was not standing in the later Moundville phases.

The evidence about the beginning date, longevity, and ending date for the northern palisade line fits together nicely. This line was probably erected sometime around the middle of the Moundville I phase, maintained diligently for 60 or more years, and then dismantled or allowed to fall into disrepair sometime around the end of the Moundville I phase. A late Moundville I date for the northern palisade line is consistent with the use of the area for residential purposes. The ceramic assemblage associated with the structures indicates that the area was most heavily occupied in late Moundville I times.

The southern palisade line appears to have been built after the northern line was gone. The radiocarbon assay and ceramics from this southern line suggest that it dates to early Moundville II times. If it was in place for 20–40 years, then a palisade of some sort may have been standing until the middle of the Moundville II phase.

The palisade system in the ECB tract is strikingly similar in plan to sections of palisade that Joseph Vogel and Jean Allan (1985) excavated on the northeast side of Moundville's plaza. In both areas, long sections of curtain wall were set in trenches about half a meter wide. The walls were constructed from pine posts 25–35 centimeters in diameter that were set at intervals of 20–40 centimeters. The curtain walls were interrupted periodically by rectangular bastions that were 4 meters wide and extended 6–7 meters out from the main palisade wall. There is some evidence that the bastions were either roofed or had elevated walkways. Given the similarities in construction techniques, it appears that the palisade walls found on the northwest and northeast edges of the plaza were part of a continuous fortification that ringed not only the mound-and-plaza complex but also residential areas.

Although the area within the ECB tract was used primarily for residential purposes, at least ten individuals were buried there (fig. 4.4). In 1948, Wimberly and Larson excavated seven burials: five were in pits that intruded the northern palisade line (burials 1–5), one was eroding from the riverbank (Burial 6, not shown on map), and one was southeast of the Conference Building (Burial 7). We found three burials: two (8 and 9) were located side by side and intruded structures 5 and 6, and the third (10) was on the eroding edge of the riverbank.

One of the graves found by Wimberly and Larson was a double interment (burials 1 and 2). The individuals in the grave were buried with a rich assemblage of goods, including a limestone effigy pipe in the form of a crouched catlike figure, a large limestone effigy in the form of a snapping turtle, two necklaces or bracelets made from human teeth, and a copper pendant attached to one of the necklaces.

Two lines of evidence suggest that the individuals in the double grave were buried in Moundville II or III times. First, the grave itself intrudes the northern palisade, which dates to late Moundville I. Second, C. B. Moore (1905: fig. 165) found a cat pipe similar to the one from the ECB tract in a grave north of Mound R at Moundville. Moore's cat pipe was in a burial (33/NR/M5) that contained Moundville III ceramics (Steponaitis 1983a: table 35). If cat pipes are late, then the presence of one in the ECB grave points to a late date for the interment.

The other burials found by Wimberly and Larson contained few grave goods. One grave (Burial 5) contained a greenstone discoidal, and another (Burial 7) yielded a scrap of copper. The others produced no artifacts. Although the graves did not yield chronologically sensitive items, most intruded the northern palisade line and thus postdate the Moundville I phase.

Like the burials found by Wimberly and Larson, the ones we found appear to date to Moundville II or III times. One (10) was located on the edge of the riverbank. Most of the burial had been lost to erosion; all that remained were the end of the burial pit and a few cranial bones. No grave goods were found in the remnants of the pit. The other two burials were found adjacent to one another in pits that cut through the wall trenches of structures 5 and 6 (fig. 4.4).

The individual in Burial 8 was supine with the face turned toward the east. The remains of what appeared to be a carbonized mat were wrapped tightly around the head. A Mississippi Plain, var. *Warrior*, bowl; a Matthews Incised, var. *Beckwith*, lobed jar; and a large Mississippi Plain, var. *Warrior*, body sherd were found above the head at the east end of the grave. At the west end of the grave there were two broken Bell Plain, var. *Hale*, pots. One was a pedestaled bottle; the other was a restricted bowl.

We submitted two samples of the matting from around the head of Burial 8 for radiocarbon dating. The calibrated average for these dates is AD 1285 (see table 4.1). This suggests a Moundville II date for the burial. The vessels, particularly the pedestaled bottle, are compatible with this date.

Burial 9 was the second of the two burials that cut through the wall trenches of structures 5 and 6. Only the teeth and fragments of temporal bones were preserved. Judging by the location of the teeth and the size of the grave, the body was probably placed in the grave in an extended position. The remains of a burned or decayed mat and a clay ball were found in the region where the chest would have been. These were underlaid by a thin layer of red clay and then white sand. A portion of a large, Moundville Incised, var. *Carrollton*, jar was used as a pillow sherd. A large Fort Payne chert core was placed at the foot of the grave.

As with Burial 8, we submitted two samples of the matting from Burial 9 for radiocarbon dating. One sample was not large enough for conventional dating methods. The other sample produced a calibrated date of AD 1433, which places the burial at the beginning of the Moundville III phase. This seems too late, given the obvious alignment of Burial 9 with Burial 8 and that the other radiocarbon date and the ceramics from the two burials suggest a Moundville II age.

The evidence from the burials indicates that the area within the ECB tract was used for interment in the Moundville II–III period. The alignment and clustering of the burial pits suggest that the northern section of the tract became a formal cemetery. The intrusion of the graves into both the wall-trench structures and the palisade trenches indicates that the use of the area changed from residential domestic in Moundville I to mortuary ceremonial in Moundville II–III.

CHRONOLOGY OF THE RIVERBANK OCCUPATIONS

In the preceding pages, I have described the PA and ECB tracts as though they were distinct entities. In reality, however, they are quite close together and their occupations are clearly interrelated. In this section, I combine the information from the two areas and examine the occupation of the northwest riverbank as a whole (fig. 4.5).

The riverbank area was first occupied in the early Moundville I phase (circa AD 1050–1150). At this time households seem to have been scattered at some distance from one another. We have more evidence

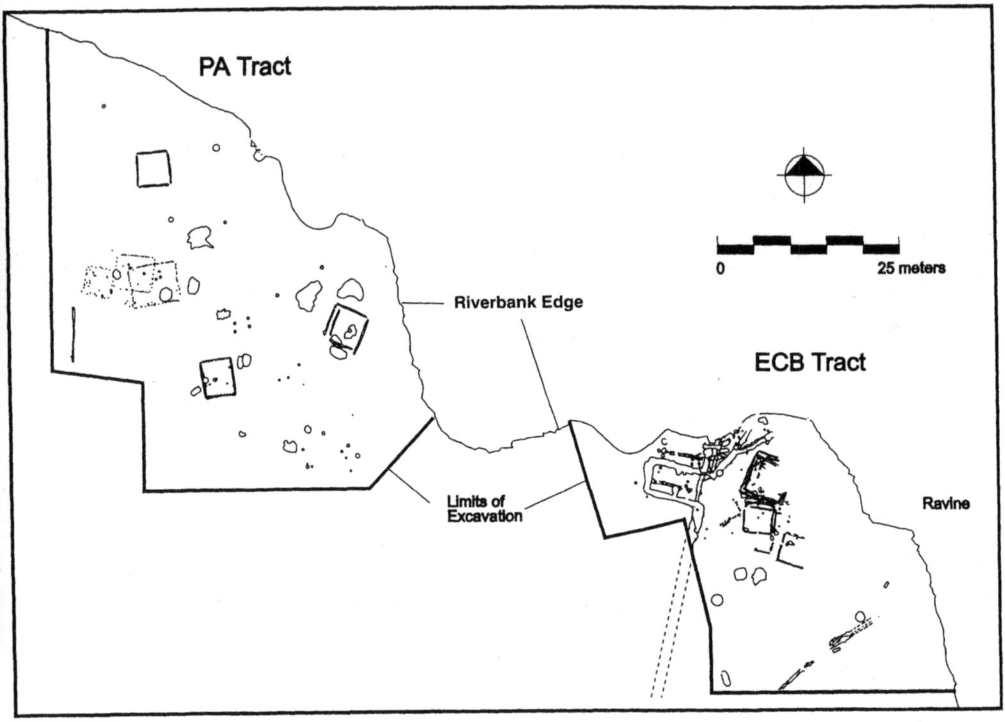

Fig. 4.5. Archaeological features in the PA and ECB tracts. Courtesy Office of Archaeological Services, University of Alabama Museums.

for this occupation from the PA tract, but this may be because later occupations in the ECB tract destroyed or obscured earlier remains. The houses that we believe were built by the early Moundville I residents of the area are the singly set post buildings in both tracts (structures 1, 2, and 6 in the PA tract and Structure 1 in the ECB tract), the semisubterranean structure (3 in the PA tract), and, perhaps slightly later, the wall-trench structure intruded by the palisade lines (2 in the ECB tract).

Sometime around the middle of the Moundville I phase, the northern palisade line was erected. Though its bastion was rebuilt at least once and its curtain walls were moved several times, it appears to have been standing in one form or another until the end of the phase. The structures that were probably occupied while the palisade was in place are 3, 4, 5, and 6 in the ECB tract. The spacing between households was undoubtedly less than before the palisade was built, but it seems unlikely that all four structures were occupied at once.

The presence of middle to late Moundville I phase structures (4 and 5 in the PA tract) outside the palisade is puzzling. It is possible that these households were occupied while the palisade was standing. The structures were certainly close enough to the palisade that their residents could have reached its protection if they had warning of attack. It seems more likely, however, that the structures were not contemporaneous with the palisade. The ceramics associated with Structure 5 suggest it was occupied before the palisade was built, rather than after it was dismantled. If so, the wall-trench structures in the PA tract may have been contemporaneous with the wall-trench structure whose remnants we found intruded by the palisade trenches.

The southern palisade line replaced the northern line and was probably built very late in the Moundville I phase or early in the Moundville II phase. Judging by the paucity of early Moundville II domestic debris and structures, people lived within the palisade and outside the excavation area at this time.

After the northern palisade line and the structures it enclosed were gone, the area within the ECB tract was used as a cemetery. It is possible that the southern palisade line was still standing when the interments took place, but this seems unlikely. More likely, the area changed from a residential zone to a mortuary precinct during the Moundville II phase.

DOMESTIC LIFE ON THE RIVERBANK

The data from the riverbank excavations can be used to investigate several aspects of domestic life during the Moundville I phase. Among other things, we can examine subsistence practices; domestic architecture; household size, composition, and distribution; craft production; and social status. Not all of these subjects can be addressed in detail, but we do have some pertinent information for each topic. Moreover, we can glean insights by incorporating information from excavations in late Moundville I deposits located south of the Conference Building (SCB) and north of Mound R (NR) (see fig. 4.1). Both these areas were excavated in the late 1970s under my direction. The SCB excavations, described earlier in this chapter, provide additional data about the riverbank area. The NR excavations, to be described presently, provide data that can be compared to those from the riverbank.

The NR excavations, part of the University of Michigan Museum of Anthropology's Moundville Archaeological Project, consisted of two units of 2 × 2 meters each. The excavations revealed nearly 2 meters of stratified deposits composed largely of superimposed structure floors interspersed with layers of midden. Radiocarbon assays and the ceramics from the structure floors and midden levels indicate that most of the deposits date to the late Moundville I phase (Scarry 1986:141–149; Steponaitis 1983a:94–106). Several lines of evidence suggest that the area north of Mound R was an elite residential zone (see Scarry 1986:141–159).

Foodways

Studies of plant and animal remains and human skeletons have provided us with a general picture of the subsistence practices of the people who lived at Moundville (chaps. 5 and 6; Michals 1981, 1990, 1992; Powell 1988; Scarry 1986, 1993a). We know that they relied on agricultural products for much of their food. Archaeobotanical data indicate that their primary crop was corn (Scarry 1986). Bone-chemistry studies of human skeletons from Moundville confirm the dietary importance of corn. Carbon-isotope ratios indicate that in Moundville I times people obtained about 40 percent of their calories from corn (chap. 6). Besides corn, the Moundville-era farmers grew small quantities of native starchy and oily seeded crops (e.g., squash, sunflower, chenopod, maygrass, little barley), but these appear to have been minor components in their agricultural strategies and diets (Scarry 1986, 1993b). Sometime during the Moundville I phase, the Moundville farmers added beans to the suite of crops that they grew (Scarry 1986:319).

People also collected and ate a variety of wild plants. They gathered substantial quantities of hickory nuts and acorns from nearby forests. Most of the hickory nuts were probably used to make oil, which was used in many recipes (Swanton 1946:364–367). Acorns were processed for their oil, and their starch was used to make a form of bread (Swanton 1946:364–367). In addition, people gathered wild fruits, such as persimmon, maypops, and grapes, which could be eaten fresh or dried and stored for later use.

As elsewhere in the prehistoric Southeast, the residents of Moundville obtained meat for their meals by hunting and fishing. They captured and ate a variety of terrestrial and aquatic animals including deer, beaver, turkey, rabbit, squirrel, opossum, turtle, and fish (Michals 1981). Deer was their principal terrestrial game (Michals 1981, 1990), and undoubtedly venison was an important source of protein. Trace-element analyses, however, indicate that about 25 percent of the protein consumed by the residents of Moundville came from fish (chap. 6).

Individual households or household groups probably managed subsistence activities, but we have no direct evidence from Moundville as to who performed which tasks. In large areas of the Southeast, women did much of the agricultural labor. Thus, it is quite likely that the Moundville farmers were women. Probably women, with the help of their children, also gathered nuts and fruits and processed and cooked most foods. Men and boys most likely cleared fields, hunted and trapped land game, and fished (Swanton 1946:304–332).

The residents of the northwest riverbank at Moundville probably captured and ate the same range of animals as did residents of other areas of Moundville. Unfortunately, bone preservation was exceptionally poor in the PA and ECB tracts. The excavations produced a few recognizable elements from deer, turkey, and fish, but there were not enough bones to warrant a formal analysis. Thus, we cannot add anything to the generic picture of meat use presented above.

Plant remains were present in the domestic debris produced by the households on the riverbank. I analyzed archaeobotanical data from refuse deposits in the PA and ECB tracts. The results indicated that the people who lived there grew, gathered, and ate the same plants as their contemporaries who lived elsewhere at Moundville and at other sites in the Black Warrior Valley. This is hardly surprising. Of greater interest is evidence that suggests that people used similar quantities of corn, hickory nuts, and acorns in early and late Moundville I times.

In a previous study of plant data from late prehistoric contexts in the Black Warrior Valley, I traced a shift from foraging and gardening to corn agriculture that occurred from West Jefferson (AD 900–1050) to Moundville I (AD 1050–1250) times (Scarry 1986). My analyses indicated that although the basic set of plants used by the West Jefferson and Moundville populations was the same, there were distinct differences over time in the relative importance of those plants in peoples' diets. The early West Jefferson assemblage suggested an economy based on foraging combined with small-scale gardening; people grew some corn and small quantities of native seed crops, but their primary plant foods were hickory nuts and acorns. During the West Jefferson phase, people increased their reliance on corn. By the end of the West Jefferson phase it appeared that they had also decreased their use of nuts. The Moundville I data indicated a highly stable pattern of plant use. Based on these results, I argued that the changes within the West Jefferson phase indicated an economy in transition and that by early Moundville I an economy focused on corn agriculture was firmly established.

Most of the Moundville I data on which these conclusions were based came from the high-status late Moundville I residential deposit north of Mound R. Thus, there was a chronological gap between late West Jefferson and late Moundville I in my data. Moreover, the late Moundville I data were biased toward the foodways of the elite.

The plant data from the riverbank excavations help to rectify this situation. They provide information about the foodways of people who lived at Moundville during early Moundville I times, and about late Moundville I people who seem to have had more modest status than the residents of the area north of Mound R.

The box plots in figure 4.6 compare the relative abundances of corn cupules, hickory nutshells, and acorn shells in contexts from early West Jefferson through late Moundville I times. The early and late West Jefferson data come from seven sites in the Black Warrior Valley (Scarry 1986:132–138). The early Moundville I data come from features associated with the singly set post and semisubterranean structures in the PA tract. The late Moundville I data come from the PA and ECB tracts, from SCB, and from NR (Scarry 1986:138–174, 1995).

The patterns shown in the box plots provide support for my earlier interpretations. Corn production, as measured by quantities of corn cupules, increased significantly within the West Jefferson phase but remained relatively stable from late West Jefferson through late Moundville I times. Nut procurement, measured by quantities of nutshells, varied somewhat within the West Jefferson phase but decreased dramatically between late West Jefferson and early Moundville I times. Though the use of acorns seems to have increased between early and late Moundville I, overall plant use within that phase was quite stable.

In sum, the people who built the first houses on the northwest riverbank at Moundville were farmers. Their foodways were more similar to those of later inhabitants of Moundville than to their Late Woodland, West Jefferson predecessors.

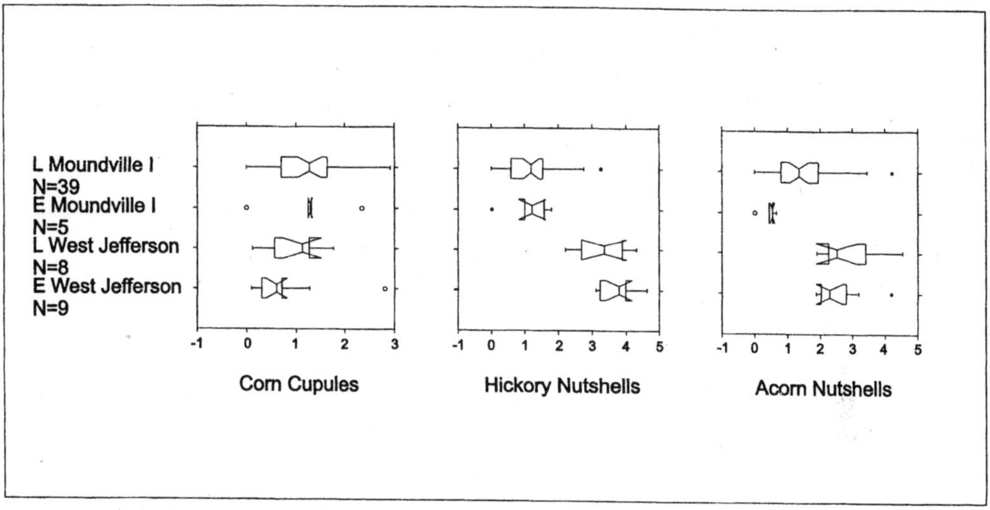

Fig. 4.6. Box plots showing abundances of major food plants in Moundville I and West Jefferson contexts. Data are plotted in $\log_n$ [(taxon count/g plant weight) + 1]. Courtesy Office of Archaeological Services, University of Alabama Museums.

Domestic Architecture

The residents of the riverbank lived in rectangular wattle-and-daub houses. In the early Moundville I phase, they used two construction techniques to build their homes. In one, they erected the walls by setting posts individually in the ground. In the other, they dug a basin and set the walls within the basin. The semisubterranean structure in the PA tract was made with two walls built with singly set posts and two walls built with the posts set in trenches. This structure, however, had two superimposed floors, and it is possible that the wall trenches were dug when repairs were made to the structure (cf. Jenkins 1982:109). Sometime around the middle of the Moundville I phase, people seem to have adopted new construction techniques. Thereafter, they built structures by setting the wall posts for all four walls in trenches. The early houses were made with closely spaced, deeply set, small-diameter posts, and the later ones had narrow, deep wall trenches. This suggests that regardless of how they erected the walls, people used flexed poles to support the roofs of their homes (see Polhemus 1987:225–233 for discussions of construction techniques).

The floor plans of these houses were quite simple. In those that had intact floors, there were puddled clay hearths near the centers of the structures. Two of the structures had small, shallow pits in the corners in which members of the household may have stored tools or other belongings. None of the structures had internal pits suitable for storing comestibles. One structure may have had benches along two walls; we found no evidence for internal partitions, covered entryways, or porticoes.

Household Size and Composition

Floor area is often used as a measure of household size and by extension household composition. The floor areas of the structures on the riverbank ranged from 10.5 to 32.5 square meters. These structures are comparable in size to ones found elsewhere at Moundville. Peebles (1978:379–380) illustrated three houses excavated southwest of Mound I and four houses found north-northwest of Mound P. The floor areas for these structures ranged from 13 to 34.7 square meters. The average floor area for 19 structures (12 from the riverbank excavations and the 7 illustrated by Peebles) is 19 square meters.

If we apply Naroll's (1962) formula for calculating household size from floor area to the houses at Moundville, we get an estimate of 1.3–3.4 people per structure. This seems unrealistically low, since ethnohistoric sources report households averaging 5–8 people for several Native American groups of the lower Southeast (Hann 1988:166; Swanton 1911:43; see also Black 1979:94–98 for a discussion of Mississippian household size). Clearly household size varied from one family to the next. Whatever the case, however, it is unlikely that the Moundville structures housed large extended families.

Several of the structures within the project area had been rebuilt and made larger or smaller. The impetus for rebuilding was probably the need to replace posts that were rotting or infested with insects. It seems reasonable to suggest, however, that the builders altered the size of the structures to accommodate changes in the number of people living in the household.

Given the small size of the structures and their apparent lack of internal furnishings, it seems unlikely that people spent much time in their homes. They probably slept in them and stored tools, pots, and other belongings there. They may also have cooked and eaten indoors when the weather was cold or wet. In good weather, however, people probably performed most of their daily activities outdoors.

Food Storage

The small size and flexed-pole construction of the houses poses a puzzle about where people stored their food. There was not enough room on the floors of the houses for people both to sleep and to store their crops. Nor could they have stored sizable quantities of food in baskets or bags hanging from the rafters or wall posts, as too much weight might threaten the structural integrity of the dwelling. We did not find any large underground storage facilities either inside or outside the houses. Where did these agricultural people store their harvest? The most likely answer is that they used aboveground granaries similar to those used by other Native Americans of the Southeast (e.g., Hann 1988:208–209). Such granaries typically were rectangular, enclosed platforms supported on 6 to 12 widely spaced posts. We did not find any post patterns that suggested the presence of granaries near the houses. This raises the possibility that crops were stored not by individual households but by kin groups or other communal groups.

Household Distribution

Even though household size and presumably composition did not change noticeably within the Moundville I phase, the spatial distribution of households did. The early Moundville I households appear to have been scattered over the project area. There would have been room for gardens and, perhaps, some fields near the dwellings. Steponaitis (chap. 2; 1991:198) has suggested that just before the mound-and-plaza complex was built, there was a dense concentration of farmsteads on the terrace at Moundville. The widely spaced early Moundville I structures in the riverbank area could easily be interpreted as support for his model.

With the building of the palisade, the distribution of households changed dramatically. People seem to have moved inside the palisade walls, and the spacing of their homes left little room for gardens, much less fields, near the dwellings. The close packing of the households may have changed patterns of social interaction. If most activities took place outdoors, then quite likely there was more casual contact between neighbors. This may have promoted closer ties, but it also would have provided more opportunities for conflicts to arise.

Craft Production

The elite members of chiefly societies typically participate in long-distance trading networks through which valued materials and finished products are exchanged. The prestige goods that are acquired through these networks or that are made from valued nonlocal materials are used as symbols of status and power both at home and abroad. Welch's (1991) study of Moundville's prestige-goods economy has demonstrated that once Moundville's dominance over other sites in the valley was established, the elite residents of Moundville controlled both the production and distribution of status goods. The overwhelming majority of prestige goods that have been found at sites in the Black Warrior Valley come from Moundville itself. Moreover, virtually no evidence for production of status-related items has been found at any site other than Moundville.

Knight's (1992) recent excavations of Moundville II phase deposits on Mound Q have produced abundant evidence, in the form of tools and raw materials, for the production of various goods almost certainly destined for use outside domestic contexts. Tools recovered from the mound deposit include sandstone saws, pottery trowels, microblades made from Fort Payne chert, and small greenstone adzes. Raw materials from the same deposits include, but are not limited to, mica, galena, and several pigments. There can be little doubt that craft production was among the activities that took place on the mound.

The domestic areas on the riverbank did not produce evidence for craft production on anything near the scale or intensity of that Knight reports for Mound Q. Nevertheless, there are indications that some of the households engaged in at least low-level production of prestige goods.

Concentrations of scrap mica were found in Structure 5 in the PA tract and in structures 4 and 6 and Feature 13 in the ECB tract. Insofar as we know, mica, which comes from the South Appalachian Mountains, was used not for any day-to-day domestic purposes but rather to make paraphernalia associated with the Southeastern Ceremonial Complex. The presence of mica scraps in the structures near the riverbank suggests that people were making something destined for distribution beyond the household. The puzzling thing is that there were no obvious tools or utilized flakes associated with the mica. Be that as it may, presumably the mica was being made into ornaments that were used with regalia and sometimes found their way into burials (cf. Moore 1907:395).

There are two things that should be noted in respect to the possibility of craft production involving mica in the riverbank area. First, the mica comes from middle to late Moundville I contexts. There is no mica from the early Moundville I phase structures. Second, the SCB excavations recovered a large quantity of mica (207 grams) from a pit that intruded a middle to late Moundville I phase floor (Scarry 1986:165). Excavations in the high-status, late Moundville I NR deposit, however, produced virtually no mica (Scarry 1986:156). The presence of mica in other deposits near the Conference Building but not in contemporaneous domestic deposits elsewhere on the site provides support for the suggestion that the riverbank area was a special locus for some form of craft production involving mica.

Palettes made from fine gray micaceous sandstone were exchanged as prestige goods throughout the Southeast (Welch 1991:166–167). The source of the sandstone from which the palettes were made was probably the Pottsville formation located above the fall line at Tuscaloosa (Steponaitis 1992:8). It seems likely that the palettes were made at sites in the Black Warrior Valley and traded elsewhere as finished products. Four fragments of finished or nearly finished palettes were recovered from the riverbank excavations. In addition, pieces of unworked fine gray micaceous sandstone were relatively abundant, and 31 pieces of this material that had been ground, sawn, or polished were recovered. This suggests that palettes or some other items were being manufactured in the area. Unfortunately, other than the palettes themselves, we have little information about the distribution of unworked or modified fine gray micaceous sandstone elsewhere at Moundville or at other sites in the valley. Thus, it is difficult to know whether the presence of this material in the riverbank collections is evidence for craft production.

Social Status

In both early Moundville I and late Moundville I the riverbank area was a residential zone. An issue I have not yet addressed is the status of the people who lived there.

Structure size, internal complexity, and location with respect to other structures in a community are measures that have been used to investigate status differences (Peebles 1978:375–381; Sykes 1989). The structures on the riverbank were similar in size range and floor plan to structures found on the west and south side of Moundville's plaza

(Peebles 1978:379–380). There were larger structures at Moundville (e.g., Peebles 1978:377–378 describes a structure with a floor area of 49 square meters on the edge of the plaza northwest of Mound Q), but those that are known appear to have been public rather than residential buildings. Thus the size of the houses on the riverbank tells us little about the status of the people who lived in them.

Our models of social status at Moundville propose that the northern part of the site was generally a higher status area than the southern end (chap. 3; Peebles 1978:381; Steponaitis 1991:200). This proposition is based on the larger size of the mounds on the north side of Moundville's plaza, the concentration of elite burials in areas on the north side of the plaza, and the distribution of status goods at Moundville. Following this line of argument, the residents of the riverbank area, while not among the highest elite at Moundville, would have been higher in status than people who lived at the southern extremities of the site. We should, however, note a caveat here. If distance from the plaza was also a measure of status, then, despite living on the northern end of the site, the residents of the riverbank may not have been of particularly high rank.

Another avenue we can use to explore status is an examination of the material culture associated with the structures. The distribution of nonlocal materials can provide clues to status. There was very little nonlocal material of any kind associated with the early Moundville I structures on the riverbank. Nonlocal chert and greenstone, however, were relatively abundant in the late Moundville I deposits. There were also concentrations of mica associated with several households, but if we are going to argue that these indicate craft production, it is problematical to use them as indicators of high status as well. That is, unless we can say that craft production is itself an indicator of status (which it might well be), we should be careful about using the presence of mica as evidence of both craft production and high status. Other, presumably high-status, nonlocal materials are rare in the riverbank deposits; they are limited to a single galena crystal from Structure 6 in the ECB tract and several scraps of copper from midden deposits in the ECB tract.

Except at the early Moundville I mound center at the Asphalt Plant mound (1Tu50), nonlocal materials are uncommon at other Moundville-era sites in the Black Warrior Valley (chap. 7; Steponaitis 1992:7–9; Welch 1991:134–176). Nonlocal chert and greenstone are far more abundant in the riverbank assemblage than at most single-mound sites or farmsteads. The question is, does this indicate that the residents of the PA and ECB tracts had higher status than those who lived at outlying sites? In comparison to people who lived on farmsteads away from Moundville, the answer is probably yes. With respect to the people who lived at single-mound centers, the answer is equivocal. It could be that simply living at Moundville gave people, regardless of their status, greater access to nonlocal goods.

The preceding discussions are rather convoluted, but they make it abundantly clear that it is difficult to evaluate status without comparative data. Setting aside the thorny issue of the relative status of the riverbank inhabitants vis-à-vis people living at sites other than Moundville, we can assess their status relative to late Moundville I residents of the area north of Mound R.

The distribution of nonlocal resources in the residential deposits at Moundville can be used as one indicator of status. Both in the various riverbank assemblages and in those from the deposits north of Mound R, nonlocal cherts constitute significant portions of the flaked-stone assemblages. There are, however, clear differences between the two areas in the relative frequencies of nonlocal cherts (fig. 4.7). The assemblage from the PA tract, which we believe to be predominantly early Moundville I, has lower frequencies of nonlocal chert than do the late Moundville I SCB, ECB, and NR deposits. The difference between the PA assemblage and the others is probably largely chronological. (Here we should note that most of the nonlocal chert in the PA assemblage appears to be associated with the later features in this area.) Insofar as we can tell, however, the SCB, ECB and NR deposits are roughly contemporaneous. The differences in the relative frequencies of nonlocal and local cherts in these deposits suggest differential access to imported materials. By this measure, it would seem that the residents of the riverbank had lower status than the residents of the area north of Mound R.

Besides the apparent differences in access to nonlocal goods, there are also indications that the social role of food consumption varied between the residential areas on the riverbank and that north of Mound R. Moundville ceramics can be divided into two broad groups: there are unburnished jars and bowls that were probably used for cooking, storage, and perhaps for serving, and there are burnished bottles and bowls that were primarily serving wares. We can use a comparison of the relative frequencies of unburnished cooking wares to burnished serving wares as a crude measure of the social role and prominence of food consumption. In the residential deposits from the

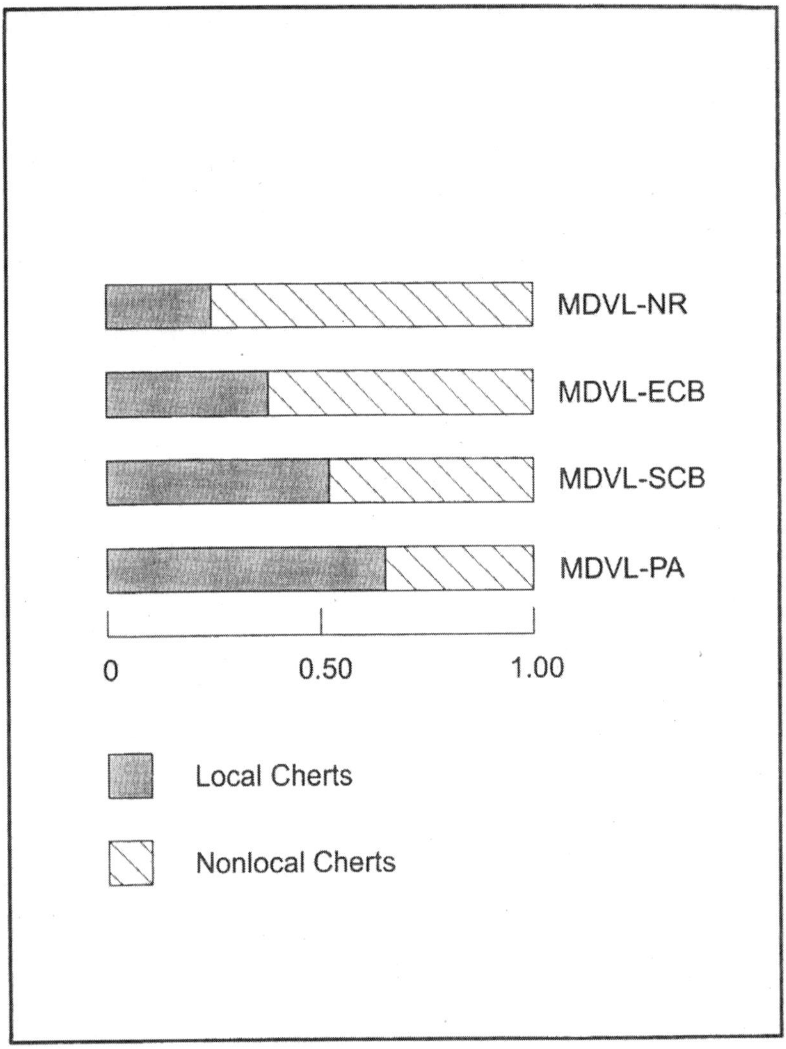

Fig. 4.7. Relative frequencies of local and nonlocal chert in Moundville I contexts. Courtesy Office of Archaeological Services, University of Alabama Museums.

riverbank, the frequency of serving wares is slightly higher in the ECB tract than it is in the PA and SCB deposits (fig. 4.8). The frequency of serving wares in the deposits north of Mound R, however, is dramatically different. Serving wares are almost twice as common in the NR deposit as they are in those on the riverbank. It appears that the presentation of food played a more prominent role in the activities of the people who lived north of Mound R than it did in the lives of the river-

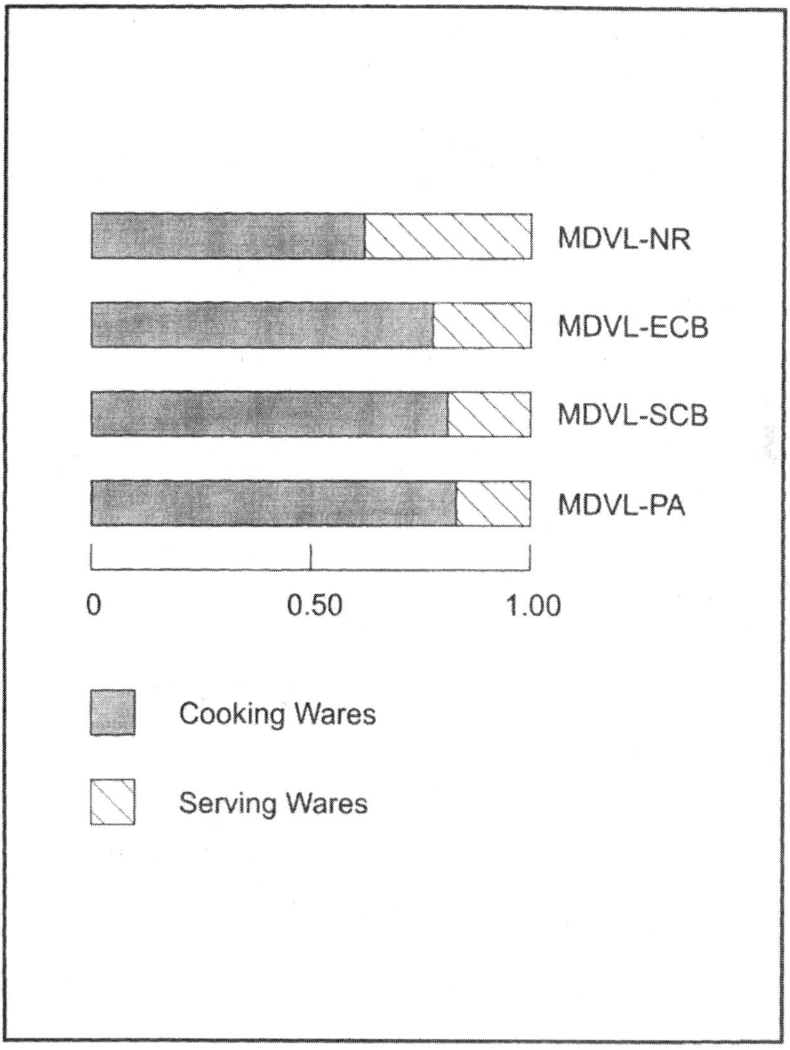

Fig. 4.8. Relative frequencies of cooking and serving wares in Moundville I contexts. Courtesy Office of Archaeological Services, University of Alabama Museums.

bank residents. We believe the area north of Mound R was occupied by members of the elite. The high proportion of serving wares can be interpreted as a reflection of the obligation of the elite to offer hospitality, including food, to their guests (Drennan 1975:135; Sahlins 1972: 268–270; Welch 1991:57).

Based on our comparisons of the distributions of nonlocal cherts and serving wares between the late Moundville I occupations on the riverbank and north of Mound R, there do appear to be status-related differences between the two areas. The residents of the riverbank area appear by both measures to be lower in status than the people who lived north of Mound R. Were the residents of the riverbank commoners? We cannot answer this question without comparable data from other Moundville I domestic deposits at Moundville.

THE RIVERBANK OCCUPATION IN CONTEXT

The Moundville I phase was a dynamic period. It was during the two centuries encompassed by this phase (AD 1050–1250) that social differentiation developed between communities and people and that Moundville gained dominance over the Black Warrior Valley.

Until recently, we thought that the mound-and-plaza complex at Moundville was built incrementally and did not reach its final configuration until sometime around the beginning of the Moundville III phase (Steponaitis 1983a:151–261). It is now evident, however, that the entire mound-and-plaza complex was laid out and probably in use by late Moundville I (chaps. 2 and 3).

Evidence from several sources also indicates that Moundville's resident population probably peaked in late Moundville I and early Moundville II times (chap. 2; Steponaitis 1991:198–200; Welch 1989). Steponaitis has proposed that in early Moundville I there was a dense concentration of farmsteads on the terrace at Moundville. Population seems to have been most concentrated and nucleated in late Moundville I. This would correspond to the period when the elite were consolidating their power and while the labor force was most needed for construction of the mound-and-plaza complex and the palisade. Sometime after the Moundville I–II boundary, the resident population at Moundville declined. Thereafter, it seems to have become home for the highest elite and a mortuary site not only for the population of Moundville but also for residents from other sites in the valley (chap. 2).

The occupations on the northwest riverbank fit comfortably in this model of Moundville's development. The evidence for domestic use of the area spans the Moundville I phase. Occupation may have continued into early Moundville II, but if so it was less intense. The early Moundville I households near the riverbank were scattered and could be interpreted as part of a dense concentration of farmsteads. The palisade was first erected sometime around the middle of the Moundville I phase. This corresponds to the time when the mound-and-plaza complex was laid out and begun. It would appear that the fortification was part of the deliberate community plan. It was in place and protected people when construction activity at Moundville was most intense and when the elite were consolidating their power. Finally, the mortuary use of the area near the riverbank correlates with Moundville's shift from a teeming community to a home for the elite and a burial place for the dead.

ACKNOWLEDGMENTS

The riverbank excavations summarized here were conducted as a result of a cooperative agreement between the United States Army Corps of Engineers, Mobile District, and the University of Alabama, Alabama Museum of Natural History. Vernon J. Knight was principal investigator for the project. Eric Gilliland, an undergraduate student at the University of Alabama, was the field supervisor. I helped VJK design the excavation strategy, visited the site four times during the fieldwork to become familiar with the deposits and help with decision-making, analyzed the artifacts and notes, and with the assistance of John Scarry prepared the report on the excavations.

5. Of Time and the River: Perspectives on Health during the Moundville Chiefdom

MARY LUCAS POWELL

A PREVIOUS SYNCHRONIC STUDY of elite and nonelite burials from Moundville indicated that minor variations in adult stature, childhood stress, dental health, trauma, and infectious disease owed more to age and sex than to differences in ranked status. A diachronic reevaluation of these dimensions of health suggests several trends from Moundville I through Moundville III: small increases in stature and diet-related dental disease for adults of both sexes, a decline in severe chronic iron-deficiency anemia among children, and the first clear appearance of endemic treponematosis and tuberculosis in Moundville II. The overall picture conforms logically to the site's changing role from a major population center to the paramount regional mortuary site, as the growing population gradually spread throughout the Black Warrior Valley in secondary- and tertiary-level communities rather than remaining concentrated at Moundville itself. This dispersed distribution would have minimized (a) localized depletion of animal protein resources through overhunting, (b) contamination of living areas by parasite-infected human wastes, and (c) pathogen exchanges promoted by crowded living conditions. The increasing reliance on maize (documented by bone chemistry and archaeobotanical evidence reported elsewhere in this volume) produced more dental caries and antemortem tooth loss. The dating of numerous burials by phase provides a secure pre-Columbian context for the paleopathological diagnosis of New

World endemic treponematosis and tuberculosis in the Black Warrior Valley.

Over the past quarter century, archaeologists have focused intensive study on many aspects of the Mississippian ranked polity centered at Moundville: its internal social organization, external trade and political relations, diet, and domestic economy. The bioarchaeological study presented here examines another critical feature—the relationship between social status and people's health in that successful chiefdom. The first section summarizes an earlier synchronic analysis of status and health in 564 Moundville burials divided into elite and nonelite mortuary segments (Powell 1988, 1992b). The second section reports a new diachronic study of health based on examination of all Moundville burials currently seriated and represented by skeletal remains ($N = 144$). This reanalysis incorporates changing views of Moundville's history as a regional mortuary center (chap. 1).

Analyses of this sort have two essential prerequisites if they are to be grounded in biocultural reality. First, the population sample must be divided into contemporaneous status-distinct subgroups, based on mortuary criteria. Second, modeled expectations of status-associated differences in health must explicitly link related aspects of biology and behavior, such as superior nutrition of elite families and smoother growth trajectories for elite subadults. The inclusion of a diachronic dimension extends this dynamic linkage through time: the coevolution of society and health in microcosm.

STATUS AND HEALTH AT MOUNDVILLE: A SYNCHRONIC VIEW

Excavations at Moundville in 1905 and 1906 by C. B. Moore uncovered approximately 800 human burials within and around the mounds (Moore 1905, 1907). The Alabama Museum of Natural History (AMNH) uncovered some 2,400 additional interments from 1929 to 1941, all from nonmound locales, for a total of 3,200 reported burials at the site (Peebles 1979). Peebles's analysis of mortuary data from the Moore and AMNH excavations divided a sample of the 2,000 best-documented burials into a series of clusters on the basis of associated grave goods and burial location (Peebles 1971, 1974, 1983; Peebles and Kus 1977). He interpreted these groupings as representing different sociopolitical aggregates: (a) an elite sector, distinguished by access to certain artifacts, design motifs, exotic materials, and special burial locales primarily in mounds (Segment A), and (b) a nonelite sector interred near mounds or village areas (segments B and C), with the majority of individuals (Cluster XI) lacking any reported associated artifacts. The association of elite items with both sexes and all ages (including infants) suggested to Peebles that social rank was to some degree ascribed at birth, although achievements in adult life probably played an additional role.

Ethnographic evidence from historic southeastern chiefdoms indicates that in some circumstances, elite individuals enjoyed varying degrees of preferential access to selected foods as well as to material items and ceremonial privileges (Bourne 1904; Du Pratz 1972; Swanton 1911, 1946; Garcilaso de la Vega 1951). If foods of high nutritional value (e.g., meat) were in short supply either seasonally or episodically, the biological consequences of elite preferential access could be profound. Normal growth and development depend heavily on adequate maternal and child nutrition (Acheson 1960; Albanese and Orto 1964; Dubos 1965; Garn 1966). Differential exposure to pathogens sets the stage for differential disease experience within populations, but the nutritional status of infected hosts is critical for adequate immunoresistance and therefore greatly influences the ultimate adaptive response to prevalent stresses (Deo 1978; Hoeprich 1977; Scrimshaw et al. 1968). All other things being equal, poorly nourished individuals grow more slowly and unevenly and resist disease less effectively than do well-nourished individuals in the same population.

A preliminary analysis of strontium levels in bone samples from Moundville (Peebles and Schoeninger 1981) had suggested that elite individuals consumed more meat than nonelites, with male meat consumption predominating in both groups. Therefore, the synchronic study hypothesized that elite individuals would show less evidence of iron-deficiency anemia than nonelites. A more recent comprehensive analysis of Moundville diets, however, based on stable carbon and nitrogen isotope levels revealed no patterned dietary differences by status or sex, although a substantial increase in reliance on maize from Moundville I to Moundville II–III times was indicated (chap. 6). Consumption of fish, a significant source of protein, remained fairly consistent throughout the subphases, by status and by sex.

The modeled expectations for variability in the biological dimensions of ranked status at Moundville focused on six biological features (Powell 1988:79–80). Adult body size reflects not only the individual's genetic potential for growth but also the quality of nutrition during growth. Better nourished individuals typically display smoother physical development (i.e., fewer dental and skeletal defects from systemic growth disruption) than poorly nourished individuals. Dental pathology (caries, antemortem tooth loss, and wear) reflects the inverse relationship of cariogenicity and texture in a diet featuring starchy plant foods such as maize and squash. Diets low in available iron, heavy intestinal parasite loads, and recurrent bacterial infections may prompt chronic severe iron-deficiency anemia.

Trauma and infectious disease experience are both affected by habitual behavior patterns. Given the important role of warfare as a means for social advancement for males in late prehistoric southeastern chiefdoms (Brown 1976), it seems reasonable to predict more skeletal evidence of war-related trauma among elite males than in their lower-status contemporaries. If elite females did not regularly perform tasks that entailed considerable physical stress, such as the cultivation of agricultural fields, they might display less evidence of trauma. The exemption of elite adults from responsibilities for hunting and the dressing of carcasses would spare them frequent exposure to traumatic stress and zoonotic diseases. An elite diet superior in high-quality protein would enhance elite immunologic resistance to infectious disease, as evidenced by differential patterns of skeletal pathology.

The Synchronic Sample

Approximately 1,500 skeletal individuals excavated from Moundville by the Alabama Museum of Natural History are curated at the Laboratory for Human Osteology (Department of Anthropology) at the University of Alabama in Tuscaloosa. All mortuary areas at the site are represented, except for the mound and perimound areas excavated by C. B. Moore. When Moore's archaeological collections were transferred in the late 1920s from the Philadelphia Academy of Natural Sciences to the Museum of the American Indian (Heye Foundation) in New York, the human skeletal remains were apparently deaccessioned, and attempts to locate these skeletons for study have been unsuccessful (C. S. Peebles, M. J. Schoeninger, personal communications). As a consequence, the highest echelon of elite status at Moundville (Peebles and Kus's Cluster I-A) is not represented in the skeletal sample, although burials from Cluster I-B are present.

Only individuals with well-documented intrasite provenience were included, to minimize the probability of sampling individuals from the pre-Mississippian West Jefferson phase (Powell 1988:80–103). The majority of burials were single primary interments of extended, articulated individuals, with multiple burials a distinct minority (Peebles 1979). Each individual was scored for degree of skeletal completeness. Of the 564 selected for the synchronic study, 144 (25.6 percent) are represented solely by cranial elements and 98 (17.4 percent) solely by postcranial elements. One-fifth (119, or 21.1 percent) are scored as "poorly represented" (less than one-fourth of the skeleton), leaving only 203 (35.9 percent) rated as "fair to good" (more than one-fourth of the skeleton).

In the synchronic study sample, 80 (12 percent of the total) met Peebles's criteria for elite burials (Peebles and Kus 1977). Those in a second group (190 individuals, or 33 percent) were buried with nonelite grave goods. The final group (294, or 55 percent), those with no recorded grave goods, were placed in a residual category (Peebles and Kus's Cluster XI) to differentiate them from the other nonelite burials. No assumption was made that the third group of individuals had necessarily held status inferior to the individuals in the second group (Powell 1988:81–83).

The respective proportions of these three groups, termed elite, subelite, and residual in the synchronic study, do not correspond exactly with the proportions reported in Peebles's analysis. An attempt was made to include only reasonably well-represented individuals in the two nonelite groups. The elite group, however, included all available individuals, even those minimally represented skeletally, to increase its size relative to the two other groups for analytical purposes.

Young subadults (particularly infants) are underrepresented in the total sample but, when present, are typically more skeletally complete than adults. Given that the bones of infants and young children decay more rapidly than adult bones buried under the same conditions because of thinner cortex and incomplete mineralization, this pattern of representation at first appears enigmatic. Many of the field burial forms, however, note that bones were present in a particular grave but were not recovered because of poor preservation. It seems likely that excavators did not attempt to recover young subadult skeletons unless they were well preserved. This policy would have selectively minimized inclusion of the youngest age segments in the available sample.

The proportion of 140 subadults (23 percent) and 424 adults (77 percent) reflects the proportion of these two broad age categories in the total available series (Peebles 1974). Individuals 15 years or younger comprise only 19.5 percent (110 of 564), in contrast to 30–50 percent in the anthropological population samples utilized by Weiss (1973) in his construction of model life tables. In particular, infant mortality (25 of 564, or 4.4 percent) is well below the 20–35 percent reported by Weiss. The next oldest portion of the sample, however, does approximate "the general shape of human juvenile mortality . . . declining from ages 1 to 5, then decreasing steadily until those from 10 to 15 years have the lowest mortality" (Weiss 1973:26).

Adult females outnumber males 221 to 172, but no statistically significant difference ($p > .05$) in skeletal representation by sex is indicated (Powell 1988:89–94). The sex estimates for the present study match in almost all cases those by M. J. Schoeninger and C. S. Larsen made in 1977 (personal communication), based on the same osteological criteria. Thus it seems unlikely that observer error is responsible for the discrepancy between expected (roughly 1 : 1) and observed (1.29 : 1) female-to-male ratios. Possible contributing factors are disproportionate representation of younger males and older females in mound burials not available for analysis, and additional loss of younger males to the sample through mortality in warring raids and hunting accidents.

Age and sex differences among the three sample segments designated by status were assessed by chi-square analysis as not significant ($p > .05$). Given the constraints of subsample construction, no conclusions could be reached regarding differential mortality experience for the two sexes or the three status groups.

ADULT BODY SIZE. Six skeletal measurements (maximum diameter of humerus and femur head, femur midshaft circumference and anterior-posterior diameter, and maximum length of femur and tibia) were taken on all complete bones of adult females and males. Analysis of sexual dimorphism by Student's t-test and one-way analysis of variance indicated significant differences ($p < .001$) within each status group. Separate comparisons by sex across status boundaries using the same analytic methods, however, revealed no significant differences ($p > .05$). On average, elite females were slightly larger than nonelite females only for humerus-head maximum diameter. Elite males averaged slightly higher values than nonelite males for the five remaining measurements (Powell 1988:105–108).

PHYSICAL DEVELOPMENT. The patterning of nonspecific developmental stress was assessed through observation of linear enamel hypoplasia (LEH) (Powell 1988:108–114). This condition results from short-term episodes of arrested enamel development initiated by a variety of systemic stresses, including malnutrition, infection, and psychological stress (Goodman et al. 1980). LEH is considered a nonspecific stress indicator because determination of the specific etiology of any particular lesion is impossible. However, the individual's developmental age at the time of the lesion's formation may be calculated by comparison of the lesion location on the tooth crown with standardized charts of enamel development.

Enamel lesions visible at 10× magnification were scored on all undamaged permanent incisors and canines in the series. To eliminate false positive scores reflecting idiosyncratic developmental errors on single teeth, only cases in which synchronous lesions were observed on two or more teeth in a dentition were scored as positive instances of systemic developmental disturbance.

The prevalence of LEH was calculated as the proportion of hypoplastic to nonhypoplastic enamel segments formed during each of the 12 six-month periods during the first six years of postnatal life. The great majority of lesions reflect acute growth arrest episodes during the third and fourth years. Contributory factors probably include weaning from a protein-rich diet to one less suited to the physiological needs of the growing infant, and greater exposure to pathogens (including parasites) due to increased mobility of toddlers. The role of differential sensitivity of certain segments of the tooth crown to systemic insults during development has not been definitively assessed (Condon 1981). Chi-square analysis of both the absolute and the age-associated prevalence of hypoplasia by age, sex, and status revealed no significant differences ($p > .05$).

DENTAL HEALTH. Dental wear is not a pathological condition per se, but the presence of grit or rough-textured foods in the diet may irritate adjacent soft tissues. Scott's (1979) system for quantification of occlusal molar wear was employed on all intact molars in adult dentitions. Observed wear was moderate, with little dentine exposure evident prior to the fourth decade. This pattern agrees well with artifactual evidence from Moundville and archaeological and ethnohistoric data from the late prehistoric Southeast in general indicating that plant foods were typically processed in wooden mortars rather than in stone grinders (Hudson 1976).

Within each group, males displayed slightly heavier occlusal wear than females, but breakdown of mean wear scores by decade indicated a strong age effect. Statistical analysis of molar wear by status for age-controlled samples of females and males revealed no consistent significant patterns of differences ($p > .05$) among the three groups (Powell 1988:114–120).

The prevalence and patterning of dental caries provide a valuable index to the proportionate representation of soft-textured high-carbohydrate foods in the diet (Powell 1985). Chi-square comparisons of caries prevalence by status in samples matched for age, sex, and tooth type paralleled the patterns of molar wear: no consistent pattern of significant differences ($p > .05$) (Powell 1988:120–135). Inter- and intragroup comparisons revealed almost identical mean caries rates for both sexes, controlled for age, between and within status subgroups. The majority of carious lesions (65 percent) were located in occlusal pits and fissures of the premolars and molars. Most antemortem tooth loss, presumably from carious destruction, also occurred in the posterior dentition. These patterns closely resemble those reported for other Mississippian populations (Larsen et al. 1991).

IRON-DEFICIENCY ANEMIA. Skeletal evidence of severe chronic iron-deficiency anemia was very rare (Powell 1988:147–148). No cases of porotic hyperostosis were noted, but ten young children (10 of 47, 21 percent) and five adults (5 of 115, 4 percent) exhibited remodeled lesions of cribra orbitalia, a condition generally considered to represent a skeletal response to iron-deficiency anemia (Hengen 1971; Ortner and Putschar 1981; Steinbock 1976). The population prevalence rate of 9 percent is slightly higher than the 7 percent reported by Powell (1983) for the combined Mississippian and Protohistoric samples at Lubbub Creek but is much lower than those reported by Hill-Clark (1981) for two Protohistoric (Moundville IV) samples (24 percent at 1Tu4, 62 percent at 1Ha19) along the Black Warrior River.

Prevalence of this condition was lowest among elite individuals (1 of 40, 2.5 percent of observed orbits), intermediate among individuals in the residual category (11 of 169, 6.5 percent), and highest among subelite individuals (10 of 101, 9.9 percent). This distribution suggests that severe iron-deficiency anemia may have been less common in the elite at Moundville. Chi-square analysis revealed no statistically significant differences ($p > .05$) by status.

TRAUMA. Healed fractures were the most common traumatic injury, noted in 34 adults but no subadults (Powell 1988:144–146). Ribs, hands, feet, radii, and ulnae were most often broken. Moundville male prevalence (1 percent of observed individuals) is more than double that of females (0.4 percent). The greatest differences by sex are noted in the rates for fractured ribs (9.4 percent of males versus 1.3 percent of females) and hands (4.0 percent of males versus 2.1 percent of females).

Elite females exhibit no trauma, unlike nonelite females, but contrary to expectations, elite males show fewer fractures than nonelite males. This difference may be owed in part to the absence of the highest stratum of elite burials (those in mounds) from this sample. It most likely also reflects the less complete representation by long bones (the site of most fractures in the sample) of elite than nonelite individuals.

INFECTIOUS DISEASE. Periostitis was the most common form of skeletal pathology observed (Powell 1988:148–157). This condition represents a nonspecific inflammatory response to pathological insults from trauma or infection and is not, by itself, diagnostic for any particular disease (Hoeprich 1977; Ortner and Putschar 1981; Steinbock 1976). However, a nonrandom pattern of anatomical distribution in an individual or a population (e.g., predominantly bilateral rather than unilocal) may suggest some specific etiology.

The anterior tibia shaft was the area most often affected by periostitis, with an overall prevalence rate of 50.7 percent. Next most often affected were the shafts of the fibula (26.2 percent), femur (14.7 percent), humerus (4.7 percent), clavicle (4.4 percent), radius (3.7 percent), and ulna (3.6 percent). In the majority of cases, skeletal involvement was minor. Analysis by chi-square of associations between presence of periostitis and sex or status indicated no significant differences ($p > .05$). Rates of prevalence and anatomical patterns of involvement are almost identical for adults of both sexes and for the members of all three status subgroups (matched for age, sex, and differences in skeletal representation).

The high prevalence of well-healed periosteal lesions and their greater frequency among older adults suggest that the majority of affected individuals survived whatever pathologic or traumatic insults were responsible for this response. The majority of affected elements display localized involvement, typically affecting only a small area of cortex. These factors, taken with the lack of association with early mortality and the nonrandom anatomical distribution, suggest endemic disease that afflicted many members of each generation but rarely caused death.

Small circular or oval lesions of the cranial vault, affecting almost exclusively the outer table and appearing well remodeled at death, were noted in 23 adults, most often in association with postcranial periostitis. Careful comparison of the anatomical and demographic patterning of these two types of lesions with disease models that combine high prevalence of postcranial periostitis with low prevalence of resorptive cranial lesions suggests that the Moundville pattern of skeletal involvement resulted from an endemic treponematosis (Powell 1988, 1991). Three adult crania clearly display the characteristic stellate lesions of healed caries sicca, considered to be strongly pathognomonic of treponemal infection (Hackett 1976). They closely resemble the cranial lesions illustrated by Haltom and Shands (1938) in their appraisal of syphilis at Moundville. The majority of the other cranial lesions observed in this sample could also represent healed treponemal scalp lesions that affected underlying bone, although their form is not so clearly diagnostic as these three specimens. Several adult cases of sabre shins were also observed, tibiae grossly deformed from recurrent episodes of periosteal inflammation.

Tuberculosis, another chronic infectious disease documented in prehistoric Amerindian populations of the eastern United States (Buikstra 1981; Kelley and Eisenberg 1987; Ortner and Putschar 1981; Powell 1991; Steinbock 1976), was also present at Moundville. A young adult male of the subelite group exhibited severe anterior kyphosis (forward curvature of the spine) resulting from extensive destruction of numerous vertebral bodies by a chronic infectious process. Nine other individuals displayed rib lesions suggestive of this disease.

Summary

The results of the synchronic study suggest a population generally well adapted within its natural and social environment (Powell 1988: 175–182). The skeletal record documents developmental disturbances in early childhood and the inevitable encounters with minor trauma and endogenous pathogens, but infections that marked bone typically left only minor reactions. The age-associated distribution of linear enamel hypoplasia closely matches patterns reported for other Mississippian populations. Bone lesions suggesting anemia were rare. The diet produced moderate dental wear and widespread dental decay, similar to patterns reported for other Mississippians.

Comparisons of the three status subgroups clearly show their basic homogeneity with respect to health. Differences by age (subadults versus adults) are more generalized and strongly marked than are differences by sex. The lack of statistically significant differences in skeletal metrics by status and the very low rate of trauma among elite males, both findings contrary to expectations, may be due in part to the absence in the sample of the most highly ranked individuals, those buried in mounds.

No consistent patterned differences were evident, however, among the two nonelite population segments, which are well represented, suggesting that status differentiation at Moundville brought no substantial biological benefits and did not exact any particular penalties.

OF TIME AND THE RIVER: A DIACHRONIC VIEW

The synchronic bioarchaeological study incorporated then-current interpretations of Moundville's development, which emphasized continual steady growth of the chiefdom through the Moundville I, II, and III phases, with no decline evident until sometime after AD 1550 (Peebles 1978; Steponaitis 1983a). This chronology was based largely on Steponaitis's (1983a) seriation of whole ceramic vessels from burial contexts: the majority of the vessels dated to the Moundville II and III phases (AD 1250–1550). More recent analyses of sherd collections from midden deposits across the site, however, have prompted a radical revision of this earlier scheme (chap. 2; Welch 1989; Steponaitis 1991; Scarry and Steponaitis 1992). Nearly three-quarters of the chronologically diagnostic midden sherds represent the Moundville I phase (AD 1050–1250), quite the opposite of the chronological distribution of the grave vessels. Evidently the Moundville site retained high significance throughout the latter phases as a preferred location for the dead, despite a decline in the resident living population.

This drastic redistribution of the effective regional population throughout the landscape after AD 1250 would have had major implications for patterns of health and disease. Steponaitis's (1991) chronological assignment of 546 ceramic gravelots from Moundville provided a welcome opportunity for a diachronic reexamination of biocultural dimensions of late prehistoric life on the central Black Warrior River. Unfortunately, skeletal material is not available from all of the seriated burials, either because the associated remains were not recovered or because they were subsequently lost.

The Diachronic Sample

The analysis reported here incorporates all available seriated individuals (*N* = 144), 98 of them previously included in the synchronic study (Powell 1988) and 46 newly examined in June 1993. The series is divided into five chronological subsets: Moundville I (*N* = 6), Moundville I–II (*N* = 11), Moundville II (*N* = 12), Moundville II–III (*N* = 62), and Moundville III (*N* = 53). The increase through time in the number of individuals reflects the overall pattern of an increasing population of burials at the site, evidenced in Steponaitis's dated gravelots. The split-phase samples could not be reliably assigned to either of the two indicated phases but could be confidently excluded from earlier or later periods. The five subsets are compared for the six biological features reported in the previous study (Powell 1988) and summarized above.

Table 5.1 compares the demographic profiles of the synchronic and diachronic samples. The latter sample (*N* = 144) is one-quarter the size of the original sample. The percentages of subadults (less than 15 years old) are similar (110 of 564, 19.5 percent, and 32 of 144, 22.2 percent), as are their percentages in the two largest subsets, Moundville II–III (13 of 62, 21.0 percent) and Moundville III (11 of 53, 20.7 percent). Infants (0–1 years) are underrepresented in all samples (25 of 564, 4.4 percent; 5 of 144, 3.5 percent; 2 of 62, 3.2 percent; and 2 of 53, 3.8 percent). Both samples show biased sex ratios: in the synchronic sample, 221 females to 174 males, and in the diachronic sample, 54 females to 34 males.

ADULT BODY SIZE. Table 5.2 presents mean values for six postcranial skeletal metrics. The very small sample sizes precluded statistical comparisons, but two measurements, maximum femur length and maximum tibia length, do show a slight average increase in both sexes from Moundville I to Moundville III times.

PHYSICAL DEVELOPMENT. No consistent pattern of increase or decrease through time was evident in the numbers of individuals whose teeth displayed linear enamel hypoplasia. Table 5.3 presents the percentages of cases scored as positive or negative in each subsample. As in the synchronic sample, the majority of lesions were formed

Table 5.1.
Synchronic and Diachronic Samples: Age Profiles

	Age Categories									
	Infant (birth–1 year)	Child (1–5)	Juvenile (5–10)	Early Adoles. (10–15)	Late Adoles. (15–20)	Young Adult (20–30)	Middle Adult (30–40)	Old Adult (40–50)	Senile (+50)	Total
Synchronic Sample (*N*)	25	52	23	10	30	131	78	82	33	564
(%)[a]	4	9	4	2	5	23	32	14	6	
Diachronic Sample (*N*)	5	18	7	2	3	37	41	25	6	144
(%)[a]	5	12	5	1	2	26	28	17	4	
Moundville Phase (*N*)										
I	1	0	1	0	0	2	1	0	1	6
I–II	0	2	0	0	0	5	3	0	1	11
II	0	3	1	0	0	11	4	3	0	12
II–III	2	6	4	1	2	18	18	7	4	62
III	2	7	1	1	1	11	15	15	0	53

a. Percentages rounded to the nearest whole number. The unaged adults in both samples have been proportionately assigned to the four adult age categories.

Table 5.2.
Moundville Postcranial Metrics: Mean Values (in Millimeters)

Phase	Sex (*N*)	Humerus Head Diameter	Femur Head Diameter	Femur Midshaft Circum.	Femur Midshaft Diameter[a]	Femur Max. Length	Tibia Max. Length
I	M (1)	47.0	46.5	85.0	34.0	442.5	370.0
I–II	M (1)	—	—	92.0	31.0	—	381.0
II	M (3)	45.0	46.8	89.2	30.8	443.0	—
II–III	M (7)	45.0	46.7	91.0	32.0	452.0	356.0
III	M (10)	47.7	46.7	90.7	31.3	458.0	372.2
I	F (0)	—	—	—	—	—	—
I–II	F (2)	38.5	39.8	77.3	25.8	400.8	336.5
II	F (0)	—	—	—	—	—	—
II–III	F (7)	—	43.0	78.5	26.2	422.0	335.0
III	F (3)	39.0	41.0	80.7	27.7	413.0	342.0

a. Anterior-posterior diameter.

Table 5.3.
Linear Enamel Hypoplasia

Phase	*N*	None	Mild	Moderate	Severe	% None
I	3	1	1	1	0	33
I–II	3	2	0	0	1	67
II	1	1	0	0	0	100
II–III	12	4	6	2	0	33
III	5	2	0	3	0	40

during the third and fourth years of postnatal life. Only one case was scored as severe.

DENTAL HEALTH. Table 5.4 presents data on dental caries and antemortem tooth loss in the five chronological subsets. The sample sizes are small, ranging from 1 to 11 individuals in each category, and many of the dentitions are incomplete. Carious activity increased in younger adults from Moundville I to Moundville II, an expected result of the increase in maize consumption during that period documented by bone

Table 5.4.
Dental Caries and Antemortem Tooth Loss

		Adult Age Categories			
Phase		20–30	30–40	40–50	+50
I	N	1/24	0/21	—	16/32
	%	4.2	0	—	50.0
I–II	N	8/29	6/45	—	5/15
	%	28.0	9.0	—	33.0
II	N	—	15/41	2/23	—
	%	—	30.0	9.0	—
II–III	N	25/250	23/172	10/86	6/54
	%	10.0	13.4	11.6	11.1
III	N	15/77	16/120	15/61	—
	%	19.0	13.3	24.6	—

$N = \frac{\text{carious teeth + teeth lost antemortem}}{\text{total observations}}$

Table 5.5.
Iron-Deficiency Anemia

Phase	*N* Crania	Cases	%
I	3	1	33.0
I–II	3	0	0
II	8	0	0
II–III	36	4	11.1
III	28	1	3.6

chemistry (chap. 6) and paleoethnobotanical analysis (Scarry and Steponaitis 1992). The lower level of caries in the later Moundville adults may reflect accumulated selective pressure against particularly caries-prone phenotypes. No change in the pattern of dental wear was evident, not a surprising observation considering the lack of artifactual evidence for any significant changes in plant-food processing technology during the Moundville phase.

IRON-DEFICIENCY ANEMIA. The skeletal lesions taken as markers of severe chronic iron-deficiency anemia were notably rare in the synchronic sample, observed in only 10 subadults and 5 adults (9.2 percent, 15 of 162 crania observed). This low prevalence was surprising, considering the then-current model of high population density at the site until the very end of Moundville III. Skeletal evidence of anemia decreases radically from Moundville I to Moundville III (table 5.5). The decentralized settlement pattern observed in the later phases may provide a partial explanation: a population distributed more equitably over the landscape would be less likely to exhaust crucial food resources (particularly iron-rich meat). Smaller communities also provide, on the whole, fewer opportunities for endogenous pathogen mutation and exchange and concentrated contamination of living areas with human wastes, thereby reducing ambient bacterial and parasitic disease loads.

TRAUMA. Evidence of skeletal trauma is rare throughout the Moundville burial sample. Healed fractures were observed in 1 of the 6 individuals assigned to Moundville I (17 percent), in none of the Moundville I–II or Moundville II individuals, in 3 of 62 (4.8 percent) of the

Moundville II–III individuals, and in 1 of 53 (1.9 percent) individuals assigned to Moundville III. No particular pattern of change through time is apparent.

INFECTIOUS DISEASE. As in the synchronic sample, the most common observed cause of skeletal pathology was periostitis, inflammation of the membrane that surrounds living bone. The majority of cases showed small areas of remodeled bone cortex, predominantly on the long bones of the forearms and lower limbs. It is impossible to determine which of these minor lesions resulted from simple trauma (bruising of the periosteum), which from nonspecific bacterial infections, and which from a combination of both causes. Skeletal evidence of inflammatory reaction (from whatever cause or causes) became more common from Moundville I to Moundville III, however (table 5.6).

A minority of cases displayed evidence of specific diseases: stellate cranial lesions and grossly distorted tibia shafts characteristic of endemic treponematosis, and the destructive vertebral, sacral, and rib lesions of tuberculosis. Both of these diseases have been reported in various locales in late prehistoric eastern Woodlands (summarized in Powell 1988, 1991, 1992b). Three new cases of treponematosis, indicated by distinctive sabre shins of two adults and one child, and one new case of tuberculosis, indicated by a severely destructive lumbar vertebra lesion in an adult female aged 30–40, were identified among the previously unstudied seriated individuals included in this diachronic study. These discoveries add significantly to the documentation of these diseases in secure pre-Columbian New World contexts.

Table 5.6.
Infectious Disease

Phase	*N*	Pathologies	%	Possible Treponematosis	Possible TB
I	6	1	16.7	0	0
I–II	11	2	9.1	0	0
II	12	3	25.0	0	0
II–III	62	23	37.1	5	2
III	53	15	28.3	5	0

CONCLUSIONS

The biological evidence from these dated burials, interpreted in the context of recent dietary analyses based on bone chemistry and food remains and the revised model of site development and regional population distribution, offers some tantalizing suggestions regarding changes in the quality of life along the Black Warrior River. The increasing reliance on maize does not seem to have produced either a decrease in adult body size or an increase in linear enamel hypoplasia; skeletal evidence of severe chronic iron-deficiency anemia actually decreased. Dental caries and premature tooth loss plagued most adults throughout their lives, the result of the highly starchy Mississippian diet. Despite the gradual increase in regional population levels, skeletal evidence of trauma remained rare.

Skeletal inflammatory reaction to trauma and/or infectious disease increased through time. Though no clear evidence of endemic treponematosis appears until the Moundville II–III sample, its presence may have been covertly responsible for the dramatic increase in nonspecific skeletal lesions during Moundville II. This disease apparently maintained a typically nonvenereal mode of transmission in pre-Columbian eastern North America, to judge from the virtual absence of dental stigmata indicative of congenital transmission (Powell 1994). If that was the case, the natural fertility of the Moundville people would not have been decreased by repeated miscarriages and stillbirths, nor would they have suffered the neurological and cardiovascular complications of venereal treponematosis.

Lesions characteristic of an endemic New World form of tuberculosis do not appear until Moundville II. Elsewhere in the late prehistoric eastern Woodlands (Buikstra and Cook 1981; Milner and Smith 1990; Kelley and Eisenberg 1987) and throughout the modern epidemiological literature (Dubos and Dubos 1952; McNeill 1976), researchers have reported the severe impact of tuberculosis on populations weakened by inadequate nutrition, overcrowding, and other diseases. The people of the Moundville chiefdom seem to have been afforded some degree of protection against the disease by their healthful diet and dispersed settlement pattern.

Whatever the social causes for the post–Moundville I population dispersion throughout the Black Warrior Valley hinterlands, the net effect on health and disease patterns was beneficial, minimizing dietary stress, overcrowding of villages, and social trauma.

ACKNOWLEDGMENTS

I thank the Alabama Museum of Natural History for permission to present these data and the Department of Anthropology, University of Alabama, for support and encouragement throughout my research on the Moundville skeletal series. Patricia Bridges, Vernon J. Knight, and Margaret Scarry provided helpful comments on the manuscript. Any misinterpretations, however, are solely my own responsibility.

6. Human Subsistence at Moundville: The Stable-Isotope Data

MARGARET J. SCHOENINGER AND
MARK R. SCHURR

STABLE CARBON AND NITROGEN ISOTOPE analyses of approximately 250 human, animal, and maize samples indicate changes in human subsistence strategies during occupation at pre-Contact Moundville in Alabama. Data suggest increased maize use between Moundville I and the subsequent Moundville II phase. Most important, a decrease in $\delta^{13}C$ values between Moundville III and the subsequent Moundville IV phase ($t = 2.96$, $df = 53$, significant at the 0.01 level, two-tailed test) coupled with a lack of change in $\delta^{15}N$ values suggests a decrease in dependence on maize and an increased dependence on gathered plant foods. This supports earlier hypotheses explaining Moundville's collapse as due to internal rather than external factors.

As befits a site studied as intensively as Moundville (Peebles et al. 1982), the diet of its inhabitants deserves attention. This project was developed toward that end with several questions in mind. First, what was the pattern of change in human diet over time at Moundville? Was there a difference between the earliest period of settlement (Moundville I) and later periods (Moundville II and III)? Was there a difference between the periods of Moundville's greatest florescence (Moundville II and III) and the last period (Moundville IV, previously called Alabama River phase), during which Moundville's control of the polity along the Black Warrior River seems to have been lost (Peebles 1987b). Second, what was the pattern of human diet among status clusters previously identified by Peebles (Peebles 1974)? Did individuals of higher status have diets that differed from those identified by mortuary analysis as lower status? Third, were there any differences in diet between males and females at Moundville? Fourth, once the pattern of diet at the site is established, does it provide any information about Moundville's loss of political control?

The method used is analysis of carbon- and nitrogen-stable-isotope ratios in bone collagen to detect diets of individuals from different time periods, different status positions, and different sex. In general, the present study is complementary to the analyses of the floral (Scarry 1986) and faunal (Michals 1981) remains from Moundville. Such midden analyses are imperative for identifying diet items and indicating subsistence trends over time, but it is not usually possible to detect individual differences in diet from such studies. The attention paid to Moundville's middens since the 1970s, however, has permitted an assessment of relative importance of diet items at different periods that has been impossible at most sites. Together, the midden and stable-isotope studies should result in a more accurate reconstruction of diet in the prehistoric Moundville community.

For carbon, the stable-isotope ratios ($^{13}C/^{12}C$), represented as $\delta^{13}C$ values in per mil (‰) notation, in bone collagen reflect the $^{13}C/^{12}C$ ratio in the diet of the individual (DeNiro and Epstein 1978). The utility of this method is based on an average 1 percent (10 per mil) difference in stable carbon isotope ratios between plants that synthesize a three-carbon molecule during the first phase of photosynthesis (referred to as C_3 plants) and other plants (referred to as C_4 plants), such as tropical grasses (e.g., maize) that synthesize a four-carbon molecule in the first phase (O'Leary 1988). The difference in plant ratios is reflected in the tissues of animals, including humans, that eat them. Humans or animals such as the white-tailed deer that eat C_3 plants have tissues with a C_3 signature, because their tissues reflect the $\delta^{13}C$ values of the C_3 plants they consume. Similarly, humans who eat C_4 plants or animals that eat C_4 plants, such as bison on the Great Plains, have tissues with a C_4 signature. The majority of wild North American plants of the southeastern United States are C_3, and maize is the only major C_4 plant that was an important dietary component prehistorically in the Moundville area. For this reason, human bone collagen $\delta^{13}C$ values with a C_4 signature indicate a diet including maize or animals that ate maize.

Stable nitrogen isotope ratios ($^{15}N/^{14}N$) in bone collagen, presented as $\delta^{15}N$ values in per mil notation, also reflect the values in the individual's diet (DeNiro and Epstein 1981). Among terrestrial plants (see Delwiche et al. 1979; Virginia and Delwiche 1982), those that fix atmospheric nitrogen (such as legumes) tend to have stable-isotope values different from those that use soil nitrates. Even so, a previous study revealed, contrary to expectation, that domestic beans did not carry a diagnostic $\delta^{15}N$ signature and thus cannot be detected as a component of human diet (Spielmann et al. 1990). In contrast, a study of fish from the Great Lakes (Katzenberg 1989) indicated that they had a diagnostic $\delta^{15}N$ signature, and the presence of fish as an important protein component of human diet was readily apparent.

MATERIALS AND METHODS

Samples of human bone (provided by the Alabama Museum of Natural History) and animal bone (provided by Lauren Michals) were analyzed for stable carbon and nitrogen isotope ratios (see table 6.1). All samples were cleaned mechanically of surface debris and then ultrasonicated in double-distilled water. The organic fraction of bone was extracted in several ways and results compared on duplicate samples. Bone was ground, passed through a 0.71-millimeter mesh screen, demineralized in hydrochloric acid, and the resultant organic fraction (mainly the protein,

Table 6.1.
Stable-Isotope Data from Moundville

	$\delta^{13}C$±s.d.			$\delta^{15}N$±s.d.		
Sample	‰ (PDB)	(*N*)	Range	‰ (AIR)	(*N*)	Range
Human						
Moundville I	−15.0±4.0	(4)	−20.8, −12.1	7.0±2.0	(4)	4.6, 9.4
Moundville II	−10.4±1.0	(3)	−11.0, −9.2	8.0±0.5	(3)	7.7, 8.6
Moundville III	−10.3±1.1	(30)	−12.2, −8.3	8.3±1.0	(30)	7.1, 11.1
Moundville IV	−11.1±0.8	(24)	−12.7, −9.3	8.3±0.6	(24)	7.1, 9.6
Fauna						
Terrestrial	−20.2±1.2	(16)	−21.9, −17.2	3.8±1.5	(16)	1.4, 7.4
Aquatic	−23.5±1.5	(5)	−25.7, −22.2	7.8±1.6	(5)	6.4, 9.8
Maize	−8.4±0.1	(5)	−8.6, −8.3	4.0±0.8	(5)	3.1, 5.0

collagen) dissolved (i.e., hydrolyzed) in a weak, hot hydrochloric acid solution (following Longin 1971, with modifications for humic acid removal by DeNiro and Epstein 1981 and Schoeninger and DeNiro 1984). In addition, pieces of bone were demineralized in weak hydrochloric acid (HCl) at room temperature (Sealy 1986). Because some of the human bone samples appeared poorly preserved, some samples were demineralized (following Tuross et al. 1988; Schoeninger et al. 1989) in cold ethylenediaminetetraacetic acid (EDTA). (EDTA has an affinity for calcium, thereby removing calcium from the bone mineral; its advantage over HCl is that it doesn't destabilize proteins, thus the recovery rate of collagen from bone is higher.) Comparison of results from samples and controls demineralized both by HCl and EDTA revealed no differences among preparation methods. In those cases where more than one preparation was made, the average value was used in the calculations presented below.

In all cases, dried organic material was weighed into clean quartz tubing with excess cupric oxide, elemental copper, and elemental silver. The tubing was sealed under vacuum, combusted at 800°C, and allowed to cool to room temperature. The resulting H_2O, CO_2, and N_2 were separated cryogenically in a glass vacuum line and the carbon dioxide and nitrogen gas were analyzed mass spectrometrically. The N_2 was prepared in Schoeninger's laboratories at Harvard University and the University of Wisconsin and measured in Jim McCarthy's laboratory at Harvard University on a V.G.602E mass spectrometer and in Schoeninger's laboratory at the University of Wisconsin using a Finnegan MAT 251 mass spectrometer. The CO_2 was prepared both at Harvard University and at the University of Wisconsin and was measured in John Hayes's laboratory at Indiana University (by Schurr) and in Schoeninger's laboratory at the University of Wisconsin on Finnegan MAT Delta E mass spectrometers. Duplicate samples indicated nonsystematic variation and were within 0.4 per mil, on average. The calculations presented below were made on the average of duplicate preparations.

RESULTS

The results are shown in table 6.1 and in figures 6.1, 6.2, and 6.3. The $\delta^{13}C$ values for maize are approximately –8 per mil, which agrees with analyses of other prehistoric maize samples and with expectations of atmospheric CO_2 composition prehistorically (Marino and McElroy

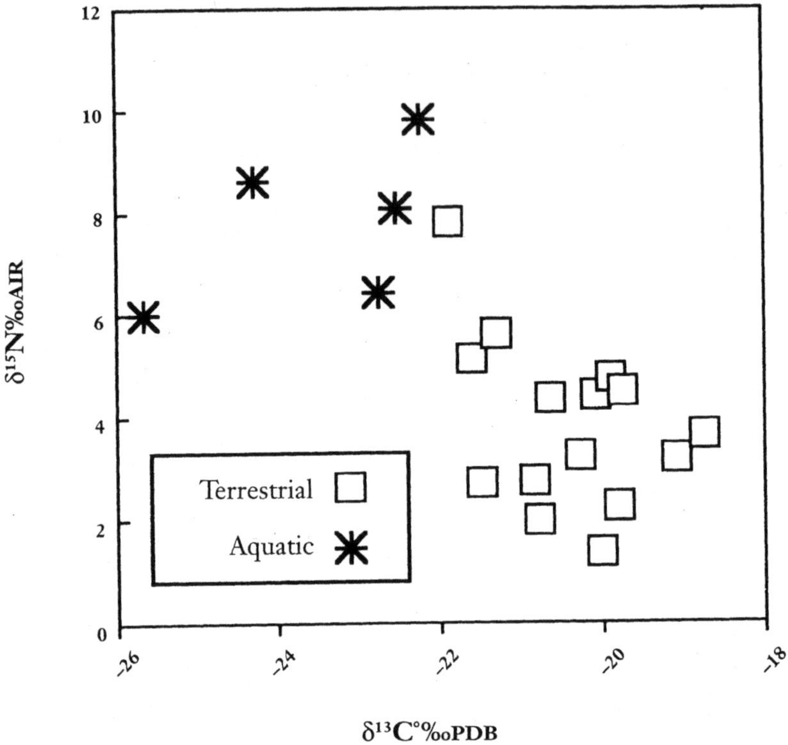

Fig. 6.1. Plot of stable-isotope data from fish and terrestrial fauna recovered from middens at Moundville. All show a strong C_3 signature in $\delta^{13}C$ values. The fish also display $\delta^{15}N$ values that are distinctly more positive than those in the terrestrial fauna.

1991; Tieszen and Fagre 1993; Schoeninger and Schurr 1994). Modern maize samples have $\delta^{13}C$ values closer to −11 per mil because of the increase in the amount of atmospheric CO_2, produced by large-scale burning of forests and of fossil fuels, which are the product of early plants. Both sources are C_3 plants with a $\delta^{13}C$ value of around −26 per mil; the addition of large amounts of CO_2 with values around −26 per mil has resulted in a reduction of atmospheric CO_2 $\delta^{13}C$ values by 2 to 3 per mil over the last 100 to 200 years. The remaining pattern for carbon isotope ratios in flora and fauna is as expected, except that some of the fish samples have extremely negative values. All of them are at the most negative end of the range of the faunal samples. None of the animals had eaten enough maize to modify a basically C_3 signature in their bone collagen.

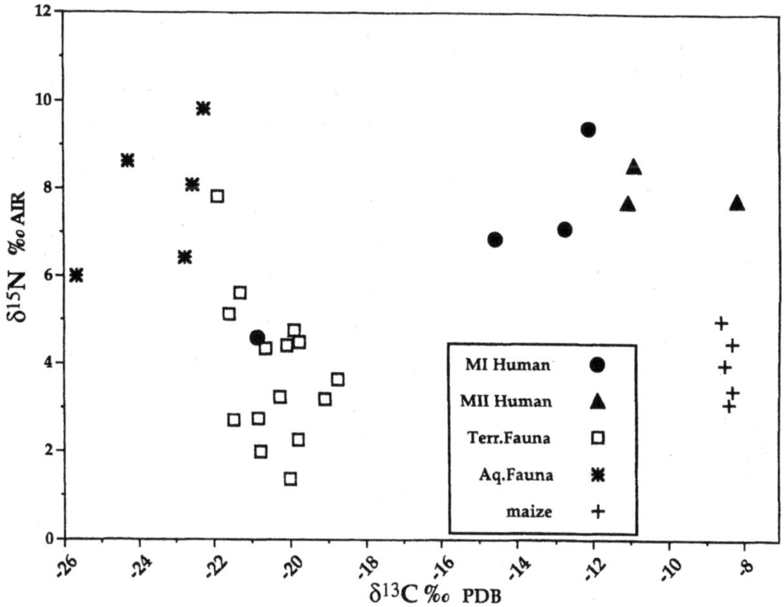

Fig. 6.2. Plot of stable-isotope data from human samples taken from the early phases of Moundville occupation compared with data from the fauna and maize. Sample sizes are very small, but the increase in $\delta^{13}C$ values indicating increased maize use between Moundville I and Moundville II is distinct.

There is a difference in the $\delta^{13}C$ values of the human samples through time. Moundville I presents an average of −14 per mil (excluding the individual at −21 per mil), Moundville II and III are identical at −10 per mil, and Moundville IV is −11 per mil (figs. 6.2 and 6.3). The sample size in Moundville I is too small for testing the apparent difference statistically, but in the absence of sampling error as an explanation, there is a distinct difference in $\delta^{13}C$ values (in the direction of increasing dependence on maize) in Moundville II compared to Moundville I. Of particular interest is that the samples from Moundville IV differ significantly in a statistical sense from those of the preceding Moundville III phase in terms of the amount of maize in the diet. Even though there is overlap between the two samples, the average $\delta^{13}C$ value of −10.3 per mil in Moundville III differs from the average value of −11.1 per mil in the Moundville IV sample at the 0.01 level in a two-tailed test of significance.

In terms of the nitrogen isotope data, the fauna present an interesting pattern (fig. 6.1). The fish $\delta^{15}N$ values are significantly more positive

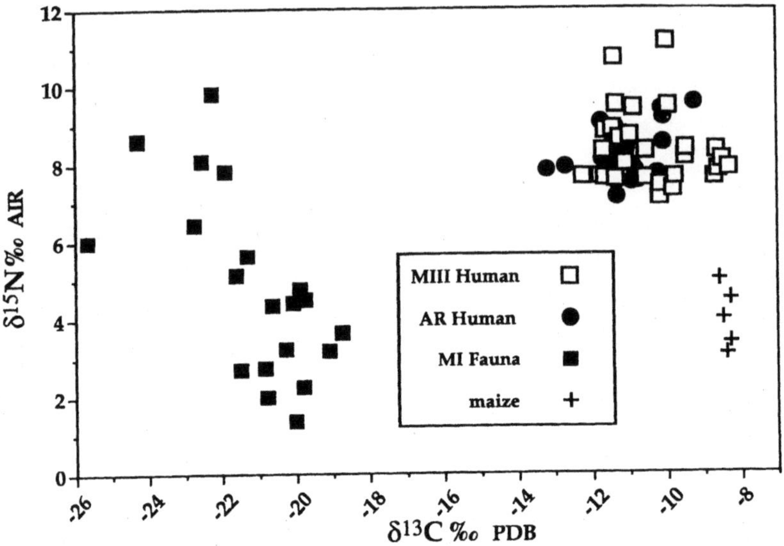

Fig. 6.3. Plot of stable-isotope data from human samples taken from the later phases of Moundville occupation compared with data from the fauna and maize. The latest phase of occupation (Moundville IV, labeled AR on the figure) shows a decrease in $\delta^{13}C$ values, indicating a decrease in the use of maize. The difference in means is statistically significant.

than those in the terrestrial fauna or in maize. This is a pattern previously observed in fish samples from the Great Lakes (Katzenberg 1989) and appears to reflect the fish fauna's dependence on degraded terrestrial organic material. Both maize and the terrestrial fauna have $\delta^{15}N$ values that are on average around +4 per mil, whereas the fish are, on average, about +8 per mil. The human bone collagen is also about +8 per mil. There is no change through time in the $\delta^{15}N$ values of human bone collagen.

DISCUSSION AND CONCLUSIONS

In order to address the first question regarding diet over time at Moundville, a series of mass balance equations was used to provide rough estimates of human diet. Beginning with nitrogen isotope ratios, we assume that the bone collagen has $\delta^{15}N$ values that are offset by 3 per mil from the diet δ values, which translates to a diet value of about +5 per mil. This assumption is based on numerous studies of animals, both experimentally fed and in natural habitats (DeNiro and Epstein 1981; Schoeninger and DeNiro 1984; Hare et al. 1991). The studies indicate that an animal's synthesized proteins are approximately 3 per mil more positive than the animal's diet protein source. A simple mass balance equation provides a rough estimate of the relative contributions of fish on the one hand and terrestrial fauna and/or maize on the other:

$$8‰ (x) + 4‰ (1-x) = +5‰$$

where x refers to the proportion of protein from fish and 1–x refers to the proportion of protein from terrestrial fauna and/or maize. Solving the equation results in x = 0.25; approximately 25 percent of the human diet protein came from fish on average. This accords well with Bruce Smith's suggestion that Mississippian populations exploited both agriculture and wild species of plants and animals, of which fish from rivers adjacent to the sites were an important resource (B. D. Smith 1978). With the exception of one individual who has a $\delta^{15}N$ value of around +5 per mil, the range of variation in $\delta^{15}N$ values (+7 to +10 per mil) translates to a range of zero to almost 75 percent of the protein coming from fish. Most of the individuals in the samples, however, ingested around 25 percent.

A mass balance equation similar to that for nitrogen can be set up for carbon, although there is less agreement regarding the offset between diet and synthesized proteins for carbon isotope ratios than there is for nitrogen isotope ratios. In this report we have chosen to use an offset of 3 per mil, based on the observed offset between diet and bone collagen in experimental rats (DeNiro and Epstein 1978) and pigs (Hare et al. 1991). If a larger offset were used, the implication would be that less maize was incorporated in the diet. Others (e.g., van der Merwe and Vogel 1978; Bumsted 1984) have estimated that the carbon isotope ratio offset is as high as 5 to 6 per mil.

Assuming an offset of 3 per mil implies that on average the human diet was around −17 per mil in the Moundville I period (the outlier of −21 per mil is not used in this estimate; this individual obviously had no maize in her/his diet during the period when most of the bone collagen was synthesized) and around −13 per mil during the Moundville II phase. The two equations are as follows:

Moundville I

$$-8‰ (x) + -22‰ (1-x) = -17‰$$

$$x = 0.36$$

Moundville II

$$-8‰ (x) + -22‰ (1-x) = -13‰$$

$$x = 0.65$$

where x is the proportion of calories provided by maize and 1−x is the proportion of calories provided by wild plants and animals.

Solving the two equations results in an estimate of about 40 percent of calories provided by maize in Moundville I and closer to 65 percent of calories provided by maize in Moundville II. Of particular interest is the lack of overlap between the two admittedly small samples and also the individual in Moundville I who ate no maize at all during the time of bone collagen synthesis. This individual may have eaten maize as an older adult but not during the bulk of her or his lifetime. This low level of maize ingestion was somewhat surprising but probably reflects the transition from the West Jefferson phase of the terminal Woodland period in which the bulk of the diet consisted of wild plants and animals (Scarry 1981b). Both estimates of 40 percent and 65 percent of calories from maize in Moundville I and II permit the inclusion of 25 percent of protein coming from fish, thereby providing an indirect confirmation of the nitrogen equation. Within the Moundville II sample the range of variation indicates differential intake of maize from 60 to almost 80 percent of total calories.

The results of the later periods (Moundville III and IV) are shown in figure 6.3. The range of $\delta^{15}N$ values is similar to that found in the earlier periods, although there are some individuals who appear to have been eating more fish than in the earlier periods. It is possible, however, that this merely reflects the differences in sample size between the two groups. In any case, the data suggest that fish provided a large fraction of the protein in the later periods, a continuation of the Mississippian pattern. The range of variation in $\delta^{13}C$ values is also similar to that for the earlier periods, with the exception that values indicating distinctly low levels of maize ingestion are not present. The samples from Moundville III are virtually identical to those from the preceding Moundville II, a result consistent with the archaeological evidence that Moundville II and III were the periods of the site's florescence, when it controlled surrounding areas with its economic base dependent on maize agriculture (Peebles 1978; Steponaitis 1978).

Using the same mass balance equation as above, dependence on maize in Moundville IV times appears to have dropped by around 10 percent from the Moundville II and III periods. We discuss the implications of this drop in comparison to other data later in this chapter.

In terms of the second question addressed in this project, there appears to be no patterning in the distribution of maize or of fish associated with any of the status clusters (table 6.2). This suggests that if

Table 6.2.
Stable-Isotope Data by Status Cluster

	$\delta^{13}C\pm$s.d.			$\delta^{15}N\pm$s.d.		
Cluster	‰ (PDB)	(*N*)	Range	‰ (AIR)	(*N*)	Range
1	−10.7	(1)	—	—		—
2	−12.2±1.1	(3)	−13.4, −11.3	8.6	(2)	7.6, 9.5
3	−9.7±1.4	(14)	−12.2, −7.3	8.1±0.7	(15)	7.1, 9.5
4	−9.9±1.2	(7)	−11.6, −8.3	8.5±1.4	(6)	7.3, 11.1
5	−9.3±0.8	(5)	−10.5, −8.5	8.3±0.5	(5)	7.8, 8.9
6	−9.9±0.7	(7)	−11.2, −9.2	8.2±0.4	(6)	7.7, 8.8
7–10	−10.3±1.1	(28)	−12.0, −8.0	8.3±0.6	(25)	7.3, 9.6

there was differential distribution of food within the population, it occurred along lines that cannot be identified isotopically. For example, based on bone strontium concentrations, it was suggested previously that elites ate more meat than did nonelites (Peebles and Schoeninger 1981), and although it is possible that elites consumed more terrestrial animals, such as deer, such dietary differences cannot be discerned isotopically because the isotopic signatures of deer are similar to those of maize. Although fish should be discernible because they have distinct isotopic signatures, the isotope data do not support a conclusion of differential consumption of fish along status lines.

In terms of the third question, there appears to be no difference between females and males in the Moundville sample at any period. The sample sizes of known-sex individuals within each status cluster are not large, and thus the possibility that within some clusters there may have been differences in diet along sex lines cannot be excluded. Even so, the data do not support such differences.

The final question can now be addressed by the data presented here. That question concerns the final abandonment of Moundville. When De Soto took his famous trip through the southeastern United States, no mention of Moundville was made. This has raised various questions concerning the nature of the collapse of the Moundville polity. One of the earlier suggestions was that European diseases (especially influenza and smallpox) preceded actual contact by Europeans and that the population at Moundville had been decimated by disease prior to De Soto's trip (Curren 1984). Alternatively, it was suggested that the collapse was due to declines in the economic and political systems (Peebles 1987b).

A set of studies considered in combination with the stable-isotope data lend credence to the notion of internal collapse. An instability study of the region suggests that there were several stages of unstable climate and ecology during the Mississippian period that would have adversely affected the agricultural systems (Baden 1987), especially if this resulted in a decline in the area's ability to support the size and type of population that existed in the region during Moundville II and III. Recent work by Steponaitis (chap. 2; 1991) suggests that the resident population at Moundville was small during Moundville II and III. If correct, this implies that the Moundville IV period burials represent a difference in mortuary patterns but not in settlement patterns. In other words, people had lived at the outlying sites since Moundville II times, but they buried their dead in their home settlements only in later Moundville III and Moundville IV times. This does not negate the collapse of Moundville as a political center, but such a scenario considered in conjunction with the stable-isotope data, recent assessments of pathology at the site (chap. 5; Powell 1992a), and a new perspective on anemia (Kent 1992) strongly tilts the explanation for Moundville's loss of control away from Spanish influence and toward an internal collapse with a fairly straightforward biological explanation.

Powell has argued convincingly that tuberculosis predates European contact in the southeastern United States (Powell 1992a). She has identified ten individuals, nine of which precede Moundville IV, in whom the disease is apparent from bony lesions. As she points out, these ten cases probably underestimate the prevalence of the disease because diagnostic skeletal areas are often not preserved. In addition, because the general level of health of an individual is crucial in determining the level of disease expression, it is likely that multiple individuals suffered from the disease at a level below that of skeletal involvement. She states that in populations stressed by malnutrition, individuals are at greatest risk of death. In contrast, populations like those near Moundville, where malnutrition was less common, provided the organism a congenial environment because most infected hosts would survive. Most important, this disease can be maintained in "very small populations even if reinfection from outside sources is rare," because the encapsulated organisms have an extremely long viability without destroying their host. This is particularly significant for Moundville I, II, and III populations, who probably lived in very small settlements surrounding Moundville.

Powell has also documented numerous cases of individuals infected with treponematosis. The general level of health of the host is not important for the survival of this parasite in human populations, and her studies indicate that infection was endemic among the Moundville populations prior to European contact. In the case of treponematosis and of tuberculosis, the overall viability of most individuals was probably not in question, but it is more significant that the reproductive capacity of individuals and therefore of the population overall could have been severely compromised.

Another line of evidence supports the argument being developed here. Other studies of skeletal pathology from individuals buried at Moundville and at adjacent sites have noted the presence of cribra orbitalia and porotic hyperostosis (Hill-Clark 1981) and suggested that the frequency of these pathologies was higher during Moundville IV times. Recent reassessment of the significance of such anemias requires a reevaluation of their presence throughout the Moundville sequence. Kent (1992) argues that anemia is an organism's defense against various pathogens because it results in the sequestering of iron, which is critical for the survival and reproduction of those pathogens. In other words, the anemias evidenced by such pathologies as cribra orbitalia and porotic hyperostosis are not a response to iron-deficient diets but rather are responses to pathogen load. Tuberculosis and treponematosis—already identified as pathogens that were tolerated at a less-than-critical level among the Moundville populations—are obvious possibilities as the perpetrators of these anemias. This explanation does not require any increase in maize or a decrease in animal protein. Such pathogens can be maintained in small dispersed populations such as those along the Black Warrior River.

In contrast, the distribution of population in the valley, especially if Steponaitis's suggestions are correct, does not provide support for the proposal that influenza and smallpox arrived prior to Spanish contact. Sattenspiel (1990) points out that for diseases like influenza (and smallpox, which is more or less similar), transmission of the virus requires person-to-person contact. The required number of infectious individuals and the number of potential recipients is much higher than any estimates that have been proposed for the population of the Black Warrior Valley settlements. Moundville itself was the only town that could have provided enough people, and even it was probably below the size necessary for maintenance of a good epidemic. If Steponaitis is correct, this virtually removes such an explanation from the realm of possibility.

On the other hand, the loss of soil productivity has a lot to recommend it as a factor, and it is supported by the stable-isotope data. During Moundville IV times the people were increasing their dependence on wild foods, as evidenced by the decrease in $\delta^{13}C$ values. Lack of control by Moundville is not a reasonable explanation for the switch from a highly productive source of energy toward wild foods, which require more in terms of collection and processing costs when considered in terms of dependable per-acre yield. The lack of soil productivity suggested by Baden's study, coupled with decreasing population and associated labor, is a more likely culprit. Individuals, such as specialized craft producers, who were not directly involved in production could no longer be maintained. The loss of exotics and other trade items in the record is probably a dependent variable resulting from a change in the biological base. The base involved a lessening of a dependable nutrient source coupled with a pathogen load that had been in place since the inception of the system. In sum, this line of reasoning points to an internal collapse of the Moundville system.

ACKNOWLEDGMENTS

We thank the organizers of this volume and the Society for American Archaeology symposium that preceded it for inviting us to participate. We also thank Margaret Scarry and Lauren Michals for providing the midden samples and Gail Wagner for discussions and for providing the maize samples. The project was funded by BNS-8607659 to MJS and BNS-9004063 to MJS and MRS. Finally, we would like to give a special thanks to Chris Peebles, our teacher, who first involved us in Moundville studies.

7. Outlying Sites within the Moundville Chiefdom

PAUL D. WELCH

THE MOUNDVILLE CHIEFDOM consisted not just of the people living at the political center at Moundville but also of the population living at outlying mound and nonmound sites. Archaeological survey and test excavations at outlying sites during the past twenty years have considerably improved our knowledge of the chronology, geographic distribution, size, and social composition of these outlying sites and of the kinds of activities that were undertaken at them. Coupled with our revised understanding of the chronology of occupation and construction at Moundville, our current understanding of the chiefdom's settlement pattern—its political geography—has changed from interpretations offered in previous publications.

This chapter summarizes current knowledge about the outlying sites within the Moundville chiefdom and concludes with a review of the Moundville polity's changing settlement pattern. Because of its multiple, large mounds and abundant, exotic grave goods, the Moundville site has attracted much more archaeological attention than the other, far smaller sites occupied by members of this polity. Although we still know more about the Moundville site than about any one other site in the polity, our knowledge about these other sites is substantially better than it was a decade ago and vastly improved from the situation in the 1970s.

Before proceeding, it is necessary to define the geographic and chronological limits of the Moundville polity. Since the mortuary analysis by Peebles (1974; Peebles and Kus 1977), it has been generally accepted that Moundville was the center of a society similar to historically described southeastern chiefdoms and that smaller sites up and down the Black Warrior River were also members of that chiefdom. Precisely where archaeologists thought the geographic limits of the Moundville chiefdom lay, however, has shifted through time. Twenty years ago, Peebles (1971; see also McKenzie 1966:38) argued that sites as distant as the Tennessee River valley in northwestern Alabama were components of the chiefdom. More recently, Peebles and other archaeologists have limited the chiefdom's extent to the 5-kilometer-wide floodplain of the Black Warrior River, from 25 kilometers north to 15–35 kilometers south of Moundville (e.g., Bozeman 1982: fig. 1.; Steponaitis 1983a: fig. 1; Peebles 1987b: fig. 2; Welch 1991:23).

There are three reasons for the more recent, reduced limits for the Moundville chiefdom. First, contemporary sites are densely clustered in the floodplain for 25 kilometers north of Moundville, but beyond that distance there is a gap of 50 kilometers upriver. The nearest sites east and west of the floodplain are 45 and 50 kilometers away, respectively. It is not so clear where the southern boundary is. Sites are abundant in the floodplain as much as 13 kilometers downriver, but then there is a gap of at least 12 kilometers before the next possibly contemporary site (Minter Creek) and another 10 kilometers to the next site (Stephens Bluff) that is definitely contemporary with Moundville. Beyond that is a gap of at least 25 kilometers, so the southern boundary of the chiefdom is no more than 35 kilometers south of Moundville. Second, the chronology and variety of pottery decoration at the sites within 25 kilometers of Moundville appear to be indistinguishable from the chronology and variety of pottery decoration at Moundville, but this is not true for sites farther afield, for example, Lubbub (Mann 1983) and Bessemer (Welch 1994). I take this as an indication that at about 25 kilometers from Moundville there is a shift in the nature of social ties to Moundville. Third, historically and archaeologically documented chiefdoms elsewhere in the world generally seem to be no wider than the distance that can be traveled in one day, about 56 kilometers if travel is by foot (Spencer 1982:6–7, 1990:7). Thus, a neat match can be found between ethnological expectation about a chiefdom's size and the 30–50-kilometers-long cluster of sites in the Moundville area.

Some settlements beyond the boundaries of the Moundville chiefdom may well have been strongly connected to it by kin, political, and other ties. For some of these communities, such as Lubbub in the Tombigbee River valley (see Blitz 1993), the ties may have amounted to a more or less permanent alliance to Moundville's chiefs. Nevertheless, I think that such communities were not part of the Moundville chiefdom in the same way that the communities in the Black Warrior floodplain were. These more distant communities should be thought of as allied, tributary, or perhaps even dependent polities. It is also worth mentioning that no community or group of communities within 100 kilometers of Moundville had sufficient population that it could have stood alone as an enemy of the more populous Moundville polity. Moundville had no nearby competitors (for discussion of Moundville's external relations, see Steponaitis 1991 and Welch 1991:183–190).

The chronological limits for the Moundville chiefdom are the beginning of the Moundville I phase (around AD 1050) and the end of the Moundville III phase (around AD 1550). Sites of the preceding West Jefferson phase (AD 900–1050) and subsequent Moundville IV phase (AD 1550–1700) are not covered here, but a review of those phases provides the chronological context for the developments described herein. There has been very little excavation of West Jefferson material in the Moundville vicinity, essentially just isolated features at several sites. As explained in detail by Welch (1990:210–212), West Jefferson settlements were mostly small (<0.5 hectare), may have been abandoned or partially abandoned in late winter–early spring, and were occupied by foragers who also grew small-scale gardens that included some maize along with smaller-seeded plants. There is no evidence for institutionalized social ranking in this society, though like all conclusions based on negative evidence, this one is not secure. Few nonlocal materials have been found at West Jefferson sites, suggesting that external exchange either was infrequent or primarily involved perishable goods. We do not know how the settlements were laid out, whether they were palisaded, or whether there was much violent conflict. Overall, West Jefferson society apparently consisted of small egalitarian communities.

Much the same can be said of Moundville IV communities. We know of them mostly from excavations of burials; Sheldon (1974:140–151) and Curren (1984:89–193) review the available data. Artifact scatters of up to 2.2 hectares, and up to 45 burials per site, indicate nucleated villages. Most of the burials were inside large pottery urns, and there were few grave goods. The burials display no evidence of social inequalities, either within or between sites. The skeletons do demonstrate that this population was unhealthy, suffering from high rates of infant mortality, malnutrition, infection, and degenerative diseases (see sections by M. C. Hill et al. in Curren 1984:104–110, 172–191). A few of the mounds at Moundville were used early in the Moundville IV phase (Steponaitis 1983a:159–160; V. Knight, personal communication), and possibly but not certainly the mounds at two or three of the secondary mound sites (see below) were used as well. In short, during Moundville IV people in the Black Warrior Valley seem to have been nucleated in small, independent, egalitarian villages where they led short, unhealthy lives.

DESCRIPTION OF OUTLYING SITES

There were at least dozens, more likely hundreds, of sites within 25 kilometers north and south of Moundville. The vast majority of these sites were isolated farmsteads or several houses clustered in a hamlet. Currently we do not even have an estimate of how many such non-mound sites there were at any given time. There were also at least ten sites with one or more mounds. These secondary mound centers will be described after the farmsteads are dealt with. The locations of all sites described in the text are shown in figure 7.1.

So few chronometric dates are available for any of the outlying sites that in all instances their chronological assessment is based on their pottery assemblage. Some pottery modes are tightly restricted in time, and others are found in two or more phases. Choosing to rely only on the most chronologically specific modes would yield site occupation assessments that might understate the duration of occupation at a given site and underestimate the number of sites occupied at any given time. Conversely, basing chronological assessments on modes that occur in more than two phases might overstate the duration of a site's occupation and the number of contemporary sites. In this paper I use a fairly inclusive strategy, basing my assessments on all those modes that occur in no more than two phases. In each site description I state which of these modes are present, so that readers who desire to make narrower assessments may do so.

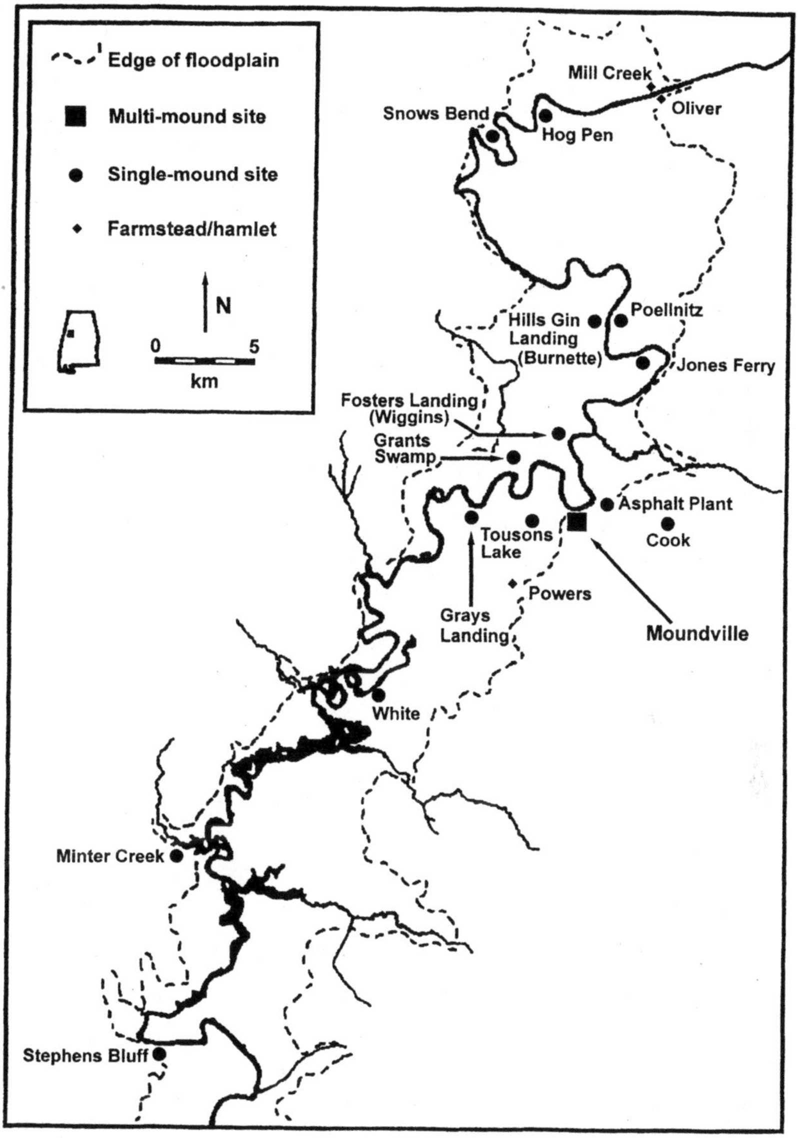

Fig. 7.1. Archaeological sites of the Moundville chiefdom.

Farmsteads and Hamlets

The reason we do not have an estimate of the number of farmsteads and hamlets is simple. Until the late 1970s we were unaware of their existence, and nobody has yet done the kind of field survey necessary for an estimate of their number and distribution. The only systematic survey in the Black Warrior floodplain was conducted in the mid-1970s by John Walthall and Ben Coblentz. In an area of almost 6 square kilometers along the course of Big Sandy Creek, a tributary of the Black Warrior, they found 20 small Moundville-age sites. Two sites were 0.4–0.5 hectare in extent, but most of the sites were smaller than 0.05 hectare (Bozeman 1982:157–159). Similarly, we found two dozen tiny sherd scatters in 1978 and 1979 when I had crews intensively survey several large plowed fields. Until this survey work in the late 1970s, archaeologists had believed that the population outside the Moundville site lived entirely or principally in nucleated towns at the secondary mound centers. As I explain below, we also discovered in the late 1970s that there is little evidence of such nucleated towns; it appears that most of the population living outside Moundville lived in scattered farmsteads and hamlets.

Based on the limited surveys done so far, we can tentatively identify a pattern in the distribution of these sites. They are found in considerable numbers in areas that (a) have a water source within 0.5 kilometer, (b) have easily tilled loamy soils, and (c) are above the 3–5-year flood level. Areas that lack one or more of these characteristics have very few or no farmsteads. We do not yet know whether the small sites are clustered in neighborhoods around the secondary mound centers or whether the small sites are evenly distributed on all geomorphologically suitable parcels of land. There have been excavations at only three of these sites: Mill Creek, Big Sandy Farms, and Oliver.

MILL CREEK (1TU265). This site is located on the first terrace levee of the Black Warrior River at its juncture with Mill Creek. The confluence is a kilometer or two below the fall line of the river, and thus it is not surprising that the levees on both sides of the river here are linear middens with artifacts of many periods. Construction of a new lock and dam facility in the 1980s led to testing (Alexander 1982; Mistovich 1986) and subsequent excavation (Mistovich 1987, 1988) of an area roughly 60 × 60 meters at the Mill Creek locale. The excavations revealed midden roughly 75 centimeters thick, in which grog-tempered and shell-

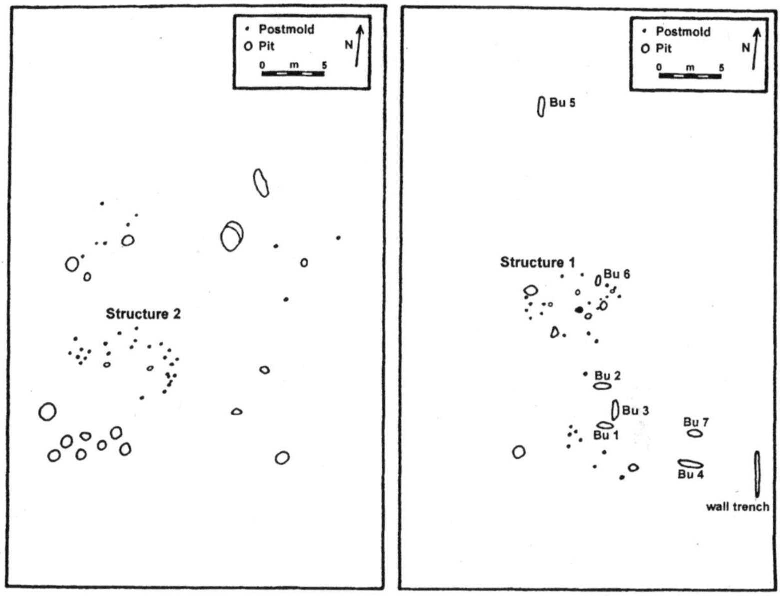

Fig. 7.2. Features at the Mill Creek site, 1Tu265 (after Mistovich 1987): *left*, Structure 2; *right*, Structure 1.

tempered pottery predominated. There were also pit features, post molds, and burials associated with two buildings.

The two buildings were nearly identical in shape, as described by Mistovich (1987:15–134). The putatively earlier building, Structure 2 (see fig. 7.2), consisted of 11 singly set posts at 1-meter intervals, forming an oval of 6 × 5 meters with an opening on the southwest side. Ten small, interior postholes near the northern and eastern sides of the house may have supported sleeping benches along the wall. A feature at the center of the building may be the basal remnant of the hole for a large central roof support post. No preserved floor surface or hearth was encountered, though there was a hearth 2 meters in front of the building's doorway. Another 2 meters beyond the hearth lay eight cooking and storage pits. The postholes of Structure 2 contained a mixture of sand-tempered, grog-tempered, and shell-tempered pottery. There are no radiocarbon dates for the structure itself. Three of the features in the cluster in front of Structure 2 yielded calibrated radiocarbon dates of AD 90–120, 1680 BC, and 1740 BC. (See table 7.1 for laboratory numbers and calibration details for all radiocarbon dates cited in this chapter.) The two

Table 7.1.
Radiocarbon Dates from Outlying Sites

Site	Context	Lab number	Age rcybp	$\delta^{13}C$ ‰	Uncalibrated $\delta^{13}C$-adjusted date	Calibrated[a] date or dates (1 σ date range)
Mill Creek	burial pit, Structure 1	Beta 21124[b,c]	630±90		AD 1320	AD 1310, 1350, 1390 (1290–1410)
	posthole, Structure 1	Beta 21123[b]	570±70		AD 1380	AD 1400 (1310–1430)
	Feature 37, near Structure 2	Beta 21128[b]	3440±110		1490 BC	1740 BC (1880–1620)
	Feature 32, near Structure 2	Beta 21125[b]	3380±110		1430 BC	1680 BC (1860–1520)
	Feature 40, near Structure 2	Beta 21127[b]	1910±100		AD 40	AD 90, 100, 120 (10–240)
Powers	Structure 2 post	Beta 36154[d]	590±50		AD 1360	AD 1400 (1310–1410)
Hog Pen	primary mound fill	DIC 1244[e]	510±105		AD 1440	AD 1430 (1320–1470)
	primary mound summit	DIC 1245[e]	610±95		AD 1340	AD 1320, 1340, 1390 (1290–1420)
	near-mound refuse deposit	Beta 68121	870±60	–27.5	AD 1120	AD 1230 (1170–1280)
	near-mound refuse deposit	Beta 68122	650±50	–29.3	AD 1370	AD 1400 (1310–1420)

Snows Bend	late-stage mound fill	Beta 1111[e]	945±85	−25.39	AD 1010	AD 1050, 1100, 1120, 1140, 1150 (1020–1220)
Hills Gin Landing	burned structure, late mound stage	Beta 1290[e]	3020±70		1070 BC	1260 BC (1390–1130)
		Beta 1483[e]	380±65		AD 1570	AD 1480 (1450–1640)
		DIC 1247[e]	260±50		AD 1690	AD 1650 (1640–1950)
		Beta 1484[e]	245±65		AD 1705	AD 1660 (1640–1950)
Poellnitz	primary mound fill	DIC 1248[e]	430±170		AD 1520	AD 1450 (1330–1650)
Jones Ferry	bell-shaped pit under mound	Beta 1109[e]	810±70		AD 1140	AD 1250 (1170–1280)
White	primary mound summit	Beta 1110[e]	570±80		AD 1380	AD 1400 (1310–1430)
	refuse deposit, village area	Beta 9951[f]	400±50		AD 1550	AD 1470 (1440–1620)
	smudge pit below refuse deposit	Beta 9952[f]	670±50	−27.38	AD 1320	AD 1310, 1350, 1390 (1300–1400)

a. Calibrated using Method A, CALIB version 3.0.3 (Stuiver and Reimer 1993), calibration data from Stuiver and Pearson (1993).

b. Mistovich 1988.

c. Accelerator (AMS) date.

d. V. Knight, personal communication.

e. Bozeman 1982.

f. Welch 1991.

earliest dates may well be accurate, since they came from features that lacked pottery or any other chronologically diagnostic artifact. The AD 90–120 date is clearly inaccurate, since it came from a pit whose fill contained 152 sherds, 91 percent of which were shell-tempered.

Structure 1 (fig. 7.2) consisted of eight singly set posts 1–2 meters apart, forming an oval of 6.75 × 5.5 meters, with an opening on the southwest side. Five interior posts may have created a partition, and a large feature at the center of the structure may have been the hole for a central roof support post. Inside the northern wall of the house a grave, oriented north-south, contained the very poorly preserved bones of an extended burial with the head to the north. No hearth was found inside the structure, nor was a preserved floor surface encountered. The fill of the postholes and features associated with Structure 1 contained a mixture of grog-tempered and shell-tempered pottery. Two radiocarbon samples, one from the fill of the grave and the other from an interior posthole, yielded calibrated dates of AD 1310–1390 and AD 1400, respectively.

The site's excavator, Tim Mistovich, argued that Structure 2 was of West Jefferson date, while he assigned the other structure to an early Moundville I date (Mistovich 1987, 1995). I disagree with those chronological assessments, in part because we now know more about early Moundville I pottery assemblages than was known at the time Mistovich prepared his reports. The hundreds of West Jefferson phase sherds in the plowzone at Mill Creek make it clear that there is a West Jefferson phase component here, but there is no evidence of an early Moundville I component. I believe Structure 2 dates no earlier than late Moundville I, with Structure 1 probably being of Moundville II or early Moundville III date.

The only evidence bearing on the date of Structure 2, which Mistovich assigned to the West Jefferson phase, is the pottery included in its postholes. These sherds all appear to be incidental inclusions in the posthole fills and could thus include sherds from pottery contemporary with the structure as well as earlier sherds from the soil of this multicomponent site. Therefore, Structure 2 could substantially postdate the West Jefferson phase.

The features in the cluster in front of Structure 2 provide no support for a West Jefferson phase date, either. Five of the eight features in the cluster were aceramic and lacked any chronologically diagnostic stone tools; two of these five yielded radiocarbon dates in the second millennium BC. Those dates are consistent with pits elsewhere on the site whose only chronological diagnostics are Late Archaic stone tools. Of the three features that had pottery in their fills, one had only two sherds and the other had three; all five sherds were West Jefferson phase types, but they could easily be accidental inclusions in the fill of substantially later pits. In the only feature that had plentiful pottery, 91 percent of the pottery was shell-tempered. None of the shell-tempered pottery was of chronologically diagnostic varieties, but three sherds had engraved decoration, a decorative technique infrequent or absent in early Moundville I. Overall, the feature cluster in front of Structure 2 seems to be an accidental juxtaposition of several Late Archaic pits, with one pit that probably postdates early Moundville I. If Structure 2 is associated with this latter pit, then Structure 2 is of late Moundville I or later date.

Mistovich's (1987:202–204) attribution of Structure 1 to the early Moundville I phase is also questionable. That attribution was based on the structural and ceramic similarities between Structure 1 and Structure 2 and on the presence of grog-tempered, shell-tempered, and grog-and-shell-tempered sherds in the postholes of Structure 1. Mistovich argued that this combination of tempering agents indicated that Structure 1 was occupied during the transition from West Jefferson phase pottery to Moundville I phase pottery. Both of the radiocarbon dates associated with this structure, however, are in the Moundville II range, and in the features associated with Structure 1 the only chronological diagnostics among the shell-tempered pottery are a beaded-rim bowl and a Moundville Engraved, var. *Hemphill*, bowl, both of which are markers of late Moundville II or Moundville III times at Moundville (Steponaitis 1983a:128–131). Nowhere at the site are there any Moundville Incised, var. *Moundville*, or Barton Incised, var. *Oliver*,[1] sherds, nor did Mistovich note any folded-flattened jar rims or folded jar rims, all of which are typically found in early Moundville I components (chap. 8; Steponaitis 1983a:99–106, 1992; Welch 1994; Scarry 1995). I have already pointed out that posthole fills in a multicomponent site are likely to contain artifacts from earlier components, which accounts for the grog-tempered sherds in the postholes. Finally, the infrequent grog-and-shell-tempered sherds in Structure 1 postholes have little chronological significance, since such mixed-temper pottery occurs as a minority throughout the period from AD 1050 to at least 1550. In short, the radiocarbon dates and associated pottery point to a Moundville II or even Moundville III date for Structure 1.

In addition to the burial inside Structure 1, elsewhere at the site there were four burials that had shell-tempered pottery as intentional grave inclusions and two burials that had no preserved grave goods.

There were shell-tempered sherds in the fill of each of the burials, indicating that all of them date within the Moundville era. Only one of the included vessels was chronologically diagnostic, a Moundville Engraved, var. *Hemphill* (hand-and-eye motif), small cylindrical bowl with a single lug. This combination of pottery modes dates the pot to late Moundville II or early Moundville III, with late Moundville III being possible but less likely. The fill of three of the other burials contained Moundville Incised, var. *Carrollton*, sherds, which establish these burials as no earlier than the late Moundville I or early Moundville II date of this variety. Little can be said about the nonpottery artifacts, since they include Middle Archaic, Late Archaic, Middle Woodland, and Late Woodland diagnostics as well as, presumably, nondiagnostic artifacts from all these time periods.

Preservation of bone in the seven burials at Mill Creek was so poor that the only available biological information is that one was probably adult, three were definitely adult, and one of the definite adults was probably male.

OLIVER (1TU459). Since Michals reports on this site in more detail in the next chapter, little will be said here. Portions of two rectangular wall-trench structures were observed while the site was rapidly being stripped away for landfill. The emergency salvage nature of the excavation precluded detailed recording of house dimensions or construction details. Fill from six large midden-filled pits was salvaged and was later screened and analyzed by Michals. Aside from a small admixture (8 percent) of Late Woodland sherds, the pottery is uniformly of early Moundville I date, with Barton Incised, var. *Oliver*, being the principal decorated variety and 67 percent of the jar rims ($N = 57$) being folded-flattened.

BIG SANDY FARMS (1TU552). Archaeological mitigation along a gas pipeline in 1990 exposed features (see fig. 7.3) dating to a variety of periods (Ensor 1993). Among the features were two rectangular structures (1 and 2) that had floor surfaces sunken below the then-prevailing ground level (i.e., semisubterranean houses). Structure 1 measured 5.2 × 3.6 meters, with singly set posts forming the northern and southern walls and posts in wall trenches forming the eastern and western walls. There was a hearth near the center of the floor. Structure 2 measured 3.0 × 2.3 meters, and there was a central hearth. No wall trenches and few postholes were seen during the excavation, so the nature of the

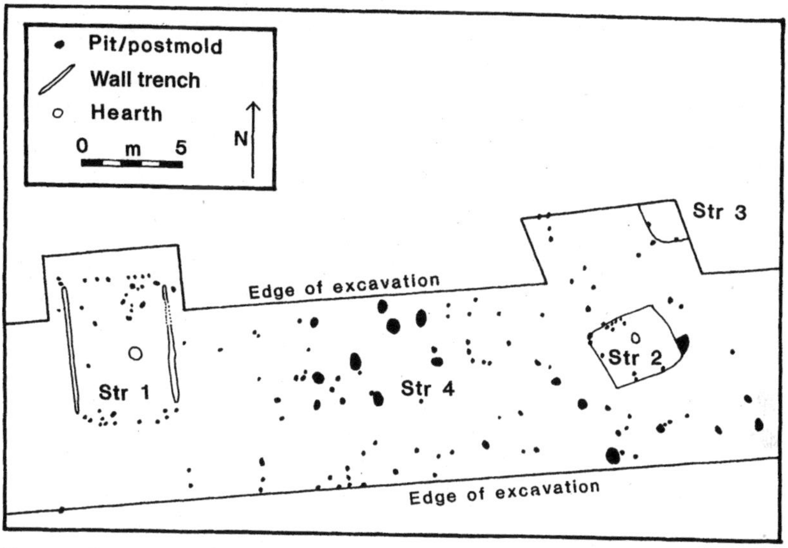

Fig. 7.3. Features at the Big Sandy Farms site, 1Tu552 (after Ensor 1993).

building's walls is unknown. A corner of what appeared to be a third semisubterranean house (Structure 3) was encountered at the edge of the right-of-way and was not further excavated. The site report also defines another structure (Structure 4), composed of single postholes encompassing a D-shaped area roughly 6 × 5 meters with the linear side facing northwest. There was no intact floor surface for Structure 4, presumably because it (and perhaps additional features and postholes) had been removed by the plowzone.

The semisubterranean style of building construction has been encountered at Moundville in early Moundville I contexts (Scarry 1986, 1995). Thus it is not surprising that the shell-tempered pottery from Big Sandy Farms includes folded-flattened rims. There is also a much later component, however, represented by hemispherical bowls with beaded rims, part of a Carthage Incised, var. *Lupton*,[2] short-neck bowl, a diminutive sherd of red-painted pottery, and what appears to be one of the handles from an arcaded row of handles on a jar rim. These diagnostics are all late Moundville II or later. No radiocarbon dates were obtained. My interpretation is that the semisubterranean buildings at Big Sandy Farms date to early Moundville I. At least some of the features in the vicinity of Structure 4 are of late Moundville II or Moundville III date, since the short-neck bowl rim was found in one of the Structure 4 features. By implication Structure 4, if it was indeed a structure, would also be of late Moundville II or Moundville III date.

No faunal remains were recovered from the site, but botanical remains were recovered by flotation and were analyzed by Scarry (1993c). She concluded that the Big Sandy Farms residents ate the same kinds of plant foods as other members of the Moundville society, but that maize was not quite as important during early Moundville I as it was from late Moundville I through Moundville III. Nuts, by contrast, were slightly more important in early Moundville I than they were later. Beans were found in the central hearth of Structure 1 as well as in two midden-filled pits 3–4 meters south of this house. If Structure 1 is indeed an early Moundville I house, these are the earliest beans known in the Moundville area and among the earliest known anywhere in the eastern Woodlands (Scarry 1993c:219). The Big Sandy Farms botanical remains also contain a greater abundance of the by-products of maize and nut processing than has been found in samples from secondary mound centers or Moundville itself (Scarry 1995; Scarry and Steponaitis 1992; Welch and Scarry 1995).

POWERS (1HA11). Richard Krause directed excavations here in 1981, 1988, and 1991 and has provided the following details (Krause, personal communication). Krause excavated three rectangular, burned, wattle-and-daub houses constructed with singly set posts. Structure 1 (fig. 7.4a) was of late Moundville III or Moundville IV date, based on the presence of a red-on-white painted jar that was smashed on the floor when the burning wall fell on it. The building (5.0 × 4.5 meters) had been rebuilt or repaired once before being burned, as indicated by adjacent pairs of postholes and two superimposed hearths. Four posts formed a rectangle inside the building, presumably for roof support. The door to the building was on the north side. Pottery from the other two houses appears to be of Moundville III date (e.g., Carthage Incised, vars. *Carthage* and *Fosters*, Moundville Engraved, var. *Wiggins*). Unlike Structure 1, these two houses each had a single central roof support post and an off-center hearth. Structure 2 (fig. 7.4b) measured 6 × 6 meters and had a door on the east side. Two pottery urns were buried under the center post of Structure 2; one of them contained bones of an infant. Charcoal from a burned wall post in Structure 2 produced a calibrated radiocarbon date of AD 1400. Structure 3 (fig. 7.4c) was the largest of the buildings, at 8.5 × 8.0 meters; the door was on the east side. The bones of an adult had received secondary burial under the floor of Structure 3,

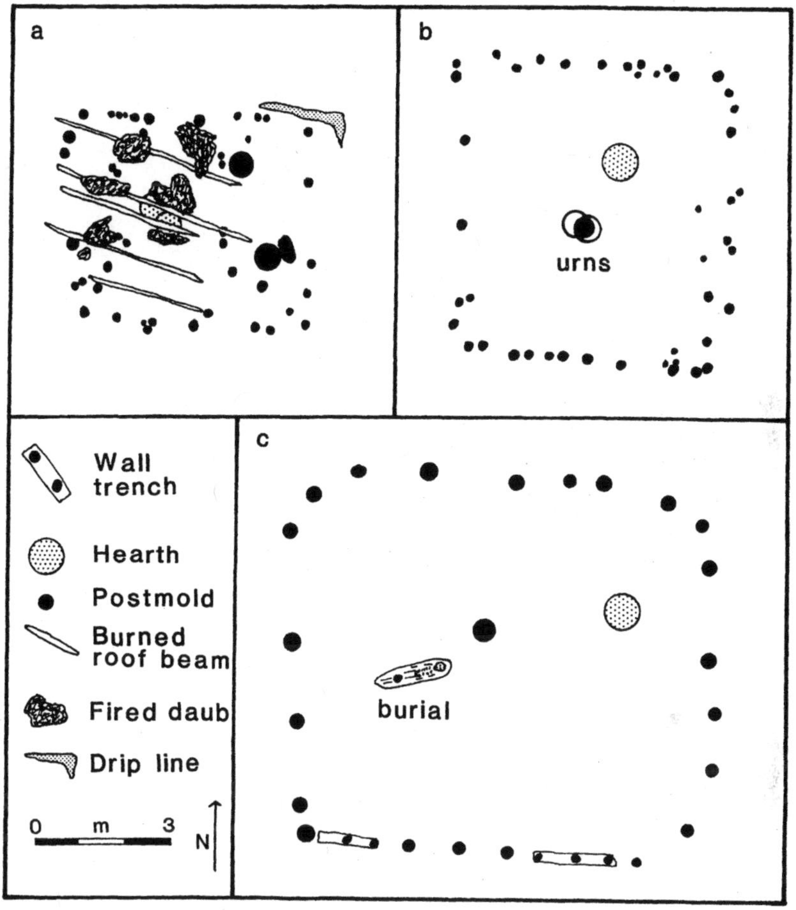

Fig. 7.4. Features at the Powers site, 1Ha11: *a*, Structure 1; *b*, Structure 2; *c*, Structure 3.

but the intrusion of a posthole through the burial indicated that the burial antedated the house.

The Powers site was described in the 1930s as having a mound, though its size and shape were not recorded. There is now a small, fresh-looking, conical pile of dirt, which I suspect is only a few decades old, and a very broad rise that may be either the plowed-down remains of a prehistoric mound or a natural topographic feature. If there was a mound at the Powers site, it was most likely of Moundville III or later date, since Moundville III is the date of the excavated houses and most of the chronological markers among the surface pottery (e.g., Moundville Engraved, var. *Wiggins*, Carthage Incised, vars. *Carthage* and *Fosters*, and red-on-white painted pottery, though there are also sherds of Moundville Incised, var. *unspecified*, which probably date to Moundville I). Krause, who excavated on and around the broad topographic rise, believes that the sediment covering the houses was not mound fill but overbank deposits from nearby Millians Creek and that the broad topographic rise at the site is natural.

Secondary Mound Sites

There are several reasons why the exact number of secondary mound sites is uncertain. Two were recorded early in this century but cannot be relocated now; it is an open question whether they were of Moundville date. Despite test excavations, we have not been able to determine the date of two other mounds. Finally, it is possible that one or more secondary mound sites may have been completely destroyed by lateral erosion of the bank of the Black Warrior River prehistorically, just as one such site was destroyed in the late 1970s. Despite these problems, our picture of the secondary mound sites is reasonably complete as a result of several distinct periods of research.

The first two episodes of investigation at the secondary mound sites took place in the first third of the century. The mound summits at several of the sites were tested by C. B. Moore in 1905. He found nothing of interest, that is, no burials and no whole artifacts (Moore 1905:127, 243–244). The secondary mound sites were visited again in the early 1930s by Walter B. Jones and David DeJarnette of the Alabama Museum of Natural History (AMNH). They excavated off-mound cemetery areas at two of the sites (DeJarnette and Peebles 1970; Welch 1991:36–37, 66–67). At all of the mound sites they visited, Jones and DeJarnette measured the mounds and also recorded the extent of the occupational debris nearby. These measurements of site size and the recorded site locations were used 45 years later by Peebles (1978) and Steponaitis (1978) in their settlement pattern analyses. Unbeknownst to them, the site size figures were badly misleading, and several of the site locations were incorrect.

At the time Jones and DeJarnette measured and recorded these sites, they knew what kinds of pottery were found at Moundville. When any of those kinds of pottery were found at outlying sites, Jones and DeJarnette quite reasonably recorded the sites as being of Moundville age. Coincidentally, both Moundville and the outlying sites have Late Woodland components. It turns out that the site sizes recorded at the outlying sites represent the extent of these Late Woodland sherd scatters, not the extent of the Moundville-age deposits. The discrepancy went undetected for almost half a century.

After the investigations by Jones and DeJarnette, the outlying sites received almost no attention until the 1970s. In 1970 the University of Alabama salvaged two burials from the village area beside the Touson Lake mound (Nielsen et al. 1973:88–89). This site and the White site, another secondary mound center, were revisited in the fall and winter of 1972–1973 (Nielsen et al. 1973:78–81). At both sites grog-tempered pottery was noted as indicating Late Woodland components, but in neither case was there a revision of the estimated size of the Moundville component. In 1976 a University of Alabama archaeological field school excavated at the Asphalt Plant site, the single-mound site 800 meters northeast of Moundville, testing the mound stratigraphy and exposing a structure adjacent to the mound. Major improvement in our knowledge of the secondary mound centers resulted from work in 1978 and 1979. In those two years field crews from the University of Michigan Museum of Anthropology visited nearly all of the secondary mound sites, making topographic maps and conducting test excavations in the mounds, as well as making gridded surface collections of the adjacent occupation areas. This was part of a multifaceted research project organized by Christopher Peebles.

It became apparent early in the 1978 field season that the outlying mound sites occupied landforms with multiple earlier occupations and that in most cases the extent of the earlier components was far larger than the very limited extent of the Moundville-era occupations. Most of these sites had only a few hundred square meters of Moundville-era occupation debris. Analysis of the first season's collections made this point even more clear, so in the second season the field crew completely surveyed a few large fields to see whether the farmsteads and hamlets found in the Big Sandy survey were present throughout the Moundville chiefdom. Strikingly, 12 such sites were found on the first afternoon this was attempted. The 1978–1979 investigations also revealed that several of the site locations recorded in the 1930s were inaccurate, in one instance by as much as 1 mile. The 1978–1979 surface collections and mound test excavations were reported by Bozeman (1982), who also recalculated the spatial analyses of Peebles (1978) and Steponaitis (1978) using the new data on site sizes and locations.

There have been excavations at two of the secondary mound sites since the days of Peebles's project. In 1983 I directed a University of Michigan Museum of Anthropology crew in the excavation of a small sample of the White site, focusing on a dense, late Moundville III midden deposit. The results of this excavation, combined with the surface collections from 1978–1979 and the 1930–1933 AMNH excavations of two cemetery areas at secondary mound sites, were the basis for a reconstruction of the economic organization of the Moundville chiefdom (Welch 1991, 1996). The other outlying mound site where there has been excavation is the Hog Pen site. Excavations in 1990 by the AMNH Summer Field Expedition and in 1992 by a Queens College crew were both under my direction. These excavations combined a stratigraphic cut into the mound and excavation of a midden deposit consisting of refuse thrown off the mound summit. Results of the Hog Pen excavations have not yet been published.

The following descriptions of recorded outlying mounds begin at the upriver end of the polity and proceed in order downriver. Some of the sites have two names, and most have at least two site numbers. In the 1930s mound-and-village sites were assigned two site numbers, one for the mound and one for the village. The first number (e.g., 1Tu56) refers to the mound and the second (e.g., 1Tu57) to the village, except for Snows Bend, where the order is reversed. There are also a few sites with multiple names or numbers as a result of duplicate entries in the official Alabama site files or inconsistent usage in published accounts.

HOG PEN SITE (1TU56/57). Like the mounds at several other secondary mound sites, the Hog Pen mound sits on the edge of a river terrace so that one slope of the mound is continuous with the terrace slope (see fig. 7.5). One of the few outlying mound sites not visited by C. B. Moore, this site was first excavated in 1978 (Bozeman 1982:59–75). Two 1 × 1-meter test units on the mound slope revealed two episodes of mound construction, the first of which had a prepared clay hearth on its surface. More extensive excavation on this side of the mound in 1990 confirmed the two-episode constructional history of the mound but revealed that the prepared clay hearth was actually off the mound summit on the sloping corner of the mound. The excavations did not reveal whether there was a building atop the summit of the first mound stage. Chronological diagnostics in the mound fill layers are mostly of Moundville I or early Moundville II date, except for two sherds from beaded-rim hemispherical bowls, a mode diagnostic of late Moundville II or Moundville III.

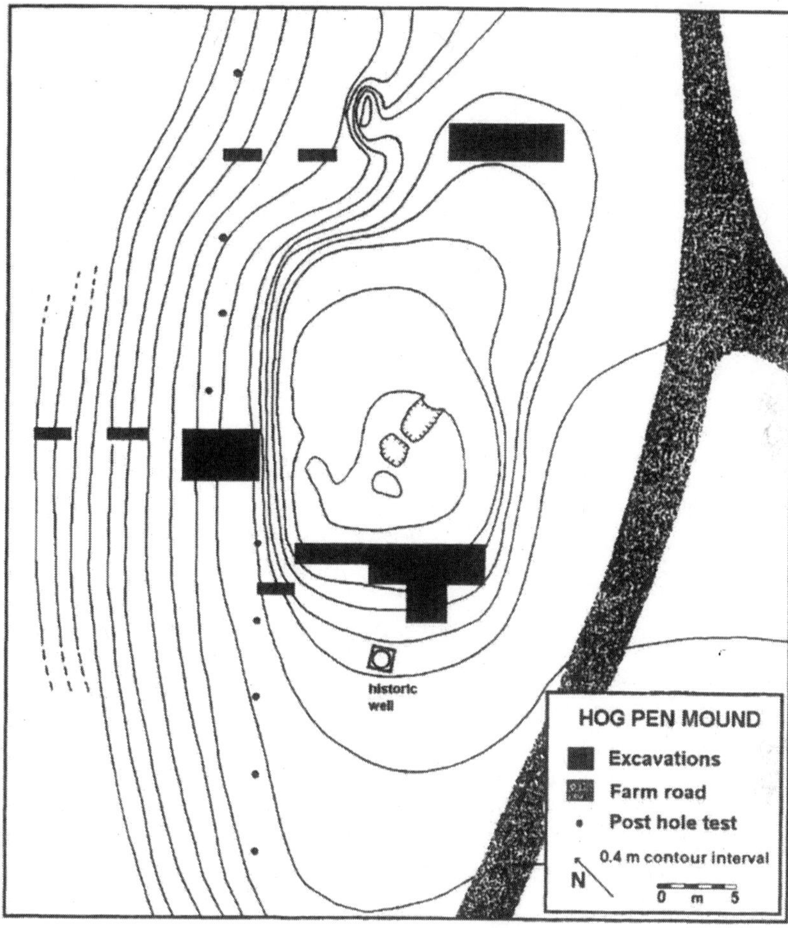

Fig. 7.5. Excavations at Hog Pen Mound, 1Tu56/57.

Charcoal lying on the mound surface associated with the hearth yielded a calibrated radiocarbon date of AD 1320–1390, which is one century more recent than the pottery suggests. Charcoal near the mound base yielded a calibrated date of AD 1430, which seems erroneously recent.

Extensive testing, both with trenches of 1 × 3 meters and with a soil auger of 7.5-centimeters diameter, showed that there was a patch of midden 3 meters in diameter on the terrace slope just beside the mound. This midden deposit was excavated in 1992. The pottery diagnostics include folded jar rims, a few folded-flattened jar rims, and sherds of Moundville Incised, vars. *Moundville*, *Carrollton*, and *Snows Bend*. There are two radiocarbon dates from the midden beside the mound. One sample yielded a calibrated date of AD 1230, which matches the associated late Moundville I and early Moundville II pottery. The other sample was stratigraphically equivalent with or below the sample dated AD 1230, but it yielded a calibrated date of AD 1400. This does not match well with the associated late Moundville I and early Moundville II pottery.

SNOWS BEND (1TU2/3). In 1930 and 1932 the Alabama Museum of Natural History excavated 47 burials from the Snows Bend site. The excavations and the burials were described decades later by DeJarnette and Peebles (1970). In 1978 we were able to determine the approximate location of the burials by examining photographs taken during the excavation. It was harder to relocate the mound at the site, for neither the report nor the site-file record mentioned that the mound is 600 meters from the village-cemetery area.

In 1979 we gridded and surface-collected the portion (0.96 hectare) of the village area that had not eroded into the river and excavated two stratigraphic tests into the mound (Bozeman 1982:94–109). One test unit, 1 × 1 meter, was located on the summit, and the other, 1 × 2 meters, was located at the foot of the mound. The unit on the summit revealed only that the deposits in the upper meter are homogeneous fill, but the lower unit revealed a sloping deposit of fired daub and charcoal flecks, probably the remains of a burned building that once stood atop the mound. The only charcoal sample large enough for radiocarbon dating yielded a δ^{13}C-corrected, calibrated estimate of AD 1050–1150. This is far too early, given that the mound fill and the burned daub-and-charcoal deposit contains Moundville Engraved and Carthage Incised, var. *Carthage*, sherds, the latter being diagnostic of Moundville III.

Most of the chronological markers in the village-area surface collections and excavated burials date to late Moundville II or later. These diagnostic modes include engraved hand-and-eye, winged serpent, and paired tail motifs; hemispherical bowls with beaded rims; a hemispherical bowl with gracile, outward-facing bird effigy; short-neck bowls; deep flaring-rim bowls; a jar with more than ten handles; and Carthage Incised, var. *Carthage*, sherds. Several of the burials, however, included jars with two handles, a mode that occurs as early as Moundville I. One burial included a two-handled jar with rectilinear incision on the neck that could be classified as Barton Incised, but the chronological significance of this jar is uncertain since the motif is typical of var. *Oliver* (a

Moundville I diagnostic), and the motif's placement and the rim shape are typical of var. *Cochrane* (a Moundville IV diagnostic). Given the uncertain date of this jar, I believe it is safest to conclude that the Snows Bend mound and village date to late Moundville II through Moundville III, with the possibility of small earlier and/or later occupations at the village.

HILLS GIN LANDING, OR BURNETTE (1TU46/47). The first recorded excavation at this site was performed by Moore (1905:243), who dug into the mound summit but found nothing to interest him. The next recorded investigation took place in 1978, when the site was mapped and gridded, a portion of the site was surface-collected, and two 1 × 1-meter stratigraphic tests were excavated in the mound (Bozeman 1982:112–128). The excavations revealed a constructional history with at least eight episodes. Charcoal from the debris of a burned wattle-and-daub building whose rubble lay on the slope of one of the later mound construction episodes yielded calibrated radiocarbon dates of 1260 BC (obviously erroneous), AD 1480, AD 1650, and AD 1660. The two later dates fall well within the Moundville IV phase, but pottery at the site indicates a Moundville III date. Diagnostics of Moundville III (Carthage Incised, var. *Carthage*, and beaded-rim hemispherical bowls) were found in mound fill, and a beaded rim from the village area also supports a late Moundville II or Moundville III date. No diagnostically Moundville IV pottery was found at the site. It is worth noting, though, that in 1931 the Alabama Museum of Natural History excavated a Moundville IV burial-urn cemetery, the Lon Robertson site, approximately 400 meters south of the mound (Curren 1984:126–132). Combined with the radiocarbon dates from the burned structure, this suggests that use of the mound in Moundville IV times is possible, though not certain.

POELLNITZ (1TU398). This mound was not known to archaeologists until the 1970s. The village area around it was gridded and surface-collected, and a 1 × 1-meter test unit was excavated in the northeast side of the mound (Bozeman 1982:129–141). The mound had at least two construction episodes. In the lower mound fill there were diagnostics of late Moundville I or early Moundville II (Moundville Incised, var. *Carrollton*); in the upper mound fill sherds of Moundville Engraved, vars. *Taylorville* and *Tuscaloosa*, date to Moundville II or early Moundville III. A radiocarbon date on wood charcoal in the lower mound fill produced a calibrated estimate of AD 1450, which is not very informative given the 170-year standard deviation. The surface collection also contains both early and late diagnostics (folded jar rims and beaded-rim bowls, respectively). Though the site may have been occupied continuously from late Moundville I through early Moundville III, it is also possible that there were two discontinuous occupations, first in late Moundville I or early Moundville II and then again in late Moundville II or early Moundville III.

JONES FERRY (1TU44/45, 1TU346). In 1905 C. B. Moore was denied permission to excavate on this mound, but in passing he noted that the mound was largely plowed away (Moore 1905:243). No further work was done at the site until 1979, by which time nearly all the mound had caved into the Black Warrior River. Two test units, each roughly 1 × 1 meter, were excavated on the eroding bluff edge. Even though most of the mound had already caved away, there was stratigraphic evidence that the mound had had at least two episodes of construction. Furthermore, the mound had been constructed atop 40 centimeters of cultural deposits. The premound deposits contained mostly shell-tempered, Moundville I pottery (folded and folded-flattened jar rims, Moundville Incised, vars. *Moundville* and *Carrollton*, hematite rubbed into engraved decoration) in the upper 20 centimeters and mostly grog-tempered West Jefferson pottery in the lower 20 centimeters. Dense foliage in the adjoining soybean field prevented surface collection of the village area. By 1981 the last remnant of the mound had eroded into the river.

Erosion of the bluff exposed at least nine burials between 1977 and 1979. Because of their location and manner of exposure we do not know which component these burials came from. Most of them were simply collected after the bones eroded out of the river bluff; only two of the burials were excavated carefully, both in 1979. One of the latter was a well-preserved individual, supine, 20–21 years old, of undetermined sex. Only the portion of the skeleton above the lumbar region was present, the rest having eroded out of the river bluff. The body had partly decomposed prior to burial; most bones were articulated but a few were clearly out of place, such as a thoracic vertebra lying atop the left humerus and the left scapula upside down and backward. No grave goods were found in the excavated portion of the grave. Though the skeleton was inside a grave whose top was beneath the Jones Ferry mound, the burial could date to either the West Jefferson or Moundville I phase. The bones of the other excavated burial were very poorly preserved, but the wide sciatic notch and diminutive stature (150–160 centimeters in the ground) suggest a female. Well-worn third molars indicate the woman was adult. No grave goods were found with this burial, either, and it could date to virtually any period. The other bones recovered from the river bluff include portions of one 20–29-year-old female, one 30–50-year-old questionable female, one male in his forties, one questionable adult male, one teenager, and two younger children (Patricia Bridges, personal communication).

There was also a bell-shaped pit below the mound. The top of this midden-filled pit appeared to be at a level where the surrounding deposits contained equal proportions of shell- and grog-tempered ceramics, but only grog-tempered pottery was included in the pit fill, along with mussel shells, animal bones, and carbonized plant remains. On the basis of the stratigraphy, the contents of the pit, and the lack of any definite instance of bell-shaped pits of Moundville I–IV date, I believe this pit was used during the West Jefferson phase, but wood charcoal from the pit yielded a calibrated radiocarbon date two centuries more recent than expected, at AD 1250.

FOSTERS LANDING, OR WIGGINS (1TU42/43). At the time Moore (1905:243) visited the Fosters Landing site it was already "almost obliterated by cultivation," and the current landowners intentionally plowed the mound down farther in the 1960s. Many burials were disturbed in this process (Curren 1984:124), and none of them can now be dated. When the site was gridded, collected, and mapped in 1978 there was no way to estimate the original mound dimensions. The spreading of the mound across the landscape raises a question about the measured extent of the "village debris": Is the 2.2-hectare site size inflated by the spreading of the mound? It is impossible to answer the question without excavations. A second question about the site is whether the mound was in use during the Moundville IV period. Moundville IV urn burials were found 200 meters south of the mound, across an ephemeral drainage line (see description of the Wiggins site in Curren 1984:124–126). Pottery from the surface collections at the Fosters Landing site includes diagnostics from late Moundville II and Moundville III (Carthage Incised, vars. *Carthage* and *Fosters;* Moundville Engraved, vars. *Hemphill* and *Maxwells Crossing;* plus beaded rims and one red-on-white painted sherd), as well as markers of the Moundville IV period (Alabama River Appliqué and Alabama River Incised).

ASPHALT PLANT (1TU50). Another mound missed by Moore in 1905, this site was tested by Richard Krause in 1975. Steponaitis (1992) recently described these excavations, concluding that the mound was built in at least two construction episodes. Immediately beside the mound there was a roughly rectangular, 3.0 × 2.1 meters, single-post building with an interior hearth. Pottery diagnostics from the mound and near-mound excavations include Moundville Incised, var. *Moundville*, folded and folded-flattened jar rims, and loop handles, indicating an early Moundville I date. Although I have listed this as an outlying site, I will argue below that it is actually part of the early Moundville I community at Moundville.

COOK (1HA1/2). As Bozeman (1982:179) noted, this is "perhaps the most interesting and perplexing" outlying mound site. A conical mound, 20 × 1.75 meters, sits just off a hill crest 4 kilometers east of Moundville's plaza. In 1979 we were denied permission to test or collect at the site, but a 1933 surface collection from 1Ha2 contains 262 shell-tempered sherds (plus one grog-tempered piece). Though some of these sherds do not fit neatly into the Moundville typology in terms of decoration and vessel shape, the overall impression is that they are of Moundville II or later date. However, the location recorded for 1Ha1/2 in 1933 is 1.6 kilometers (1 mile) from the mound we saw in 1979, and there is neither mound nor village at the location listed in 1933. Most likely this is simply a typographic error on the site form (Section 4 instead of Section 5), but nevertheless it raises the question whether the 1933 surface collection does in fact go with the mound we saw in 1979. Given the shape and location of the mound, unique among the Moundville chiefdom's settlements, the less-than-certain date of the mound is particularly nagging.

TOUSONS LAKE (1HA14/15). This site has suffered considerable disturbance. The mound itself had one side cut off by construction of a county road, and the opposite side appears to have been modified historically to permit vehicular access to the summit. Stratigraphic tests indicated two construction episodes, but the sandy mound fill was extensively leached and stratigraphy was difficult to discern. A sherd of Moundville Engraved, var. *Tuscaloosa*, in the mound fill suggests a date of late Moundville II or Moundville III. The village area, too, has been significantly altered. In 1970 a flood eroded a gully through the village area. Shortly afterward the site was visited by archaeologists from the University of Alabama, who found, "The profile of this gully showed a deposit of sandy soil approximately *2* feet thick overlying the village deposit. It was learned that this soil had been trucked in to level the surface when cultivation of the land was begun. After the flood the landowners brought in additional soil to again level the ground's surface. . . . The University of Alabama removed two burials which had been exposed and disturbed at that time" (Nielsen et al. 1973:90).

Like the mound, the village area yielded pottery indicating a late Moundville II or III date. The diagnostics included Carthage Incised, var. *Carthage*, beaded rims, and short-neck bowls. Neither of the burials contained chronologically diagnostic grave goods, and I could find no information about the skeletal material.

GRANTS SWAMP (1TU387 AND 1TU388). It is curious that both C. B. Moore in 1905 and the University of Alabama archaeologists in the 1930s were unaware of these two mounds only 4 kilometers from Moundville. Both mounds are made of sandy fill, and in 1978 both had rounded shapes (Bozeman 1982:203–215). The smaller mound, 1Tu388, was being plowed over regularly at that time, which would certainly account for its rounded contours, but the large trees on and around 1Tu387 show that its rounded shape probably is not the result of modification during the last 50–70 years. No stratigraphy was visible in a 1 × 1-meter excavation in the smaller mound. A vertical section excavated at the margin of a deep pothunter's hole in the larger mound showed that the mound consisted of a low primary mound constructed of clay that was capped by a massive sandy fill. The mound now has an oval outline with a rounded summit. This shape and construction history sound more like Middle Woodland mounds in south Alabama (e.g., McQuorquodale Mound in Wimberly and Tourtelot 1941) than the Mississippian mounds in the Moundville area. Nevertheless, shell-tempered pottery was sparsely distributed throughout the fill of the larger mound, and one shell-tempered sherd was found in the smaller mound. None of the pottery was chronologically diagnostic. There was no village debris around the mounds, though several small surface scatters indicative of farmsteads were found in the general vicinity. The Phillips site, a Moundville IV village, lies 0.6 kilometer southwest of the mounds (Curren 1984:119), but there is no direct evidence that either mound is of Moundville IV origin. The date of these mounds remains a puzzle; it is possible that both are of historic date, which could explain why there are historic artifacts near the surface of both mounds, and why neither Moore nor DeJarnette recorded this site.

GRAYS LANDING (1TU41 AND 1HA107). In 1905 Moore recorded a mound near Grays Landing. At that time it was already "so much ploughed over that a mere rise in the ground remained" (Moore 1905:127). Moore conducted "considerable digging" on the mound but found nothing to interest him. In 1933 the mound, 1Tu41, was relocated and was described as being largely obliterated by cultivation (Bozeman 1982:216). We were not able to locate the mound in 1979. We did find widely dispersed surface scatters of 10–30 meters diameter (1Ha107B-L), indicating isolated farmsteads, and part of a larger scatter of Moundville-era debris actively eroding into the river. Because it is close to the location recorded for 1Tu41, we have taken this larger scatter (1Ha107A) to be the remains of the settlement at Grays Landing.

We gridded and collected the remaining 0.6 hectare of this settlement (Bozeman 1982:216–227). Sherds from Moundville Engraved, var. *Taylorville*, and beaded-rim hemispherical bowls suggest dates ranging from Moundville II through Moundville III, but a single sherd of Moundville Incised, var. *Moundville*, suggests a date of Moundville I or early Moundville II. Since there is no chronological overlap between Moundville Incised, var. *Moundville*, and beaded rims, there may be more than one Moundville-era component at this location, for example, an early farmstead and a later village. Whether any of this is an accurate indication of the date of the now-obliterated mound is a moot point.

WHITE (1HA7/8). This is the best preserved and most thoroughly investigated of the secondary mound centers (see fig. 7.6). Moore (1905:127) dug trial holes in the mound summit in 1905 but found nothing to interest him beyond some fragments of a human skull. The site was relocated in 1933, at which time DeJarnette excavated 28 burials. Only minimal records of the excavation exist today, but the artifacts from each grave were catalogued and labeled separately. The burials are described by Welch (1991:66–67).

In 1979 three stratigraphic tests were dug on the mound, one on each of the two distinct summit levels and the third at the base of the mound slope (Bozeman 1982:246–261). The mound was built in two episodes, the earlier of which is of Moundville III date, as indicated by a sherd of Carthage Incised, var. *Carthage*, in the lower fill. Carbonized material taken from a sandy floor deposit on the summit of the primary mound yielded a calibrated radiocarbon date of AD 1400. Two sherds of Alabama River Appliqué near the surface of the mound may indicate a Moundville IV date for the later mound construction episode but could also be intrusive.

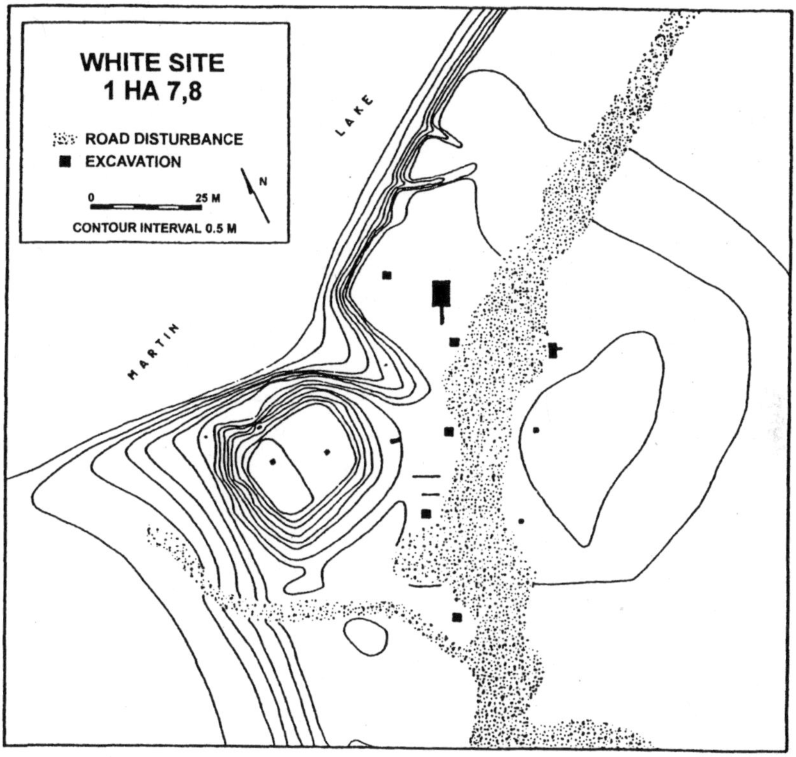

Fig. 7.6. Excavations at the White site, 1Ha7/8.

Another round of excavations took place in 1983, when I put test units of 2 × 2 meters and 1 × 1 meter throughout the village area and excavated one block of 4 × 6 meters (Welch 1991:40–75). Of roughly 20,000 shell-tempered sherds from the site, hundreds are Moundville III diagnostics and only 20 display modes that date earlier than Moundville III. There may have been one or more small occupations on this levee location in Moundville I or II times, but clearly the mound and adjacent settlement date to Moundville III. The 4 × 6-meter block was excavated in a secondary refuse deposit—an intentional trash deposit—that apparently received refuse from at least one high-status household during late Moundville III. Three absolute dates were obtained from material in this refuse deposit: a calibrated radiocarbon date of AD 1470, a thermoluminescence date of AD 1530 ± 40, and another thermoluminescence date of AD 1520 ± 50. A smudge pit stratigraphically below the refuse deposit yielded a δ^{13}C-corrected, calibrated radiocarbon date of AD 1310–1390. These dates appear to confirm that the Moundville III phase ended circa AD 1550.

MINTER CREEK (1GR76). The gap between the White site and this mound has usually been taken as indicating the limit of the Moundville chiefdom, or at least of its core. This mound lies 13 kilometers from the White site and 26 kilometers from Moundville measured in a straight line, 28 kilometers from White and 58 kilometers from Moundville along the river. The mound has a split-level summit, like that of the White mound. Auger tests suggest that the mound has at least two construction stages. Pottery recovered at or near the surface of the mound is shell-tempered, but most sherds have a brushed surface atypical for Moundville pottery. The brushed pottery is probably related to McKee Island Brushed (Heimlich 1952:28), which is found on sixteenth- and seventeenth-century sites in eastern Alabama. Possibly the latest occupants of the Minter Creek site were people displaced from their homes in eastern Alabama, one of the many groups moving around the Southeast during the Protohistoric period. The brushed pottery indicates an occupation contemporary with Moundville IV, but since this pottery was found on the surface of the mound it is not clear whether the whole mound is of that date. In short, we are confident neither of this site's construction date nor of its membership in the Moundville polity.

STEPHENS BLUFF (1GR14). This mound is also so far downriver from Moundville (35 kilometers in a straight line, 78 kilometers by river) that its membership in the Moundville polity is questionable. Surface collection near the mound has yielded mostly Late Woodland pottery (Nielsen et al. 1973; Shogren 1989), but excavation 32 meters from the mound encountered a pit feature whose fill included nearly 500 shell-tempered sherds. These sherds included pieces of Barton Incised, var. *Demopolis*, red-and-white painted pottery, short-neck bowls, deep flaring-rim bowls, frog effigy vessels, and downturned lugs (Hayward et al. 1990). At Moundville none of these modes dates before Moundville III, and some occur only in late Moundville III or Moundville IV times. There is also one sherd of Moundville Incised, var. *Snows Bend*, which in the Moundville area is diagnostic of Moundville I or early Moundville II. In the Tombigbee River valley and Mobile Bay-Delta areas, however, the *Snows Bend* motif has been found in contexts contemporary with Moundville III or later (Jenkins 1981:31–32; Fuller and Stowe 1982:62–65; Mann 1983:76). Before we conclude that Stephens Bluff was occupied during the Moundville I time span, we ought to have additional, less equivocal evidence. Excavation of a feature on the mound summit also yielded shell-tempered pottery, including two small, looplike handles of the sort found on jars with more than ten handles; this mode occurs during late Moundville III and Moundville IV times. Whether or not this site was part of the Moundville polity, it was occupied during at least the later part of the Moundville III time span and possibly in early Moundville III and Moundville IV times as well.

SETTLEMENT PATTERN

The picture we now have of the development of the Moundville chiefdom's settlement pattern is significantly different from what it was a decade ago (see fig. 7.7). At that time, we believed that there were four

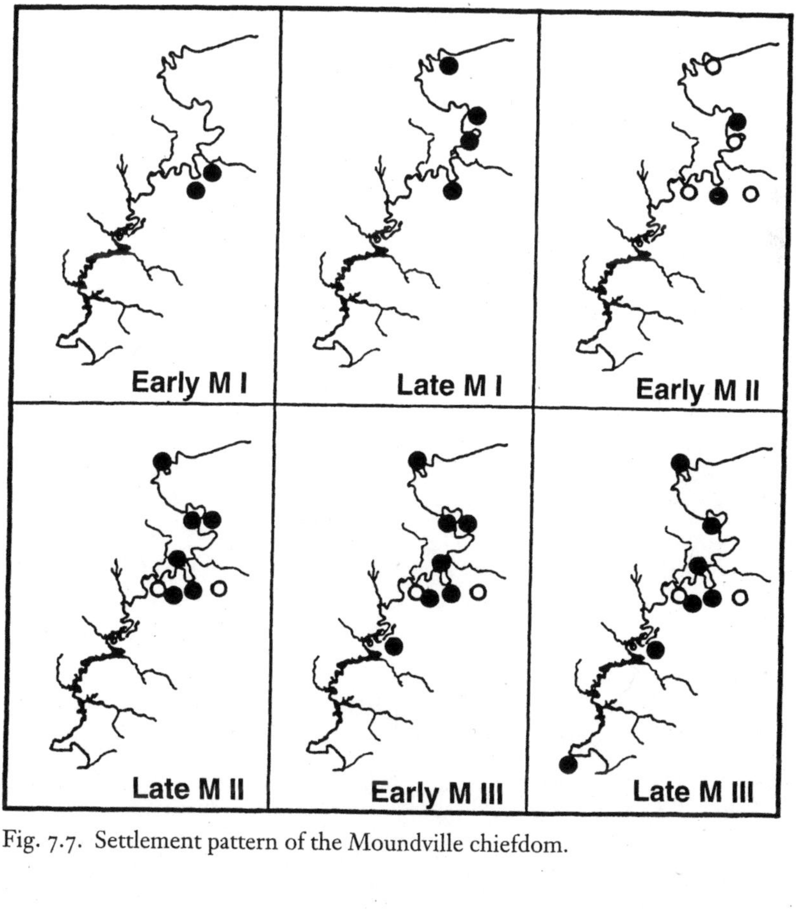

Fig. 7.7. Settlement pattern of the Moundville chiefdom.

single-mound sites during the Moundville I phase, with Moundville being one of them. We interpreted these as the centers of four separate simple chiefdoms (e.g., Bozeman 1982; Peebles 1987b:25–27; Welch 1991:212–214). By the beginning of Moundville II times, we thought, these four initially separate simple chiefdoms had coalesced into a single complex chiefdom centered at Moundville. The maximum political complexity and tightest integration of this polity seemed to occur in the Moundville II–early Moundville III time range. But a more precise dating of the occupations at Moundville and the secondary mound sites shows that the four-become-one model is no longer tenable.

Right from the beginning of the Moundville I phase, the settlement on the high, flood-free terrace at Moundville was different in kind from settlements elsewhere in the valley. The only two known early Moundville I mounds are both located here: Mound X, east of the present plaza, and the Asphalt Plant mound, 0.9 kilometer to the northeast. Some of the other mounds at Moundville may also date this early, since in general we have evidence from the outermost, latest layers of the mounds and not from the possibly deeply buried early construction episodes. Early Moundville I occupation—off-mound buildings, features, and sheet midden—is documented at the Asphalt Plant, north of Mound R, and at the Picnic Area at the northwest corner of Moundville. Early Moundville I pottery diagnostics are also widely spread throughout the excavated portions of the Roadway around the Moundville site (Welch 1989). These data suggest that the Moundville community began as an extensive but somewhat dispersed neighborhood or neighborhoods on this high terrace. Though the high terrace at Moundville was the only early Moundville I mound center, the Oliver and Big Sandy sites demonstrate that people also lived at nonmound sites elsewhere in the valley.

By late Moundville I times, the Moundville settlement had been redesigned, now having a large central plaza surrounded by mounds and enclosed by a bastioned palisade several kilometers long (Vogel and Allan 1985; Knight 1989, 1992; Scarry 1995; chap. 2). Mound X must have been abandoned, for the late Moundville I palisade went right over it. The Asphalt Plant site was also abandoned. At about the same time that Moundville was being redesigned and the Asphalt Plant mound abandoned, three new secondary mound centers were built north of Moundville. These were the Jones Ferry, Poellnitz, and Hog Pen sites, each of which date to late Moundville I. The three sites were not necessarily built at the same time; Jones Ferry may date a few decades earlier than Hog Pen, and the Poellnitz mound may actually have been no earlier than early Moundville II. What is important, however, is that Moundville was already the political center of the valley decades before there were any secondary mound centers.

The settlement pattern shows strong continuities from late Moundville I to early Moundville II, though this statement may be somewhat deceptive. Most of the pottery modes diagnostic of late Moundville I are also present during early Moundville II, though there are also modes diagnostic of early Moundville II that are absent earlier. Both Hog Pen and Jones Ferry have the late Moundville I and early Moundville II diagnostics, though neither has any of the diagnostics specific to early Moundville II. Therefore, it is possible but not certain that these two sites were occupied in early Moundville II. Poellnitz, in contrast, does have pottery modes not present before Moundville II, and we can therefore be more confident that it was occupied during this time. The Cook site, on the hill east of Moundville, and the Grays Landing site may also have been occupied during early Moundville II, though neither of these sites is securely dated. At Moundville, the palisades were no longer being maintained or rebuilt after early Moundville II times (Scarry 1995), and as Steponaitis (chap. 2) explains, there is relatively little evidence of occupation at Moundville in Moundville II despite the large number of burials dating to this time. Where all those people lived is not clear, since there is no evidence for any sizable nucleated communities elsewhere in the polity. We assume that most of the population must have lived in farmsteads and small hamlets in neighborhoods around the 4–6 secondary mound centers.

There are seven secondary mound sites that may have been occupied during late Moundville II. These are the Snows Bend, Hills Gin, Poellnitz, Fosters Landing, Cook, Touson Lake, and Grays Landing sites. Both the Hog Pen and Jones Ferry sites were abandoned, Hog Pen apparently being replaced by Snows Bend, and Jones Ferry by Hills Gin or Poellnitz. The Poellnitz and Hills Gin mounds are directly across the Black Warrior River from each other. Given the resolution of our chronological tools, it is not possible to tell whether both sites were occupied throughout the late Moundville II period or whether occupation alternated between the two. The Fosters Landing and Touson Lake sites appear in areas that had not previously had secondary mound centers. At Moundville, the number of burials increased, though there is only sparse evidence of late Moundville II occupation on or off the mounds.

All seven late Moundville II secondary mound centers continued in use during early Moundville III, and one new secondary mound center,

White, was constructed. The first (definitely dated) cemetery areas outside Moundville appear in early Moundville III at Snows Bend and White (unless the burials at Jones Ferry are of Moundville I rather than West Jefferson date). Though their dates are not known, burials at Fosters Landing and Touson Lake may also indicate Moundville III cemeteries at these sites. If this apparent change in burial patterns is not just an artifact of scant excavation, it may signal a shift in relations between outlying communities and the Moundville center. Moundville continued to be sparsely occupied in early Moundville III, though burials there are more common than ever.

The settlement pattern of late Moundville III differs from that of early Moundville III in ways that are not apparent in figure 7.7. Nearly all the same mound centers were occupied—abandonment of Poellnitz is the only change—but there was a change in the size of the occupations. At Moundville, the Roadway excavations show a small increase in the extent of occupation debris, though occupation remained spotty and not nearly as extensive as during Moundville I. Conversely, there was a decline in the number of burials at Moundville. Cemeteries at Snows Bend and White continued in use. One of the secondary mound sites, Fosters Landing, may have increased to 2.2 hectares, almost twice the size of any other secondary mound site, though as I stated above there is some doubt about both the size of the occupation and the date at which the maximum size was reached. The second, third, and fourth largest secondary mound centers (Touson Lake, Snows Bend, and White) also have abundant late Moundville III debris. Taken together, these data suggest that there was a trend toward population nucleation at the secondary mound sites in late Moundville III.

Population nucleation continued in the Moundville IV phase. Surface scatters of artifacts range from around 1 hectare up to 2.2 hectares (Curren 1984). The internal layout of these villages is not known, nor is it known whether any of them were palisaded. The mounds at Hills Gin Landing and Fosters Landing may have continued in use, along with a few of the mounds at Moundville (V. J. Knight, personal communication). Most of the known Moundville IV components, however, lack mounds. Excavations (see Curren 1984:89–193) have focused on recovering burials, many of which were secondary burials inside large pottery urns. The only excavated structure is a roughly oval (9 × 7 meters) scatter of burned daub overlying a central hearth and some postholes that form no discernible pattern (Curren 1984: fig. 62). In recent decades archaeologists (e.g., Bozeman 1982:307; Curren

1984:240–242; Peebles 1987b:9; Welch 1991:31; Steponaitis 1991:202) have taken the similarity of the sizes of Moundville IV villages, the absence of (confirmed) mound-building activity, the near-disappearance of exotic goods, and the decreased differentiation between burials as evidence of the disintegration of the Moundville chiefdom. The process of disintegration began during late Moundville III times (see Welch 1991:57–70) and clearly was in progress by the early sixteenth century, well before Hernando de Soto's expedition crossed the Black Warrior River in November of AD 1540 (Hudson et al. 1990:181–191).

Perhaps the most striking aspect of the changing settlement pattern of the Moundville chiefdom is the progressive proliferation of secondary mound sites. This proliferation could be the result of several distinct processes, acting alone or in combination. One possible explanation for proliferation of secondary mound sites is an increase in the number of lower-level chiefs appointed by the Moundville paramount, in response to growth of the chiefdom's population. Such population growth could result either from accretion of people who formerly lived elsewhere or from intrinsic population growth. Since much or most of the chiefdom's population lived in dispersed farmsteads and hamlets, and we do not yet have estimates for the number and chronology of these sites, we cannot yet say how the chiefdom's population size changed through time. A more fundamental problem is that nobody has yet stated an explicit rationale for believing that the outlying mounds were home to appointed low-level chiefs, as opposed to other plausible interpretations of the identity of the residents atop these mounds. One such plausible interpretation is that each outlying mound site was identified with, or claimed by, a particular high-status lineage, such as a cadet line descended from a past paramount chief. Since the number of cadet lines would increase through time, this could account for the increase in the number of outlying mound sites. To put it simply, there is not yet any convincing explanation of the social identity of residents of the outlying mound sites and therefore no convincing account for the proliferation of such sites. Even though important questions about the secondary mound sites remain to be answered, we do know far more about these sites than we do about farmsteads and hamlets.

The dearth of information about farmsteads and hamlets is clearly an impediment to several lines of Moundville-related research. Currently, we are in the uncomfortable position of believing that much of the chiefdom's population lived in these small settlements simply because there is so little evidence of their living at mound sites. But without knowing the number, geographic distribution, and chronology of these small sites we cannot make estimates of the population of the chiefdom as a whole, how the population size changed through time, or how the changing population size is related to changing diet, agricultural practices, regional political domination, patterns of warfare, internal political processes, and the eventual disintegration of the chiefdom. Finding out more about the small, nonmound sites is therefore one of the most obvious, and most clearly needed, directions for future research.

NOTES

1. The *Oliver* variety of Barton Incised subsumes sherds with alternating panels of slanting parallel lines incised, while the paste was wet, on the exterior shoulder of jars made of Mississippi Plain, var. *Warrior*, paste. Previously, sherds with this motif have been subsumed under Barton Incised, var. *unspecified* (e.g., Scarry 1995:24–26 and Welch 1994:19–21). Because this incised motif on unburnished jars seems to be tightly restricted to early Moundville I contexts, Moundville researchers have for several years referred informally to this material as var. *Oliver*, a usage worth formalizing.
2. Another pottery variety not previously defined, Carthage Incised, var. *Lupton*, subsumes Carthage Incised pottery that has the *Moon Lake* motif (zones of parallel, usually oblique, line segments arranged in chevronlike patterns around a vessel) on the exterior shoulder of short-neck bowls. Steponaitis (1983a:54) defined var. *Moon Lake* to include vessels with this motif on the inside rim of flaring-rim bowls as well as on the exterior shoulder of short-neck bowls. Because this motif is found on the exterior of short-neck bowls only during Moundville III, separate variety names for these two decorative treatments are warranted. In the new usage, var. *Moon Lake* would refer only to flaring-rim bowls with the parallel segments incised inside the rim.

8. The Oliver Site and Early Moundville I Phase Economic Organization

LAUREN M. MICHALS

LITTLE IS KNOWN about the economic relationship between Early Mississippian Moundville phase populations (AD 1050–1150). Various classes of material recovered from midden deposits at the Oliver site (1Tu459), an early Moundville I phase farmstead, are used to examine the relationships between outlying farmsteads, single-mound centers, and the emerging regional center of Moundville. A comparison between the Oliver site material and early Moundville I phase material from the Asphalt Plant mound (1Tu50) and Moundville shows a general lack of difference in the ceramic remains but suggests that differential access to nonlocal material may have been present by this time. As a comparison, material from Moundville II phase deposits at Moundville is also included in the discussion and indicates that clear status-related differences in material remains are evident during this later phase.

Much of the research on the Moundville polity has, out of necessity, dealt with the period as a whole or at its most complex point. With the new research presented in this volume it is possible to concentrate on more detailed aspects of this system. Although we have some idea of the economic organization of the mature Moundville polity, very little is known about the economic organization and relationships between early Moundville phase sites. The following is a presentation and discussion of material recovered from an early Moundville phase farmstead, the

Oliver site. The aim of this research is to clarify the economic relationship between early mound centers and farmsteads and to obtain an idea of the origin of the economic differences between sociopolitical classes present in later Moundville phases.

This discussion starts with a brief description of the early Moundville I phase and the material recovered from the Oliver site. The material is then compared to data from the Asphalt Plant site (1Tu50), an early Moundville I phase single-mound center (Steponaitis 1991), data from Moundville I phase deposits at Moundville, and data from two Moundville II phase deposits.

EARLY MOUNDVILLE I PHASE

During the early Moundville I phase (approx. AD 1050–1150), the settlement pattern in the river valley consisted of single-mound sites of roughly equal size in the vicinity of Moundville and a number of dispersed hamlets or farmsteads (chap. 7; Bozeman 1981). These sites may represent roughly equivalent simple chiefdoms with each single-mound site being the center of a politically independent entity. Although only one earthwork, Mound X, is known to have been in existence during this phase at Moundville, Steponaitis has shown that the area around Moundville, including the Asphalt Plant site, appears to have had a higher population density than other areas of the river valley (Steponaitis 1991, 1992).

Sometime around AD 1200, Moundville became a paramount center, with numerous mounds, a plaza, and palisade (chap. 1). Presumably, Moundville had incorporated the entire valley under its control by approximately this time.

OLIVER SITE

The Oliver site (1Tu459) is a farmstead located at the northern end of the central Black Warrior River valley. This site was located within the modern boundary of Tuscaloosa, approximately 275 meters south of the Black Warrior River and just downstream of the fall line between the Cumberland Plateau and the coastal plain.

At the time of its discovery, the site was in the process of being destroyed, and a quick salvage project was conducted by V. J. Knight

Table 8.1.
Types and Varieties of Sherds Larger Than Half an Inch from the Oliver Site

Type	Variety	*N*	%
Alligator Incised	*unspecified*	1	0.1
Barton Incised	*Oliver*	26	2.3
Barton Incised	*unspecified*	8	0.7
Barton Incised?		2	0.2
Baytown Plain	*unspecified*	1	0.1
Baytown Plain	*Roper*	93	8.2
Bell Plain	*Hale*	163	14.4
Bell Plain	*Hale?*	2	0.2
Carthage Incised	*unspecified*	1	0.1
Mississippi Plain	*Warrior*	634	56.0
Mississippi Plain	*Hull Lake*	193	17.0
Red and white		1	0.1
Unidentified sand-tempered		2	0.2
Sand/shell-tempered		1	0.1
Unidentified shell-tempered		4	0.4

(Knight 1982b; Alexander 1982). Portions of two rectangular wall-trench structures were identified but were destroyed before they could be excavated. Six large midden-filled pits were located approximately 15 meters north of the structures and were excavated. Part of each feature was dry-screened through 0.635-centimeter (0.25-inch) mesh, a 5–12-liter sample from each feature was processed by flotation, and the remainder was water-screened through 0.159-centimeter (0.063-inch) mesh.

Overall preservation was very good, although preservation of bone in each feature was variable. Two features had extremely poor bone preservation, with only calcined bones and fragments of relatively thick long bones present in the midden. The other four features had extremely good preservation, with no weathering or leaching of bones.

Chronological placement of the site is based on the recovered ceramics (table 8.1). The presence of Late Woodland, grog-tempered ceramics (comprising approximately 8 percent of the total ceramic sample), a high proportion of jars with folded rims or folded-flattened rims (38, or 67 percent, of 57 identified jar-rim sherds), a previously undescribed variety of Barton Incised (labeled var. *Oliver*), and the lack of

Fig. 8.1. Decorated sherds from Oliver: *a–e*, Barton Incised, var. *Oliver;* *f*, Barton Incised? (possibly Moundville Incised, var. *Moundville*); *g*, Alligator Incised, var. *unspecified.*

ceramic types and varieties indicative of later phases suggest that this was an early Moundville I farmstead (figs. 8.1, 8.2). There does not appear to be any difference in the ceramic types and varieties identified from each feature.

The faunal remains are similar to other Moundville deposits (tables 8.2, 8.3): deer comprise the largest percentage of the remains, both by count and weight, followed in importance by bird and fish. Other research on the Moundville polity has investigated provisioning the elite with specific portions of deer (Michals 1990; Welch 1986, 1991). Examination of the deer remains from this site shows that the greatest deviation from the expected values for deer body parts is in the low values for skull and foot bones (table 8.4). This is probably the result of differential transportation of the body parts from kill and pro-

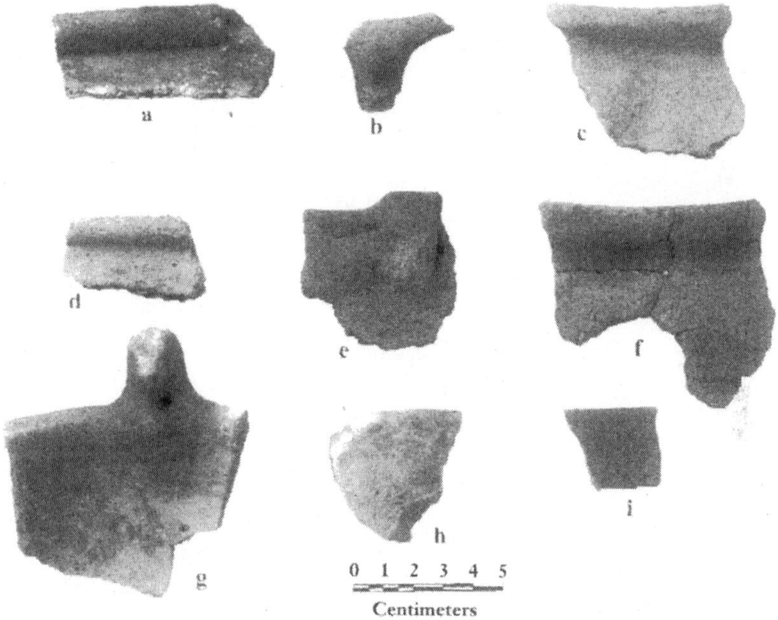

Fig. 8.2. Undecorated sherds from Oliver: *a–f*, Mississippi Plain, var. *Warrior*, jars (*a*, *d*, and *f* have folded-flattened rims; *c* has a folded rim); *g–i*, Bell Plain, var. *Hale*, bowls (*g* has an inward-facing rim effigy).

Table 8.2.
Abundance of Identified Bone Weight and Number in Each Taxonomic Category from the Oliver Site

	By Weight (% of 484.5 grams)	By Number (% of 392)
Large mammal	89.4	49.2
Medium mammal	0.4	1.3
Small mammal	0.5	3.1
Bird	5.0	11.7
Fish	3.7	30.4
Reptile	1.1	4.4

Table 8.3.
Number of Identified Specimens and Minimum Number of Individuals for Each Identified Species from the Oliver Site

Species	Identified Specimens	Minimum Number Individuals
White-tailed deer *Odocoileus virginianus*	40	3
Swamp rabbit *Sylvilagus aquaticus*	1	1
Fox squirrel *Sciurus niger*	2	1
Unidentified hawk or kite Order Falconiform	5	2
Catfish *Ictalurus* sp.	1	1
Freshwater drum *Aplodinotus grunniens*	13	2
Snake, poisonous	1	1
Snake, nonpoisonous	2	1

Table 8.4.
Percentage of Deer Bone Weight in Each Body-Part Category from Selected Moundville Phase Assemblages

	Oliver	Moundville WR	Moundville WC	Expected[a]
Skull	7.0	3.1	0.5	11.9
Axial	13.6	22.5	44.4	25.5
Limbs	73.2	69.7	50.6	44.0
Foot	6.2	4.4	4.6	18.9
Fore limb	31.4	19.1	27.6	17.2
Hind limb	5.2	19.6	18.6	26.8

Note: Includes bone positively identified as deer as well as the category "unidentified large mammal," most of which is probably deer.

a. From Scott 1983:357, calculated for a single buck, aged approximately 14 months.

Table 8.5.
Artifacts Recovered from the Oliver Site

	N	Weight (g)
Ceramics		
Sherds	1132	—
Discoidal	1	7.4
Chipped stone, total	160	250.9
Madison point (local)	3	—
Projectile point (local)	2	—
Projectile point (nonlocal)	1	—
Scraper (local)	3	—
Microdrill (local)	1	—
Blade (nonlocal)	1	—
Modified flake (local)	1	—
Flakes, shatter (local)	134	—
Flakes, shatter (nonlocal)	13	—
Flakes, shatter (unident.)	1	—
Ground stone		
Micaceous sandstone	12	124.3
Sandstone	41	2415.9
Ground hematite	1	8.9
Unidentified groundstone	1	2.6
Unmodified sandstone	31	611.0
Quartzite cobbles	2	139.4
Fire-cracked rock	3	60.1
Daub	—	253.5
Shell	—	945.0
Bone	464	503.4

cessing sites. There is a deficit of deer hind legs, which cannot be explained without comparable data from contemporaneous higher-status deposits, since higher-status late Moundville I phase deposits from Moundville do not show the expected inflated values for deer hind limbs (Michals 1990).

The botanical remains from the site were analyzed by Margaret Scarry (1993c). The assemblage is dominated by acorn, corn, and hickory remains, with small amounts of wild fruits and native crops. The corn remains were more frequent than in later Moundville I deposits at Moundville, and the nut remains more closely resemble the preceding West Jefferson phase.

The rest of the remains are presented in table 8.5 and will be discussed in the following intersite comparison.

OTHER SAMPLES

Two contemporaneous samples are available for comparison with the Oliver remains: the Asphalt Plant site (1Tu50), recently analyzed by Steponaitis (1992; see also chap. 7), and the Moundville Picnic Area (PA) remains discussed in chapter 4 by Scarry. Asphalt Plant is an early Moundville I phase single-mound center located 1 kilometer northeast of Moundville. The material from this site was recovered from mound fill on the side of the mound and from the remains of a structure on the edge of the mound. Preservation was poor, with no faunal or botanical material recovered.

The Oliver ceramics appear to be extremely similar in type and proportion to those recovered from Asphalt Plant and Moundville PA (table 8.6), confirming their similarity in chronological placement, especially in contrast to the later Moundville I phase deposits north of Mound R (NR) and east of the Conference Building (ECB) at Moundville (chap. 4; Steponaitis 1983a).

In order to provide an idea of the relation of the Oliver site to the development of the Moundville phase and to the socioeconomic differences and relationships seen between later Moundville phase deposits, two other samples are included in this analysis. These two samples are from Moundville and date, based on ceramics, from the Moundville II phase, approximately AD 1250–1400. One sample was recovered from a sheet midden and structure west of Mound R (WR), and one was from a midden-filled pit just west of Mound C (WC).

SOCIOECONOMIC DIFFERENTIATION

Four different kinds of information can be used to examine possible socioeconomic differences in the deposits: the location of the deposits, the quantity and type of ceramics, the relative abundance of religious and luxury goods, and the relative abundance of nonlocal goods and materials. It must be noted that the undifferentiated midden recovered from these deposits could have been formed by a number of different households of various statuses. In addition, all possible status levels that may have been present in the society may not be represented in the remains. As a result, the measures employed can be used only to assess the relative status that the deposits represent in relation to each other, rather than the actual status represented by the deposits.

Table 8.6.
Frequency of Shell-Tempered Ceramics in Selected Moundville I Phase Assemblages

	Total (*N*)	Barton or Moundville Incised (%)	Carthage Incised (%)	Moundville Engraved (%)	Bell Plain (%)	Mississippi Plain (%)
Oliver	1029	3.5	0.1	0	16.0	80.4
Asphalt Plant[a]	607	1.8	0.5	0	15.0	82.7
Moundville PA[b]	1843	3.3	0.7	0.5	15.1	80.4
Moundville ECB[b]	3614	4.7	1.5	1.3	18.8	73.7
Moundville NR[c]	2799	3.8	0.5	2.4	34.8	58.1

a. Data from Steponaitis 1992.

b. Data from Scarry (chapter 4, this volume).

c. Data from Steponaitis 1992, Moundville I phase material only.

The location of the deposits in relation to site type and assumed high-status areas (i.e., mounds or elite cemeteries) can be used to help assess the status of the individuals who created them. Asphalt Plant, a single-mound site, is likely to have been occupied by people in the higher level of the sociopolitical hierarchy. In contrast, the Oliver site is likely to have been occupied by the lowest rank in the society. The PA deposit from Moundville is unclear as to its locational status. Although it is from what became the paramount center, the role of Moundville during the early Moundville I phase is not clear. These assumptions about site type and status, however, are based on the sociopolitical distinctions present during Moundville's most complex stage, distinctions which may not be present during the simple chiefdoms of the early Moundville I phase. In addition, the mound sites may have been primarily vacant during portions of the year, with the majority of the population living in farmsteads, thus masking economic differences between mound sites and farmsteads.

Status determinations based solely on site type depend on the assumption that only one class of people lived at each site; Moundville may have had attached laborers living there, and the same may also be true of the minor centers. In the case of multiple-resident sites, internal placement of deposits in relation to mounds can be used to help determine status. There was no difference in the types of material recovered from each feature within the Oliver site, so it can be assumed that there was no status or economic difference between individuals at the site. The material from Asphalt Plant was recovered from the mound, suggesting that it is probably from high-status or ritual activities. Within Moundville, the PA deposits are from a residential area believed to consist of a "dense concentration" of farmsteads (chap. 4). The Moundville WC deposit is located just off the side of a mound, and the burials from Mound C have been identified as being from the highest sociopolitical level (Peebles 1974; Peebles and Kus 1977); the WR deposit is located near a mound and in an area where intermediate-status burials were recovered (Moore 1905; Peebles 1974).

Many researchers have used the presence and absence of, and the proportion of, specific artifacts as a tool to measure the relative status, or wealth, of individual households within state-level societies (M. E. Smith 1987). Five categories of items have been identified by Smith as wealth indicators in archaeological contexts: (a) tools and household equipment, (b) food preparation equipment, (c) serving ware, (d) religious items, and (e) nonutilitarian items. Several modifications in those five measures must be made in order to insure that status, rather than just wealth, is being measured and to make the measures applicable to chiefdom-level societies. The modifications are included in the following discussion.

Numerous researchers have identified differences in the relative proportion of serving to cooking vessels in relation to the socioeconomic status and function of a household (Drennan 1975; M. E. Smith 1987; Whalen 1976). That is, elites have larger quantities of serving ware in order to feed guests during ritual and festive occasions (Douglas and Isherwood 1979). Because of the increased social role that elites often play in societies, higher-status households usually have a higher ratio of serving vessels to cooking vessels than lower-status households. Serving ware can be defined based on surface treatment that could be harmed by cooking, such as burnished or painted ceramics, and on size and shape that would preclude food preparation, such as outslanting bowls and small restricted bowls. In addition, Steponaitis has demonstrated that those vessels with relatively fewer and smaller fragments of shell as a tempering agent are better able to withstand breakage (mechanical stress), and those with relatively larger and more frequent fragments of shell are better able to withstand thermal stress (1983a:33–45). Because we must deal with sherds instead of whole vessels, cooking ware can be defined as all unburnished ceramics and ceramics with large fragments of shell temper (Mississippi Plain, Barton Incised, and Moundville Incised),

Table 8.7.
Ratio of Serving-Vessel to Cooking-Vessel Fragments from Selected Moundville Phase Assemblages

	Cooking Ceramics[a]	Serving Ceramics[b]	Serving : Cooking Ratio
Oliver	863	167	0.19
Asphalt Plant[c]	512	95	0.19
Moundville PA[d]	1543	300	0.19
Moundville ECB[d]	2833	781	0.28
Moundville NR[c]	1733	1055	0.61
Moundville WR	1305	703	0.54
Moundville WC	279	223	0.80

a. Consists of unburnished local Moundville phase ceramic types: Barton Incised, Mississippi Plain, and Moundville Incised.

b. Consists of burnished and painted/filmed local Moundville phase ceramic types: Bell Plain, Moundville Engraved, Carthage Incised, Red Film, and Red and White Film.

c. Data from Steponaitis 1992.

d. Data from Scarry (chapter 4, this volume).

and serving ware can be defined as all burnished, painted, or finely engraved ceramics and ceramics with small fragments of shell temper (Bell Plain, Carthage Incised, Moundville Engraved).

Examining the ceramics in each of the samples shows that Asphalt Plant and the PA tract deposit have the same ratio of serving to cooking ware as the Oliver site (table 8.7). The later Moundville I phase deposits, ECB and NR, both have higher ratios than the early Moundville I deposits, with the NR deposit having the highest ratio. Given the limited number of samples, it is not clear whether the differences between the early Moundville I and late Moundville I phase deposits are status-related or chronological. The similarity in ratios between the early Moundville I phase deposits suggests either that these deposits represent the same status or that this indicator is not applicable during this level of political development. The Moundville II phase WC sample has a much higher ratio than the Moundville II WR sample, a difference expected given the location of the deposits within Moundville and the highly developed status differences present by that time.

The presence and relative amount of luxury, or nonutilitarian, items can be used as a measure of socioeconomic differences (M. E. Smith 1987:314–317). Many of the Moundville polity's luxury

Fig. 8.3. Micaceous sandstone artifacts from Oliver: *a* and *b*, irregular slabs, 7–10 millimeters thick; *c* and *d*, saws, 2–3 millimeters thick (the upper edge of each illustrated specimen is ground and beveled in cross-section).

items are those identified as sumptuary goods and were used as indicators of status in Peebles's mortuary analysis. These items overlap with Southern Cult artifacts and are often hard to differentiate from religious items. Because of the inability to differentiate many luxury items from religious items in chiefdom-level societies, these two categories are grouped together. However, very few of these remains have been recovered. The most common remains that may be from luxury-nonutilitarian items are micaceous sandstone artifacts—a material used in the manufacture of palettes. A comparison of the relative abundance of micaceous sandstone (number of fragments/total number of sherds) in the early Moundville I phase deposits shows that the Moundville PA deposit had the highest density (76/2345 = 0.032), followed by the Oliver site (12/1132 = 0.013) and then Asphalt Plant (2/657 = 0.003). The relatively high density at Oliver may be due to the site's proximity to the assumed source of micaceous sandstone at the Pottsville formation, located above the fall line (Steponaitis 1992:8), and may be due to the site's being a location for the production of such artifacts (fig. 8.3).

Various researchers have linked the presence and proportion of nonlocal materials and artifacts to status and wealth (e.g., Helms 1979; M. E. Smith 1987; Welch 1986). The value of these goods is based on their relative scarcity within the society and on the cost of procuring such items. The most common nonlocal materials and goods present in

Table 8.8.
Number, Weight, and Ratio of Greenstone Fragments to Sherds from Selected Moundville Phase Assemblages

	Greenstone		Sherds	
	N	Weight (g)	*N*	Ratio[a]
Oliver	0	0.0	1132	0.000
Asphalt Plant[b]	1	—	657	0.002
Moundville PA[c]	5	37.7	2345	0.002
Moundville WR	8	2.8	2106	0.004
Moundville WC	5	44.7	536	0.009

a. Ratio of number of greenstone fragments to number of sherds.

b. From Steponaitis 1992; no weight for the greenstone is available.

c. From Scarry 1993 (and chapter 4, this volume).

the Moundville polity are greenstone, various chipped stone materials, and ceramics. In the case of ceramics, it is often difficult, if not impossible, to identify nonlocal ceramics from small sherds. Because of this, the proportion of nonlocal ceramics in each deposit was not examined.

No nonlocal minerals were recovered from the Oliver site. The most common nonlocal material, outside of chipped stone, is greenstone (table 8.8). One greenstone fragment was recovered from Asphalt Plant (greenstone-to-sherd ratio of 0.002), and five fragments were recovered from the PA deposit (greenstone-to-sherd ratio of 0.002). For the Moundville II samples, WR has a greater number of greenstone fragments than the WC sample, which, as the ratios indicate, is mostly likely a function of the larger volume of material recovered from WR (greenstone-to-sherd ratio for WC is 0.009; for WR the ratio is 0.004).

Examining the abundance of local and nonlocal chipped stone material and the proportion of tools in each sample produces interesting results (table 8.9). The Oliver site contains much less nonlocal chipped stone than Asphalt Plant, and Asphalt Plant contains slightly more nonlocal chipped stone than the PA deposit. Breaking this down to the proportion of chipped stone artifacts that are flakes versus tools, more of Asphalt Plant's chipped stone artifacts are tools (12 percent versus 7.5 percent at Oliver), suggesting that less tool manufacturing was occurring at the Asphalt Plant site. Approximately 9 percent of the PA chipped stone artifacts were tools. In the Moundville II samples, WR

Table 8.9.
Abundance of Local and Nonlocal Chipped Stone Material from Selected Moundville Phase Assemblages

	Local Stone[a]		Nonlocal Stone[b]	
	(*N*)	(%)	(*N*)	(%)
Oliver[c]				
tools and debitage	144	90.6	15	9.4
(tools only)	(10)		(2)	
Asphalt Plant[d]				
tools and debitage	20	58.8	14	41.2
(tools only)	(1)		(3)	
Moundville PA[e]				
tools and debitage	83	59.3	57	40.7
(tools only)	(6)		(6)	
Moundville WR[c]				
tools and debitage	23	34.8	43	65.2
(tools only)	(2)		(4)	
Moundville WC[c]				
tools and debitage	6	50.0	6	50.0
(tools only)	(2)		(0)	

a. Local material consists of quartz, quartzite, and Tuscaloosa chert.

b. Nonlocal material consists of Fort Payne chert, Bangor chert, Mill Creek chert (identified in the 1Tu50 remains), and other nonlocal cherts.

c. Figures exclude unidentified chipped stone material.

d. Data from Steponaitis 1992.

e. Data from Scarry 1993 (and chapter 4, this volume).

contains more nonlocal chipped stone than WC, although WC also contains proportionately more tools (29 percent versus 9 percent).

The overall differences in the amounts of nonlocal material between the deposits and sites can be explained by a number of factors. For the early Moundville I deposits, proximity to Moundville or the general high density of population in the Moundville–Asphalt Plant area may have allowed greater opportunity for trading or other routes of access to nonlocal materials. The relatively higher proportion of tools in the Asphalt Plant remains and the slightly higher proportion of nonlocal chipped stone material at the Asphalt Plant mound, in comparison to the Moundville PA remains, may be a result of the materials' coming from a mound rather than residential context. This explanation for the higher proportion of tools is supported by the Moundville II phase deposits, where the mound deposit from WC has a higher percentage of finished tools.

CONCLUSIONS

In comparison to the later Moundville II phase deposits, the Oliver site appears to have been occupied by low-status people. In comparison to the early Moundville I phase material from the Asphalt Plant site and the Moundville PA tract, however, the sites appear to be relatively the same. The major difference between these early Moundville I samples is in the amount of nonlocal material. Their overall similarity in ceramics may be due to a lack of, or poorly defined, status-related differences in household possessions during the early Moundville I phase. This similarity may also be due to the residence, at least part-time, of individuals of all status levels in farmsteads. It should be mentioned that within the nearby Mississippian Lubbub Creek site, Blitz (1989) has shown that although the ceramic types are similar in mound and nonmound settings, vessel sizes do reflect status or use differences. Vessel size measurements are not, at present, available for these samples.

By the Moundville II phase, differences in material goods are much more evident. The WC sample outranks the WR sample in all measures except the frequency of nonlocal lithics. This difference in nonlocal chipped stone material can be explained by a lack of manufacturing done in elite contexts.

The greatest differences in the Moundville II samples are in the ratio of serving vessels to cooking vessels and the presence of nonutilitarian luxury items, both local and nonlocal in origin. In contrast, in the early Moundville I samples, only the presence of nonlocal goods and materials appears to reflect assumed sociopolitical differences between the sites. Steponaitis (1991) has shown that access to nonlocal material may have contributed to the establishment and maintenance of the complex Moundville chiefdom present by the Moundville II phase. The results in this analysis support his contention in that the assumed high-status sample, Asphalt Plant, has almost identical quantities of locally produced materials as the farmstead but more nonlocal material.

Welch (1991) has argued that as part of a prestige-goods economy in the mature Moundville polity, luxury items of nonlocal origin and of nonlocal raw materials were primarily restricted to residents of Moundville, while nonlocal utilitarian goods may not have been restricted. Given the results presented here, such restriction of nonlocal goods to the Moundville vicinity and to mound sites may have started early on in the Moundville phase.

In conclusion, these results indicate that socioeconomic differences in the earliest Moundville phase, during the simple chiefdom level of organization, are not reflected in everyday utilitarian material. Socioeconomic differences are reflected in nonlocal material and goods, supporting the connection between control of outside resources and sociopolitical power. Given the similarity in everyday material, it is not surprising that there is, at present, no indication of status-related differences in faunal resources during this period. Future research on early Moundville deposits may clarify the point at which we begin to see the socioeconomic differences in utilitarian remains that are present by the Moundville II phase.

ACKNOWLEDGMENTS

Access to the Oliver site material was provided by Eugene Futato and the University of Alabama, Alabama Museum of Natural History. The assistance of the staff at the Division of Archaeology, Alabama Museum of Natural History, is greatly appreciated, as are the guidance and suggestions of my colleagues in this volume, especially those of Vincas Steponaitis and V. J. Knight. Vincas Steponaitis prepared the artifact photos.

Bibliography

Acheson, R. M.

1960 Effects of nutrition and disease on human growth. In *Human growth*, ed. J. M. Tanner, pp. 73–92. Oxford: Pergamon Press.

Adair, James

1968 *The history of the American Indians.* New York: Johnson Reprint.

Albanese, A. A., and G. A. Orto

1964 The proteins and amino acids. In *Modern nutrition in health and disease*, ed. M. G. Wohl and R. S. Goodhart, pp. 125–193. 3rd ed. Philadelphia: Lea & Febiger.

Alexander, Lawrence S.

1982 *Phase I archaeological reconnaissance of the Oliver Lock and Dam project area, Tuscaloosa County, Alabama.* Report of Investigations 33. Tuscaloosa: University of Alabama Office of Archaeological Research.

Allan, Aljean W.

1984 Mound State Monument palisade excavations, 1978–1982. Paper presented at 38th annual meeting of the Southeastern Archaeological Conference, Memphis, Tenn.

Atkinson, James R.

1987 The De Soto expedition through North Mississippi in 1540–1541. *Mississippi Archaeology* 22:61–73.

Atkinson, James R., J. Phillips, and R. Walling

1980 *The Kellogg Village site investigations, Clay County, Mississippi.* Starkville: Department of Anthropology, Mississippi State University.

Baden, W. W.

1987 A dynamic model of stability and change in Mississippian agricultural systems. Ph.D. dissertation, University of Tennessee, Knoxville.

Black, Thomas K.

1979 *The biological and social analyses of a Mississippian cemetery from Southeast Missouri: The Turner site, 23Bu21a*. Anthropological Papers 68. Ann Arbor: University of Michigan, Museum of Anthropology.

Blitz, John H.

1989 Vessel size as a measure of Mississippian mound activities. Paper presented at 46th annual meeting of the Southeastern Archaeological Conference, Tampa, Fla.

1993 *Ancient chiefdoms of the Tombigbee*. Tuscaloosa: University of Alabama Press.

Bourne, E. G., ed.

1904 *Narratives of the career of Hernando de Soto in the conquest of Florida*. New York: A. S. Barnes.

Bozeman, Tandy K.

1981 Moundville phase sites in the Black Warrior Valley, Alabama: Preliminary results of the UMMA survey. *Southeastern Archaeological Conference Bulletin* 24:84–86.

1982 Moundville phase communities in the Black Warrior River valley, Alabama. Ph.D. dissertation, University of California, Santa Barbara.

Brown, James A.

1976 A reconsideration of the Southern Cult. *Midcontinental Journal of Archaeology* 1:115–135.

Buikstra, J. E., ed.

1981 *Prehistoric tuberculosis in the Americas*. Scientific Papers 5. Evanston, Ill.: Northwestern University Archaeological Program.

Buikstra, J. E., and D. C. Cook

1981 Pre-Columbian tuberculosis in west-central Illinois: Prehistoric disease in biocultural perspective. In *Prehistoric tuberculosis in the Americas*, ed. J. E. Buikstra, pp. 115–140. Scientific Papers 5. Evanston, Ill.: Northwestern University Archaeological Program.

Bumsted, M. P.

1984 *Human variation: $\delta^{13}C$ in adult bone collagen and the relation to diet in an isochronous C_4 (maize) archaeological population*. Los Alamos, N.Mex.: Los Alamos National Laboratory.

Champagne, Duane

1992 *Social order and political change: Constitutional governments among the Cherokee, the Choctaw, the Chickasaw, and the Creek*. Stanford, Calif.: Stanford University Press.

Cole, Gloria G., and Caroline H. Albright

1983 Summerville I–II fortifications. In *Prehistoric agricultural communities in west central Alabama*, vol. 1, *Excavations in the Lubbub Creek archaeological locality*, ed. C. Peebles, pp. 140–196. Report submitted to U.S. Army Corps of Engineers, Mobile District, by University of Michigan Museum of Anthropology, Ann Arbor.

Condon, K.

1981 Correspondence of developmental enamel defects between the mandibular canine and first premolar. M.A. thesis, Department of Anthropology, University of Arkansas, Fayetteville.

Cottier, John W.

1970 The Alabama River phase: A brief description of a late phase in the prehistory of south-central Alabama. In *Archaeological salvage investigations in the Miller's Ferry Lock and Dam Reservoir*. Report to National Park Service, on file at Moundville Archaeological Park, Moundville.

Curren, Caleb [Cailup]

1982a The Alabama River phase: A review. In *Archaeology in southwest Alabama: A collection of papers*, ed. Cailup Curren, pp. 103–114. Camden: Alabama-Tombigbee Regional Commission.

1982b Appendix: A classification of Alabama River phase ceramics. In *Archaeology in southwest Alabama: A collection of papers*, ed. Cailup Curren, pp. 115–131. Camden: Alabama-Tombigbee Regional Commission.

1984 *The Protohistoric period in central Alabama*. Camden: Alabama-Tombigbee Regional Commission.

DeBoer, Warren R.

1997 Ceremonial centres from the Cayapas (Esmeraldas, Ecuador) to Chillicothe (Ohio, USA). *Cambridge Archaeological Journal* 7:225–253.

DeBoer, Warren R., and John H. Blitz

1991 Ceremonial centers of the Chachi. *Expedition* 33:53–62.

DeJarnette, David L.

1952 Alabama archaeology: A summary. In *Archaeology of eastern United States*, ed. James B. Griffin, pp. 272–284. Chicago: University of Chicago Press.

DeJarnette, David L., and Christopher S. Peebles

1970 The development of Alabama archaeology: The Snow's Bend site. *Journal of Alabama Archaeology* 16:77–119.

DeJarnette, David L., and Steve B. Wimberly

1941 *The Bessemer site: Excavations of three mounds and surrounding village areas near Bessemer, Alabama*. Museum paper 17. University: Geological Survey of Alabama.

Delwiche, C. C., P. J. Zinke, C. M. Johnson, and R. A. Virginia

1979 Nitrogen isotope distribution as a presumptive indicator of nitrogen fixation. *Botanical Gazette* 140 (Suppl.): S65–S69.

DeNiro, M. J., and S. Epstein

1978 Influence of diet on the distribution of carbon isotopes in animals. *Geochimica et Cosmochimica Acta* 42:495–506.

1981 Influence of diet on the distribution of nitrogen isotopes in animals. *Geochimica et Cosmochimica Acta* 45:341–351.

Deo, M. G.

1978 Cell biology of protein-calorie malnutrition. *World Review of Nutrition and Dietetics* 32:49–95.

Dillehay, Thomas D.

1990 Mapuche ceremonial landscape, social recruitment, and resource rights. *World Archaeology* 22:223–241.

Douglas, Mary

1972 Symbolic orders in the use of domestic space. In *Man, settlement, and urbanism*, ed. P. Ucko, R. Tringham, and G. W. Dimbleby, pp. 513–521. Cambridge, Mass.: Schenkman Publishing.

Douglas, Mary, and B. Isherwood

1979 *The world of goods: Toward an anthropology of consumption*. New York: Basic Books.

Drennan, Richard

1975 Fabrica San Jose and middle formative society in the valley of Oaxaca, Mexico. Ph.D. dissertation, Department of Anthropology, University of Michigan.

Du Pratz, Le Page

1972 *The history of Louisiana*. Reprint. Trans. and ed. J. G. Tregle Jr. Baton Rouge: Louisiana State University Press. Originally published 1774, London.

Dubos, R.

1965 *Man adapting*. New Haven: Yale University Press.

Dubos, R., and J. Dubos

1952 *The white plague: Tuberculosis, man, and society*. Boston: Little, Brown.

Ensor, H. Blaine

1979 Archaeological investigations in the upper Cahaba River drainage, north central Alabama. *Journal of Alabama Archaeology* 25(1):1–60.

1993 *Big Sandy Farms: A prehistoric agricultural community near Moundville, Black Warrior River floodplain, Tuscaloosa County, Alabama*. Report of Investigations 68. Tuscaloosa: Division of Archaeology, Alabama Museum of Natural History, University of Alabama.

Fuller, Richard S., and Noel R. Stowe

1982 A proposed typology for late shell-tempered ceramics in the Mobile Bay/Mobile-Tensaw Delta region. In *Archaeology in southwestern Alabama: A collection of papers*, ed. Cailup Curren, pp. 45–93. Camden: Alabama Tombigbee Regional Commission.

Futato, Eugene M.

1983 *Archaeological investigations in the Cedar Creek and upper Bear Creek reservoirs*. Report of Investigations 29. Tuscaloosa: University of Alabama Office of Archaeological Research.

Gall, Daniel G.

1993 Greenstone artifacts at the Moundville site, Alabama: Petrography and provenance. Paper presented at 58th annual meeting of Society for American Archaeology, St. Louis, Mo.

Garcilaso de la Vega, El Inca

1951 *The Florida of the Inca*. Trans. and ed. J. G. Varner and J. J. Varner. Austin: University of Texas Press.

Garn, S. M.

1966 Malnutrition and skeletal development in the pre-school child. In *Pre-school child malnutrition: Primary deterrent to human progress*, pp. 43–62. Washington, D.C.: National Research Council.

Gatschet, Albert S.

1884 *A migration legend of the Creek Indians, with a linguistic, historic, and ethnographic introduction*. Vol. 1. Brinton's Library of Aboriginal American Literature 4. Philadelphia.

Goodman, A. H., G. J. Armelagos, and J. C. Rose

1980 Enamel hypoplasias as indicators of stress in three prehistoric populations from Illinois. *Human Biology* 52:515–528.

Graebner, Norman Arthur

1945 Provincial Indian society in eastern Oklahoma. *Chronicles of Oklahoma* 23:323–337.

Hackett, C. J.

1976 *Diagnostic criteria of syphilis, yaws, and treponarid (treponematoses) and of some other diseases in dry bones*. New York: Springer-Verlag.

Hall, Robert L.

1989 The cultural background of Mississippian symbolism. In *The Southeastern Ceremonial Complex: Artifacts and analysis*, ed. P. Galloway, pp. 239–278. Lincoln: University of Nebraska Press.

Haltom, W. L., and A. R. Shands

1938 Evidences of syphilis in mound builders' bones. *Archives of Pathology* 25:228–242.

Hann, John H.

1988 *Apalachee: The land between the rivers*. Ripley P. Bullen Monographs in Anthropology and History 7. Gainesville: University Presses of Florida.

Hardman, Clark, Jr.

1971 The primitive solar observatory at Crystal River and its implications. *Florida Anthropologist* 24:135–168.

Hare, P. E., M. L. Fogel, T. W. Stafford Jr., A. D. Mitchell, and T. C. Hoering

1991 The isotopic composition of carbon and nitrogen in individual amino acids isolated from modern and fossil proteins. *Journal of Archaeological Science* 18:277–292.

Harré, Rom

1978 Architectonic man: On the structure of lived experience. In *Structure, consciousness, and history*, ed. R. H. Brown and S. M. Lyman, pp. 139–172. Cambridge: Cambridge University Press.

Hayward, Hampton D., Caleb Curren, Ned J. Jenkins, and Keith J. Little

1990 Archaeological investigations in the proposed Pafallaya province. Unpublished MS in Paul D. Welch's possession.

Heimlich, Marion Dunlevy

1952 *Guntersville Basin pottery*. Museum paper 32. University: Geological Survey of Alabama.

Helms, Mary W.

1979 *Ancient Panama: Chiefs in Search of Power.* Austin: University of Texas Press.

Hengen, O. P.

1971 Cribra orbitalia: Pathogenesis and probable etiology. *Homo* 22:57–76.

Hill-Clark, Mary C.

1981 The Mississippian decline in Alabama: A biological analysis. *American Journal of Physical Anthropology* 54:233.

Hodder, Ian

1986 *Reading the past: Current approaches to interpretation in archaeology*. Cambridge: Cambridge University Press.

Hoeprich, P. D., ed.

1977 *Infectious diseases: A modern treatise on infectious processes.* 2nd ed. Philadelphia: Harper & Row.

Hudson, Charles

1976 *The southeastern Indians.* Knoxville: University of Tennessee Press.

Hudson, Charles, Marvin T. Smith, and Chester B. DePratter

1990 The Hernando de Soto expedition: From Mabila to the Mississippi River. In *Towns and temples along the Mississippi*, ed. D. H. Dye and C. A. Cox, pp. 181–207. Tuscaloosa: University of Alabama Press.

Huffman, Thomas N.

1981 Snakes and birds: Expressive space at Great Zimbabwe. *African Studies* 40:131–150.

Isbell, William H.

1976 Cosmological order expressed in prehistoric ceremonial centers. In Vol. 4, *Actes du 42 Congrés International des Américanistes* (Paris), pp. 269–297.

Jenkins, Ned J.

1981 *Gainesville Lake area ceramic description and chronology.* Vol. 2, *Archaeological investigations in the Gainesville Lake area of the Tennessee-Tombigbee Waterway.* Report of Investigations 12. Tuscaloosa: University of Alabama Office of Archaeological Research.

1982 *Archaeology of the Gainesville Lake area: Synthesis.* Report of Investigations 23. Tuscaloosa: University of Alabama Office of Archaeological Research.

Jenkins, Ned J., and H. Blaine Ensor

1981 *The Gainesville Lake area excavations.* Vol. 1, *Archaeological investigations in the Gainesville Lake area of the Tennessee-Tombigbee Waterway.* Report of Investigations 11. Tuscaloosa: University of Alabama Office of Archaeological Research.

Jenkins, Ned J., and Richard A. Krause

1986 *The Tombigbee watershed in southeastern prehistory*. Tuscaloosa: University of Alabama Press.

Jenkins, Ned J., and Jerry J. Nielsen

1974 *Archaeological salvage investigations at the West Jefferson Steam Plant site, Jefferson County, Alabama.* Report to the Alabama Power Company, on file at Moundville Archaeological Park, Moundville.

Jones, Walter B.

1939 Geology of the Tennessee Valley region of Alabama. In *An archaeological survey of Wheeler Basin on the Tennessee River in northern Alabama*, by William S. Webb, pp. 9–20. Washington, D.C.: Bureau of American Ethnology.

Jones, Walter B., and David L. DeJarnette

1936 *Moundville culture and burial museum.* Museum paper 13. Tuscaloosa: Alabama Museum of Natural History.

Katzenberg, M. A.

1989 Stable isotope analysis of archaeological faunal remains from southern Ontario. *Journal of Archaeological Science* 16:319–329.

Kelley, M. A., and L. E. Eisenberg

1987 Blastomycosis and tuberculosis in early American Indians: A biocultural view. *Midcontinental Journal of Archaeology* 12:89–116.

Kent, S.

1992 Anemia through the ages: Changing perspectives and their implications. In *Diet, demography, and disease: Changing perspectives on anemia*, ed. P. Stuart-Macadam and S. Kent, pp. 1–30. New York: Aldine De Gruyter.

Knight, Vernon James, Jr.

1981 Mississippian ritual. Ph.D. dissertation, Department of Anthropology, University of Florida, Gainesville.

1982a Document and literature review. In *Phase I archaeological reconnaissance of the Oliver Lock and Dam project area, Tuscaloosa, Alabama*, ed. Lawrence S. Alexander, pp. 27–102. Report of Investigations 33. Tuscaloosa: University of Alabama Office of Archaeological Research.

1982b Unpublished field notes on excavations at 1Tu459. On file at University of Alabama Office of Archaeological Services.

1986 The institutional organization of Mississippian religion. *American Antiquity* 51:675–687.

1989 Certain aboriginal mounds at Moundville: 1937 excavations in mounds H, I, J, K, and L. Paper presented at annual meeting of the Southeastern Archaeological Conference, Tampa, Fla.

1990 Social organization and the evolution of hierarchy in southeastern chiefdoms. *Journal of Anthropological Research* 46(1):1–23.

1992 Preliminary report on excavations at Mound Q, Moundville. Paper presented at annual meeting of the Southeastern Archaeological Conference, Little Rock, Ark.

1994 Evidence for the dating of mounds A, B, P, R, and S, Moundville. Paper presented at annual meeting of the Southeastern Archaeological Conference, Lexington, Ky.

Kohler, Timothy A., and Eric Blinman

1987 Solving mixture problems in archaeology: Analysis of ceramic materials for dating and demographic reconstruction. *Journal of Anthropological Archaeology* 6:1–28.

Kus, Susan

1981 The context of complexity. In *Archaeological approaches to the study of complexity*, ed. S. E. van der Leeuw, pp. 197–227. Amsterdam: University of Amsterdam.

1982 Matters material and ideal. In *Symbolic and structural archaeology*, ed. I. Hodder, pp. 47–62. Cambridge: Cambridge University Press.

Lafferty, Robert H., III
1973 An analysis of prehistoric southeastern fortifications. M.A. thesis, Department of Anthropology, Southern Illinois University, Carbondale.
Lankford, George E.
1987 *Native American legends. Southeastern legends: Tales from the Natchez, Caddo, Biloxi, Chickasaw, and other nations.* Little Rock, Ark.: August House.
Larsen, C. S., R. Shavit, and M. C. Griffin
1991 Dental caries evidence for dietary context: An archaeological context. In *Advances in dental anthropology*, ed. M. A. Kelley and C. S. Larsen, pp. 179–202. New York: Wiley-Liss.
Lathrap, Donald W., Jorge M. Marcos, and James A. Zeidler
1977 Real Alto: An ancient ceremonial center. *Archaeology* 30:3–13.
Lawrence, Denise L., and Setha M. Low
1990 The built environment and spatial form. *Annual Review of Anthropology* 19:453–505.
Lévi-Strauss, Claude
1963 Do dual organizations exist? In *Structural anthropology*, by C. Lévi-Strauss, pp. 132–163. New York: Basic Books.
Little, Keith J., and Caleb Curren
1995 The Moundville IV phase on the Black Warrior River. *Journal of Alabama Archaeology* 41(1):55–77.
Longin, R.
1971 New method of collagen extraction for radiocarbon dating. *Nature* 230:241–242.
MacArthur, Robert H., and Edward O. Wilson
1967 *The theory of island biogeography*. Monographs in Population Biology 1. Princeton: Princeton University Press.
Mann, C. Baxter
1983 Classification of ceramics from the Lubbub Creek archaeological locality. In *Prehistoric agricultural communities in west central Alabama*, vol. 2, *Studies of material remains from the Lubbub Creek archaeological locality*, ed. Christopher S. Peebles, pp. 2–137. Report submitted to U.S. Army Corps of Engineers, Mobile District, by University of Michigan Museum of Anthropology, Ann Arbor.
Marino, B. D., and M. B. McElroy
1991 Isotopic composition of atmospheric CO_2 inferred from carbon in C_4 plant cellulose. *Nature* 349:127–131.
Marshall, Richard A.
1977 Lyon's Bluff site (22OK1) radiocarbon dated. *Journal of Alabama Archaeology* 23:53–57.
McKenzie, Douglas
1964 The Moundville phase and its position in southeastern prehistory. Ph.D. dissertation, Department of Anthropology, Harvard University.
1966 A summary of the Moundville phase. *Journal of Alabama Archaeology* 12:1–58.

McNeill, W. H.

1976 *Plagues and peoples*. New York: Anchor Books.

Michals, Lauren M.

1981 The exploitation of fauna during the Moundville I phase at Moundville. *Southeastern Archaeological Conference Bulletin* 24:91–93.

1990 Faunal exploitation and chiefdom organization at Moundville. Paper presented at 55th annual meeting of Society for American Archaeology, Las Vegas, Nev.

1992 The nature of faunal exploitation in Mississippian societies. Paper presented at 57th annual meeting of Society for American Archaeology, Pittsburgh, Pa.

Milner, G., and V. G. Smith

1990 Oneonta human skeletal remains. In *Archaeological investigations at the Morton Village and Norris Farms 36 cemetery*, by S. S. Santure, A. D. Harn, and D. Esary, pp. 111–153. Reports of Investigations 45. Springfield: Illinois State Museum.

Mistovich, Tim S.

1986 *Excavations at sites 1Tu265 and 1Tu423, Oliver Lock and Dam, Tuscaloosa, Alabama*. Report of Investigations 51. Tuscaloosa: University of Alabama Office of Archaeological Research.

1987 *The Mill Creek site, 1Tu265, Black Warrior River, Alabama*. Report of Investigations 54. Tuscaloosa: University of Alabama Office of Archaeological Research.

1988 Early Mississippian in the Black Warrior Valley: The pace of transition. *Southeastern Archaeology* 7:21–38.

1995 Toward an explanation of variation in Moundville phase households in the Black Warrior Valley, Alabama. In *Mississippian communities and households*, ed. J. Daniel Rogers and Bruce D. Smith, pp. 156–180. Washington, D.C.: Smithsonian Institution Press.

Moore, Clarence B.

1905 Certain aboriginal remains of the Black Warrior River. *Journal of the Academy of Natural Sciences of Philadelphia* 13:125–224.

1907 Moundville revisited. *Journal of the Academy of Natural Sciences of Philadelphia* 13:337–405.

Morgan, William N.

1980 *Prehistoric architecture of the eastern United States*. Cambridge, Mass.: MIT Press.

Nairne, Thomas

1988 *Nairne's Muskogean journals: The 1708 expedition to the Mississippi River*. Ed. Alexander Moore. Jackson: University of Mississippi Press.

Naroll, Raoul

1962 Floor area and settlement population. *American Antiquity* 27:187–189.

Nielsen, Jerry J., John W. O'Hear, and Charles W. Moorehead

1973 *An archaeological survey of Hale and Greene counties, Alabama*. Report submitted to Alabama Historical Commission by University Museums, University of Alabama.

O'Hear, John W.

1975 Site 1Je32: Community organization in the West Jefferson phase. Master's thesis, Department of Anthropology, University of Alabama, Tuscaloosa.

O'Hear, John W., Clark Larsen, Margaret Scarry, J. Phillips, and E. Simons

1981 *Archaeological salvage excavations at the Tibbee Creek site (22Lo600), Lowndes County, Mississippi*. Starkville: Department of Anthropology, Mississippi State University.

O'Leary, M. H.

1988 Carbon isotopes in photosynthesis. *Bioscience* 38:328–336.

Ortner, D. J., and W. G. J. Putschar

1981 *Identification of pathological conditions in human skeletal remains*. Smithsonian Contributions to Anthropology 28. Washington, D.C.: Smithsonian Institution.

Panshin, A. J., and Carl de Zeeuw

1970 *Textbook of wood technology*, vol. 1, *Structure, identification, uses, and properties of the commercial woods of the United States and Canada*. 3rd ed. New York: McGraw-Hill.

Pauketat, Timothy R.

1994 *The ascent of chiefs: Cahokia and Mississippian politics in Native North America*. Tuscaloosa: University of Alabama Press.

Peebles, Christopher S.

1971 Moundville and surrounding sites: Some structural considerations of mortuary practices. In *Approaches to the social dimension of mortuary practices*, ed. James A. Brown, pp. 68–91. Memoir 15. Society for American Archaeology.

1973 Moundville: Multivariate analysis and settlement organization. Paper presented at 50th annual meeting of Alabama Academy of Sciences.

1974 Moundville: The organization of a prehistoric community and culture. Ph.D. dissertation, University of California, Santa Barbara.

1978 Determinants of settlement size and location in the Moundville phase. In *Mississippian settlement patterns*, ed. Bruce D. Smith, pp. 369–416. New York: Academic Press.

1979 *Excavations at Moundville, 1905–1951*. Microfiche. Ann Arbor: University of Michigan Press.

1981 Archaeological research at Moundville, 1840–1980. *Southeastern Archaeological Conference Bulletin* 24:77–81.

1983 Moundville: Late prehistoric sociopolitical organization in the southeastern United States. In *The development of political organization in Native North America*, ed. Elizabeth Tooker, pp. 183–201. Washington, D.C.: American Ethnological Society.

1986 Paradise lost, strayed, and stolen: Prehistoric social devolution in the Southeast. In *The burden of being civilized: An anthropological perspective on the discontents of civilization*, ed. Miles Richardson and Malcolm Webb, pp. 24–40. Southern Anthropological Society Proceedings 18. Athens: University of Georgia Press.

1987a Moundville from 1000 to 1500 AD as seen from 1840 to 1985 AD. In *Chiefdoms in the Americas*, ed. Robert D. Drennan and Carlos A. Uribe, pp. 21–41. Lanham, Md.: University Press of America.

1987b The rise and fall of the Mississippian in western Alabama: The Moundville and Summerville phases, AD 1000 to 1600. *Mississippi Archaeology* 22:1–31.

Peebles, Christopher S., and Susan M. Kus

1977 Some archaeological correlates of ranked societies. *American Antiquity* 42:421–448.

Peebles, Christopher S., and Margaret J. Schoeninger

1981 Notes on the relationship between social status and diet at Moundville. *Southeastern Archaeological Conference Bulletin* 24:96–97.

Peebles, C. S., M. J. Schoeninger, V. P. Steponaitis, and C. M. Scarry

1982 A precious bequest: Contemporary research with the WPA-CCC collections from Moundville, Alabama. In *The research potential of anthropological museum collections*, ed. A. M. Cantwell, J. B. Griffin, and N. A. Rothschild. *Annals of the New York Academy of Sciences* 376:433–447.

Polhemus, Richard R.

1987 *The Toqua site: A late Mississippian Dallas phase town*. Report of Investigations 41. Knoxville: Department of Anthropology, University of Tennessee.

Pope, Melody

1989 Microtools from the Black Warrior Valley: Technology, use, and context. M.A. thesis, Department of Anthropology, State University of New York, Binghamton.

Powell, Mary Lucas

1983 Biocultural analysis of human skeletal remains from the Lubbub Creek archaeological locality. In *Prehistoric agricultural communities in west central Alabama*, vol. 2, ed. C. S. Peebles, pp. 430–447. Washington, D.C.: National Technical Information Service.

1985 The analysis of dental wear and caries for dietary reconstruction. In *The analysis of prehistoric diets*, ed. R. I. Gilbert Jr. and J. H. Mielke, pp. 307–388. Orlando, Fla.: Academic Press.

1988 *Status and health in prehistory: A case study of the Moundville chiefdom*. Washington, D.C.: Smithsonian Institution Press.

1991 Endemic treponematosis and tuberculosis in the prehistoric southeastern United States: The biological costs of chronic endemic disease. In *Human paleopathology: Current syntheses and future options*, ed. D. J. Ortner and A. C. Aufderheide, pp. 173–180. Washington, D.C.: Smithsonian Institution Press.

1992a Health and disease in the late prehistoric Southeast. In *Disease and demography in the Americas*, ed. J. W. Verano and D. H. Ubelaker, pp. 41–54. Washington, D.C.: Smithsonian Institution Press.

1992b In the best of health? Disease and trauma among the Mississippian elite. In *Lords of the Southeast: Social inequality and the Native elites of southeastern North America*, ed. A. W. Barker and T. R. Pauketat, pp. 81–97. Archaeological Papers of the American Anthropological Association 3. Washington, D.C.

1994 Treponematosis before 1492 in the southeastern United States: Why call it syphilis? In *L'Origine de la syphilis en Europe: Avant ou après 1493*, ed. O. Dutour, G. Palfi, J. Berato, and J.-P. Brun, pp. 158–163. Paris: Centre Archaeologique du Var. Editions Errance.

Prezzano, Susan Carol

1992 Longhouse, village, and palisade: Community patterns at the Iroquois southern door. Ph.D. dissertation, State University of New York, Binghamton.

Romans, Bernard

1775 *A concise natural history of east and west Florida: Containing an account of the natural produce of all the southern part of British America*. New York: Printed for the author.

Sahlins, Marshall D.

1972 *Stone age economics*. Chicago: Aldine.

Sattenspiel, L.

1990 Modeling the spread of infectious disease in human populations. *Yearbook of Physical Anthropology* 33:245–276.

Scarry, C. Margaret

1980 Excavations at Moundville, 1978–1979: The University of Michigan Museum of Anthropology Moundville Archaeological Project. Manuscript in possession of Vincas P. Steponaitis.

1981a The University of Michigan Moundville excavations, 1978–1979. *Southeastern Archaeological Conference Bulletin* 24:87–90.

1981b Plant procurement strategies in the West Jefferson and Moundville I phases. *Southeastern Archaeological Conference Bulletin* 24:94–96.

1986 Change in plant procurement and production during the emergence of the Moundville chiefdom. Ph.D. dissertation, Department of Anthropology, University of Michigan, Ann Arbor.

1993a Agricultural risk and the development of the Moundville chiefdom. In *Foraging and farming in the Eastern Woodlands*, ed. C. Scarry, pp. 157–181. Gainesville: University Press of Florida.

1993b Variability in Mississippian crop production strategies. In *Foraging and farming in the Eastern Woodlands*, ed. C. Scarry, pp. 78–90. Gainesville: University Press of Florida.

1993c Plant remains from the Big Sandy Farms site (1Tu552), Tuscaloosa County, Alabama. In *Big Sandy Farms: A prehistoric agricultural community near Moundville, Black Warrior River floodplain, Tuscaloosa County, Alabama*, by H. B. Ensor, pp. 205–233.

1995 *Excavations on the northwest riverbank at Moundville: Investigations of a Moundville I residential area*. Report of Investigations 72. Tuscaloosa: University of Alabama Museums, Office of Archaeological Services.

Scarry, C. Margaret, and Vincas P. Steponaitis

1992 Between farmstead and center: The natural and social landscape of Moundville. Paper presented at 57th annual meeting of Society for American Archaeology, Pittsburgh, Pa.

Schoeninger, M. J., and M. J. DeNiro

1984 Nitrogen and carbon isotopic composition of bone collagen from marine and terrestrial animals. *Geochimica et Cosmochimica Acta* 48:625–639.

Schoeninger, M. J., K. M. Moore, M. L. Murray, and J. C. Kingston

1989 Detection of bone preservation in archaeological and fossil samples. *Applied Geochemistry* 4:281–292.

Schoeninger, M. J., and M. R. Schurr

1994 Interpreting carbon stable isotope ratios. In *Corn and culture in the prehistoric New World*, ed. S. Johannessen and C. A. Hastorf, pp. 55–66. Boulder, Colo.: Westview Press.

Schoolcraft, Henry Rowe

1851–1857 *Historical and statistical information respecting the history, condition, and prospects of the Indian tribes of the United States*. 6 vols. Philadelphia: Lippincott, Grambo.

Scott, E. C.

1979 Dental wear scoring techniques. *American Journal of Anthropology* 51:213–218.

Scrimshaw, N. S., C. E. Taylor, and J. E. Gordon

1968 *Interactions of nutrition and infection*. World Health Organization Monograph 57. Geneva.

Sealy, J.

1986 *Stable carbon isotopes and pre-historic diets in the southwestern Cape Province, South Africa*. British Archaeological Reports International Series 293. Cambridge: Cambridge Monographs in African Prehistory.

Sheldon, Craig T.

1974 The Mississippian-historic transition in central Alabama. Ph.D. dissertation, University of Oregon, Eugene.

Shogren, Michael G.

1989 *A limited testing program at four mound sites in Greene County, Alabama*. Alabama De Soto Commission Working Papers 11. Tuscaloosa: Alabama Museum of Natural History.

Smith, Adam, and Nicholas David

1995 The production of space and the house of Xidi Sukur. *Current Anthropology* 36:441–471.

Smith, Bruce D.

1978 Variation in Mississippian settlement patterns. In *Mississippian settlement patterns*, ed. B. D. Smith, pp. 479–503. New York: Academic Press.

Smith, Marvin T., and Mark Williams

1994 Mississippian mound refuse disposal patterns and implications for archaeological research. *Southeastern Archaeology* 13(1):27–35.

Smith, Michael E.

1987 Household possessions and wealth in agrarian states: Implications for archaeology. *Journal of Anthropological Archaeology 6:297–335*.

Solís, Carlos, and Richard Walling

1982 *Archaeological investigations at the Yarborough site (22Cl814), Clay County, Mississippi*. Report of Investigations 30. Tuscaloosa: University of Alabama Office of Archaeological Research.

Speck, Frank G.

1907 Notes on Chickasaw ethnology and folk-lore. *Journal of American Folk-Lore* 20:50–58.

1913 European tales among the Chickasaw Indians. *Journal of American Folk-Lore* 26:292.

Spencer, Charles S.

1982 *The Cuicatlan Canada and Monte Alban: A study of primary state formation*. New York: Academic Press.

1990 On the tempo and mode of state formation: Neoevolutionism reconsidered. *Journal of Anthropological Archaeology* 9:1–30.

Spielmann, K. A., M. J. Schoeninger, and K. Moore

1990 Plains-Pueblo interdependence and human diet at Pecos Pueblo, New Mexico. *American Antiquity* 55:745–765.

Steinbock, R. T.

1976 *Paleopathological diagnosis and interpretation*. Springfield, Ill.: C. C. Thomas.

Steponaitis, Vincas P.

1978 Location theory and complex chiefdoms: A Mississippian example. In *Mississippian settlement patterns*, ed. B. D. Smith, pp. 417–453. New York: Academic Press.

1980a Some preliminary chronological and technological notes on Moundville pottery. *Southeastern Archaeological Conference Bulletin* 22:46–51.

1980b Ceramics, chronology, and community patterns at Moundville, a late prehistoric site in Alabama. Ph.D. dissertation, Department of Anthropology, University of Michigan, Ann Arbor.

1983a *Ceramics, chronology, and community patterns: An archaeological study at Moundville*. New York: Academic Press.

1983b The Smithsonian Institution's investigations at Moundville in 1869 and 1882. *Mid-Continental Journal of Archaeology* 8:127–160.

1986 Prehistoric archaeology in the southeastern United States, 1970–1985. *Annual Review of Anthropology* 15:363–404.

1991 Contrasting patterns of Mississippian development. In *Chiefdoms: Power, economy, and ideology*, ed. Timothy Earle, pp. 193–228. New York: Cambridge University Press.

1992 Excavations at 1Tu50, an early Mississippian center near Moundville. *Southeastern Archaeology* 11:1–13.

Steponaitis, V. P., R. P. S. Davis, Jr., and H. T. Ward

1994 Field evaluation of two subsurface augering methods at Moundville. Report submitted to the Alabama Museum of Natural History, Tuscaloosa.

Stuiver, M., and G. W. Pearson

1993 High-precision bidecadal calibration of the radiocarbon time scale, AD 1950–500 BC and 2500–6000 BC. *Radiocarbon* 35:15–23.

Stuiver, M., and P. J. Reimer

1993 Extended ^{14}C database and revised Calib radiocarbon calibration program. *Radiocarbon* 35:215–230.

Swanton, John R.

1911 *Indian tribes of the lower Mississippi Valley and adjacent coast of the Gulf of Mexico*. Bulletin 43. Washington, D. C.: Smithsonian Institution, Bureau of American Ethnology.

1928 Social and religious beliefs and usages of the Chickasaw Indians. In *44th annual report of Bureau of American Ethnology*, pp. 169–273. Washington, D.C.

1939 Final report of the U.S. De Soto Expedition Commission. House Document 71. 76th Congress, 1st session. Washington, D.C.: Government Printing Office.

1946 *The Indians of the southeastern United States*. Bulletin 137. Washington, D.C.: Smithsonian Institution, Bureau of American Ethnology.

Sykes, Kay

1989 The chief's house: Symbol of power. In *Households and communities*, ed. S. MacEachern, D. Archer, and R. Garvin, pp. 490–501. Calgary: University of Calgary.

Tieszen, L. L., and T. Fagre

1993 Carbon isotopic variability in modern and archaeological maize. *Journal of Archaeological Science* 20:25–40.

Tuross, N., M. L. Fogel, and P. E. Hare

1988 Variability in the preservation of the isotopic composition of collagen from fossil bone. *Geochimica et Cosmochimica Acta* 52:929–935.

van der Merwe, N. J., and J. C. Vogel

1978 ^{13}C content of human collagen as a measure of prehistoric diet in woodland North America. *Nature* 276:815–816.

Virginia, R. A., and C. C. Delwiche

1982 Natural ^{15}N abundance of presumed N_2-fixing and non-N_2-fixing plants from selected ecosystems. *Oecologia* 54:317–325.

Vogel, Joseph O., and Jean Allan

1985 Mississippian fortifications at Moundville. *Archaeology* 38(5):62–63.

Walthall, John A., and Steve B. Wimberly

1978 Mississippian chronology in the Black Warrior Valley: Radiocarbon dates from Bessemer and Moundville. *Journal of Alabama Archaeology* 24:118–124.

Wardle, H. Newell

1906 The treasures of prehistoric Moundville. *Harpers Monthly Magazine* 112:200–210.

Warrick, Gary A.

1988 Estimating Ontario Iroquoian village duration. *Man in the Northeast* 36:21–60.

Weiss, K. M.

1973 *Demographic models for anthropology*. Memoirs 27. Washington, D.C.: Society for American Archaeology.

Welch, Paul D.

1981 The West Jefferson phase: Terminal Woodland tribal society in west-central Alabama. *Southeastern Archaeological Conference Bulletin* 24:81–83.

1986 Models of chiefdom economy: Prehistoric Moundville as a case study. Ph.D. dissertation, Department of Anthropology, University of Michigan, Ann Arbor.
1989 Chronological markers and imported items from the Roadway excavations at Moundville. Paper presented at annual meeting of Southeastern Archaeological Conference, Tampa, Fla.
1990 Mississippian emergence in west central Alabama. In *The Mississippian emergence*, ed. Bruce D. Smith, pp. 197–225. Washington, D.C.: Smithsonian Institution Press.
1991 *Moundville's economy*. Tuscaloosa: University of Alabama Press.
1994 The occupational history of the Bessemer site. *Southeastern Archaeology* 13:1–26
1996 Control over goods and the political stability of the Moundville chiefdom. In *Political structure and change in the prehistoric southeastern United States*, ed. John F. Scarry, pp. 69–91. Gainesville: University Presses of Florida.

Welch, Paul D., and C. Margaret Scarry
1995 Status-related variation in foodways in the Moundville chiefdom. *American Antiquity* 60:397–419.

Whalen, Michael
1976 Excavations at Santo Domingo Tomaltepec: Evolution of a formative community in the valley of Oaxaca, Mexico. Ph.D. dissertation, Department of Anthropology, University of Michigan, Ann Arbor.

Wimberly, Steve B.
1956 A review of Moundville pottery. *Southeastern Archaeological Conference Newsletter* 5(1):17–20.

Wimberly, Steve B., and Lewis Larson
1948 Field notes on file at Moundville Archaeological Park, Moundville.

Wimberly, Steve B., and Harry A. Tourtelot
1941 *The McQuorquodale Mound: A manifestation of the Hopewellian phase in South Alabama*. Museum Paper 19. University: Geological Survey of Alabama.

Wylie, Alison
1985 The reaction against analogy. In *Advances in archaeological method and theory*, vol. 8, ed. M. B. Schiffer, pp. 63–111. New York: Academic Press.

Index

Pages numbers in **bold** indicate pages with figures and tables.